INTO THE GREAT WHITE SANDS

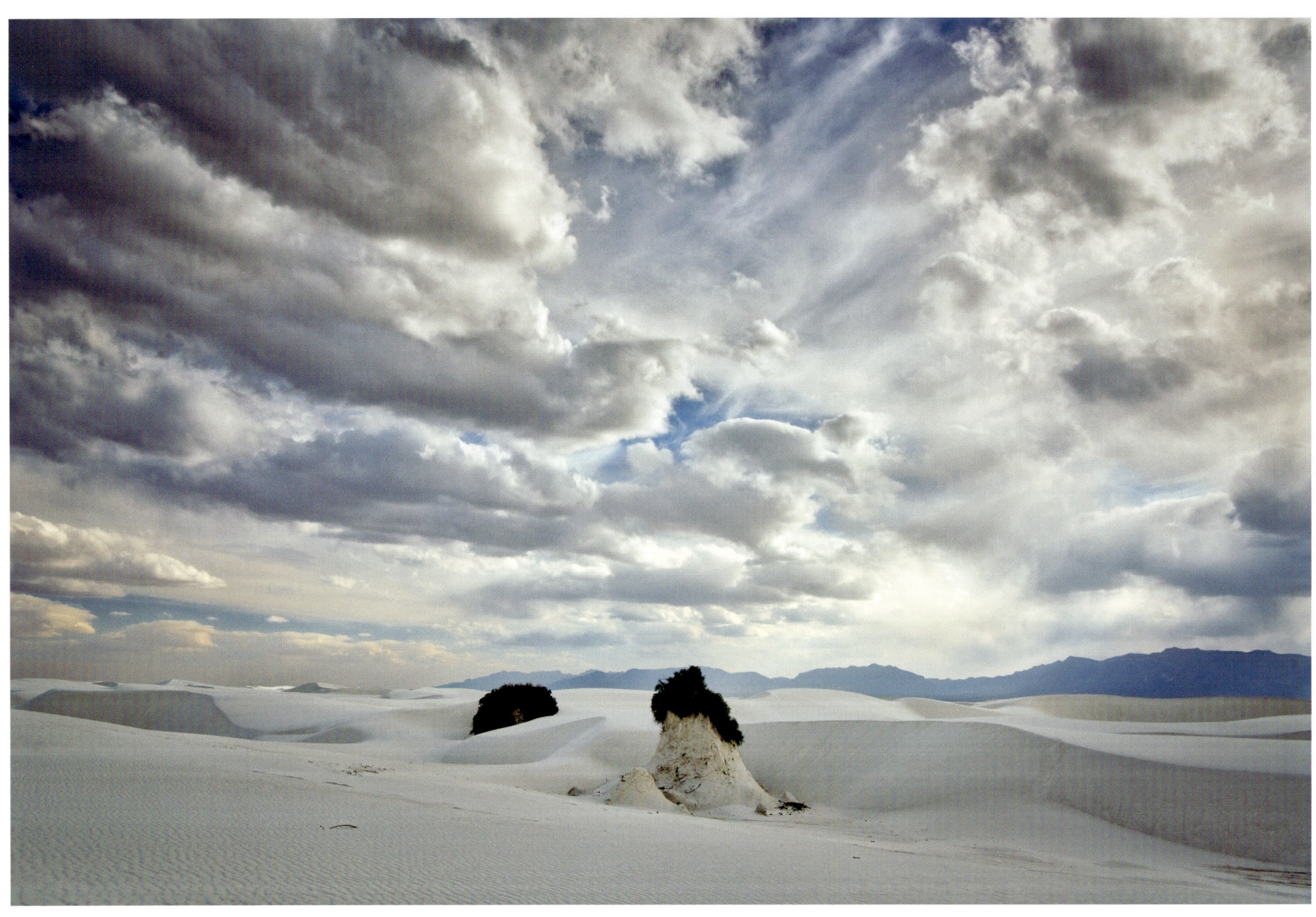

Salt Cedar Pedestals and Clouds. Pedestal dunes are erosional landforms that owe their origins to temporary stabilization of dune sediments by trees or other deep-rooted plants. When the dune moves on, the "Pedestal" dune remains, commonly with the plant still in place and growing.

INTO THE GREAT WHITE SANDS

PHOTOGRAPHS BY CRAIG VARJABEDIAN

Essays by

Jeanetta Calhoun Mish, Dennis Ditmanson,
and Jim Eckles

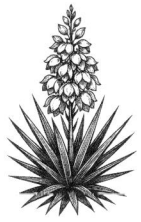

UNIVERSITY OF NEW MEXICO PRESS | ALBUQUERQUE

In 1933, White Sands was set aside as a national monument; in 2019, it became a national park—
a change that carries more than a shift in name. It is a promise, renewed and strengthened,
to safeguard this rare landscape for generations yet to come.

While these are milestones in human history, the dunes mark time in their own way.
Wind moves across them in a steady breath, carrying grains of gypsum that gleam under sun and moon alike.

For a moment, a beetle's trail may lace the surface, delicate as a thread, before it is gathered back into the shifting sands.
Here, life endures by listening to the rhythms of the earth—by bending to wind, rain, and heat, by taking only what is needed.

To protect such a place is to understand that our greatest gift is to let it remain as it has always been,
a world apart, alive with its own ancient voice.

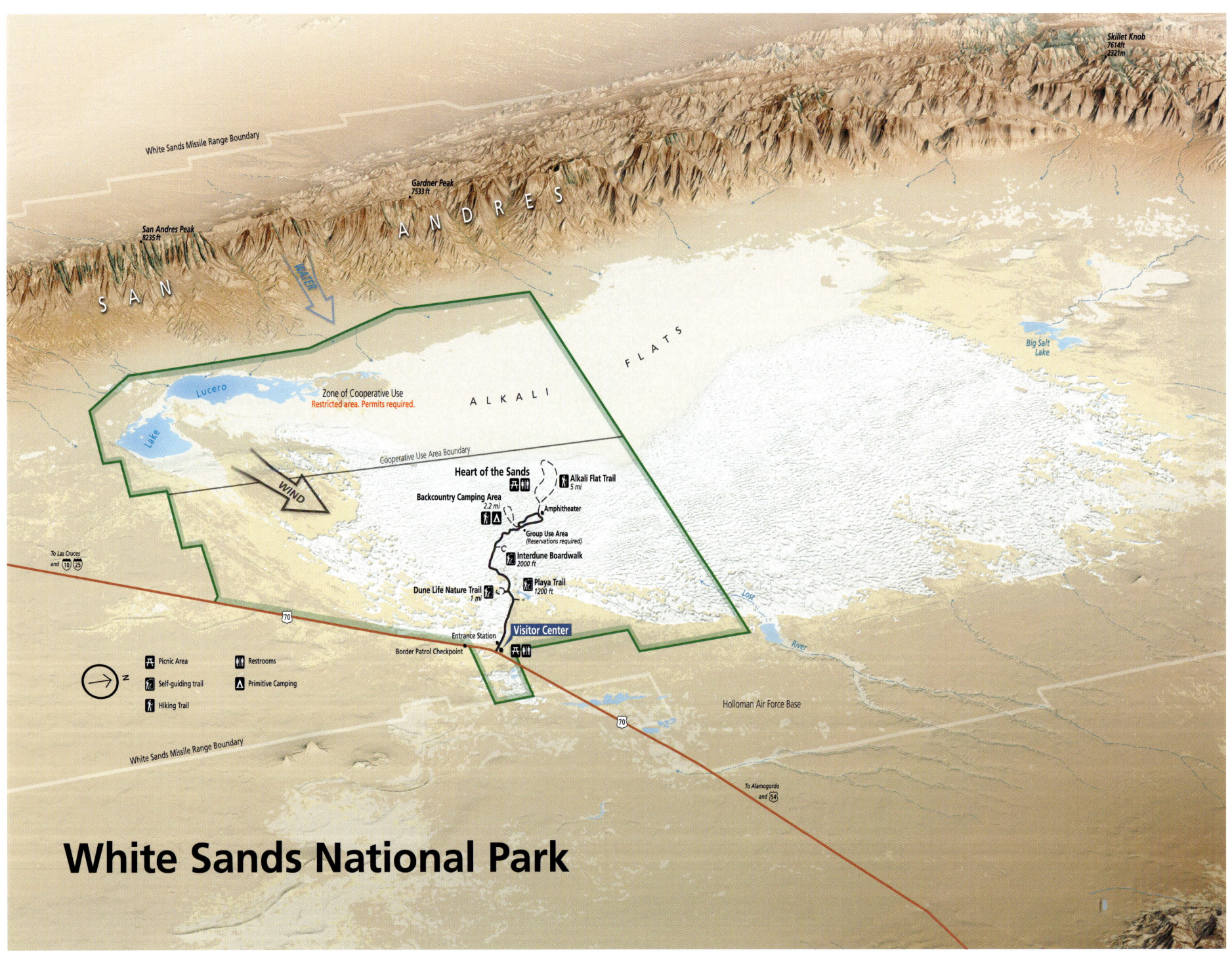

White Sands National Park

CONTENTS

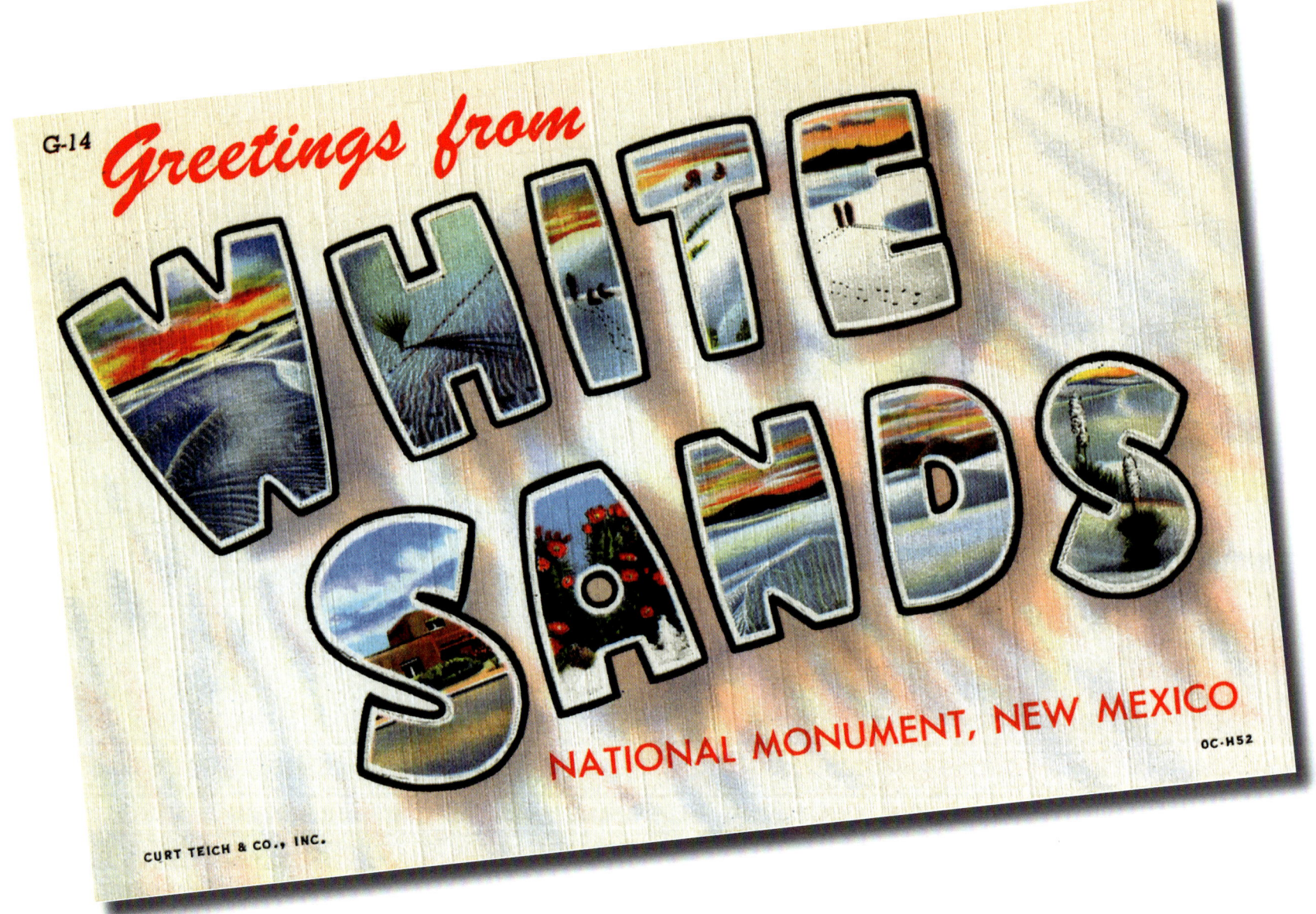

Greetings from White Sands National Monument, New Mexico.
Postcard published in 1950 by Curt Teich & Company, Inc.

AN INVITATION

To you who have never seen the Sands, I want to invite you to come and I hope that you see them on an evening just as the setting sun breaks through a canopy of clouds above the rugged San Andres, painting the points of the hills in yellow and gold; with here and there a burning ball of fire; that the mountains themselves are purple and the blue and the deep shadows of the Sands stand out against the snow white hills. For it was on such an evening that Dr. Gilbert Grosvenor[1] visited the Sands and said, "This is one of the Natural Wonders of the World. I place it on a par with Carlsbad Caverns and the Grand Canyon."

And as you linger in the twilight I hope that a gust of wind will come up the long slope and sweep up an eddy of swirling sand, and as it reaches the summit it will stand erect, almost in human form, and then stop and bend as if peering into the shadows, and run along the rippled ridge and stop and bend again, then disappear into the darkness. For then you will have seen the Pavlo Blanco, the White Wraith, the ghost of the beautiful woman who, according to Spanish Legend, comes nightly, dressed in the flowing white robes of her wedding gown and looks and hunts and searches for her lover, lost and buried in the Great White Sands. And as you stand peering into the darkness, listening to the silence of the desert, without the whisper of a single leaf, I hope that you turn, half frightened, and face the full red moon as it rises over the Sacramento mountains, scattering its millions of diamonds over every rippled dune, and you will have seen the Great White Sands.

TOM CHARLES, First Custodian of White Sands
National Monument, 1938
from Story of the Great White Sands

---

1 Gilbert Grosvenor served as chairman of the board and president of the National Geographic Society and editor of its magazine from 1899 to 1954.

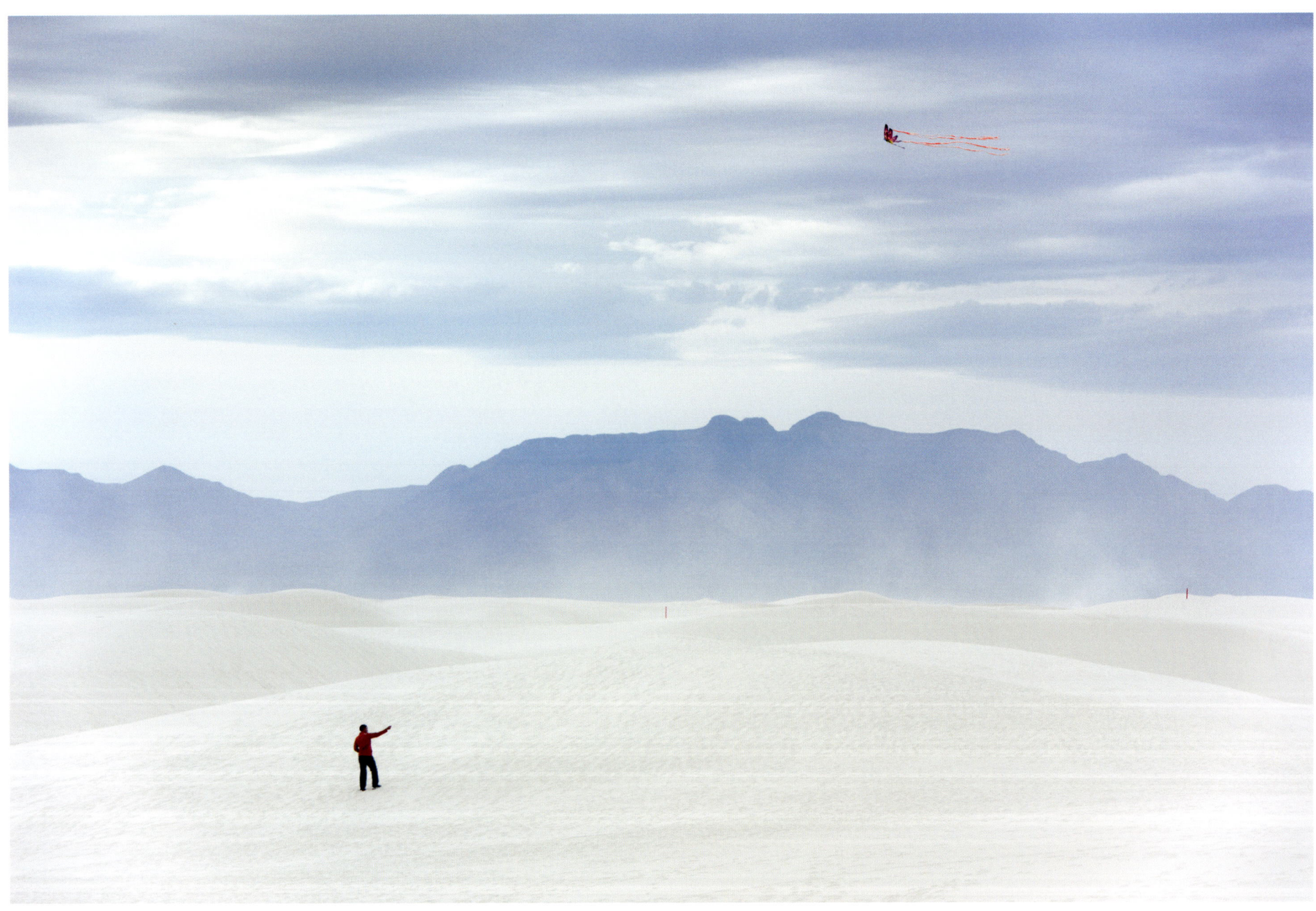

Flying a Kite on the Dunes, Spring.

Changeless Yet Ever-Changing

Dennis Ditmanson

My introduction to Craig Varjabedian came in the form of a phone call. He explained that he was working on a book, a photographic essay, on the White Sands and that a mutual friend had suggested he talk to me about my experiences while serving as superintendent at the park. Intrigued, I agreed to meet for breakfast and was soon drawn into the project by Craig's enthusiasm and his sincere and genuine dedication to his craft. Through subsequent conversations I've come to admire his concern for getting to the core of whatever project he is working on, and I've found myself drawn into this story through his probing questions and desire to make this publication an authentic—as he put it—representation of this landscape. Craig's photographs speak so eloquently of the spirit of the White Sands that I was at a loss as to what I might contribute until I thought about the mix of people and place that, for me, sets the White Sands apart.

As a career National Park Service (NPS) manager, my introduction to White Sands National Park was not the usual first view experienced by an incoming park superintendent. When Regional Director John Cook appointed me to the position early in 1989, it was with the caveat that I be on hand for the Easter Weekend activities at the park, even though my official reporting date was a bit later in the spring. He explained that this particular weekend was a big deal for the park and it would be important that I see the situation for myself in order to better understand the issues I'd face once I was ensconced in the position. Striving to make the best first impression on my soon-to-be staff, I headed for the park at what I thought was an early hour only to find traffic backed up out onto the highway. Good, I thought. People enjoying their national park. What I

found was pretty much chaos—a smaller version of the spring break mayhem usually associated with Fort Lauderdale or South Padre Island. After spending the day wading through a sea of beer cans and paper cups with the park rangers while making contacts with the revelers, Director Cook's message was clear—we had to find a way to balance use with visitor safety and resource protection. White Sands was an area set aside for the protection of a pretty special environment, but people also had a place in that landscape. In retrospect, I find most of the memories of my time there revolve around that interplay between the visitors and the resource.

I think Tom Charles had that same thought in mind. A local businessman, Mr. Charles was also a local "booster" who worked tirelessly to have the White Sands set aside as a unit of the National Park System. He saw economic potential in the dune field but recognized that its value lay in being promoted, as he put it, "by the inspiration rather than by the railcar load." Beginning in 1933 as the first caretaker of the new monument, he pressed for roads and other improvements that would get visitors into the landscape. Early on in my time at White Sands I happened on the bound copies of the Monthly Superintendent's Reports prepared by Johnwill Faris, who served as superintendent there longer than anyone—from November of 1939 until January of 1961. If Tom Charles is to be considered the father of White Sands, then Johnwill Faris has to be its hero. Coming on the scene when he did, just at the beginning of the war years, he guided the fledgling monument through that period when the growth of the military presence in the Tularosa Basin threatened its very existence.

Johnwill's reports stayed on the corner of my desk throughout my tenure.

Having seen the abuse of the park on that first Easter, I wanted to get a grasp of how visitor use occurred on a more typical day. Going into "covert" mode—causing much snickering among the staff—I donned shorts and a T-shirt, grabbed a lawn chair, and found a tall dune from which I could observe the visitors' behavior. Unlike my previous experience, I saw families picnicking, kids surfing the dunes, a volleyball game or two, an artist set up with a sketchpad, and others like myself, alone on a dune, just absorbed with a sense of place. It occurred to me that here was the challenge of the NPS mission in a microcosm: "To conserve the scenery and the natural and historic objects and the wild life therein and to provide for the enjoyment of the same in such manner and by such means as will leave them unimpaired for the enjoyment of future generations" (16 USC, Sec. 1). Linking people and place occupied me for the next eight years, but this session ended when it dawned on me that sitting in a metal lawn chair on the highest point around probably wasn't the best idea, given the rapidly approaching thunderstorm.

My friend Jim Eckles has also contributed to this volume. I worked closely with Jim in his capacity as chief of public affairs for White Sands Missile Range (WSMR). He talks about the relationship between the National Park and the overwhelming presence of its neighbors, WSMR and Holloman Air Force Base. By the time of my arrival, the situation was very different from that experienced by Johnwill Faris and some of his successors. Years of having to make this odd-couple relationship work had resulted in a process of long- and short-range planning and notification that made the occasional closure, evacuation, or delayed opening almost routine. We usually worked with a thirty-day calendar, but we sometimes found ourselves reacting to events on the world stage. During the first Iraq war, for example, I'd get calls at home asking for a next-day closure as weapons systems being tested at WSMR were adapted based on events occurring in real time. Being former military myself, I very much appreciated the important work being done at the missile range, but I did have to smile at the incongruity of this ex-enlisted man engaging with the top leadership on the range. In terms of the threat of inappropriate development on our boundaries, we couldn't have had a better neighbor, but life with the range added a whole new definition of "park impacts."

The balancing act between use and protection had another aspect. As a unit of the National Park System, White Sands belonged to the nation as a whole and had to be managed as such, but our local community considered the dunes to be their park, and over the years use patterns had developed that were not always in keeping with NPS practices. There was some validity to this belief, as studies indicated that the majority of visitors were local or at least regional. Early on, events such as the "Play Days" attracted thousands of schoolchildren and others to the park and contributed to the recreational reputation of the site. The excesses I observed in that first visit to the park were the outgrowth of that situation, but the root of the problem wasn't the number of people, it was the behavior fueled in large part by the alcohol. Now, I enjoy a beer with a burger as much as the next person, but we were seeing pickups entering the park with the entire bed filled with liquor, and underage drinking

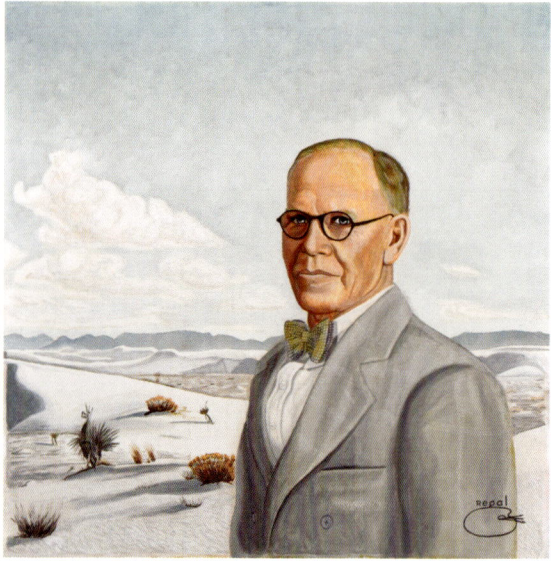

Tom Charles and White Sands. Painting by Regal Leftwich. Courtesy of the National Park Service. This painting of Tom Charles, first custodian of White Sands National Monument, was painted by local Alamogordo artist Regal Leftwich. The painting was displayed in the White Sands Visitor Center lobby from 1960 until 1989.

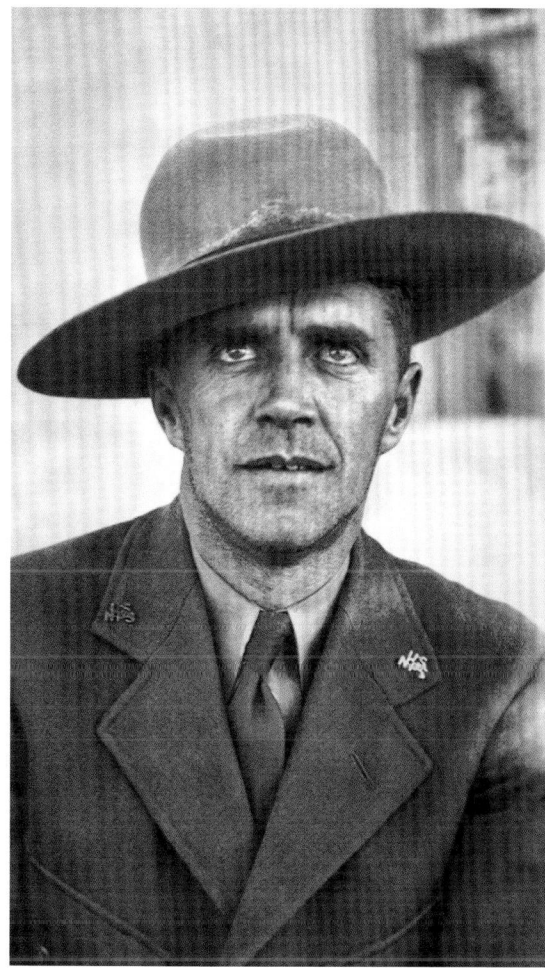

Johnwill Faris, Personnel file photo, 1937. Courtesy of the National Park Service. Johnwill Faris was the second custodian and later first superintendent of White Sands National Monument.

was a real problem. For me, the logical solution seemed to be to simply close the park to alcohol. But cooler heads, led by Regional Director Cook, prevailed, and a seasonal ban resulted, effective during the problematic spring break months. This made the dunes experience much calmer and safer for all, and we were still able to maintain the close relationship between the park and our local communities.

Aubrey L. Dunn Sr., a local businessman and longtime member of the New Mexico legislature, was a "booster" in the best tradition of Tom Charles. One of his favorite questions was, "What if?" I well remember him asking me one day, "What if we put on a hot-air balloon event over the dunes?" I answered in my best bureaucratic voice that there were issues of airspace restrictions, and traffic, and permits, and the next thing I knew we were in the car on the way to WSMR headquarters, where he put the same question to the post commander. In 1992 we hosted the first annual White Sands Balloon Festival. This event—and others sponsored by local businesses and organizations, ranging from concerts to volleyball tournaments— helped to reinforce the idea that while some activities were inappropriate in a national park, there were many ways that visitors could enjoy the place and still protect park resources. After all, the environment is by nature very forgiving. As an early brochure put it, "Throw paper and refuse in the trash box. With a little assistance the wind will do the rest."

My time with the NPS ran some thirty-five years, and I'm often asked about my favorite park. The assignment to White Sands always resonates as the highlight of my NPS years. Thanks to the relationship with our military neighbors I was able to monitor the resource in ways that would not otherwise have been possible. In particular, professional cultural- and natural-resource management staff from WSMR were available for consultation and willingly shared data from studies conducted on resources common to both the range and the park. Community leaders came to value the park as a significant element of the local economy and would include visits to NPS officials as a part of their annual trips to congressional offices in Washington, DC. I was able to experience this place in every way imaginable: on foot, on horseback, on an ATV, by helicopter, through satellite imagery, and through the eyes of the many visitors who shared their experiences. For the most part, however, what made the difference were the many opportunities to get out of the office and to see firsthand the interplay between people and resource. I'd like to think that exposure helped me to make a difference—or, to echo Jim Eckles, to make this bit of the country worth defending.

Craig's lens has captured the stunning beauty of the White Sands, but the absolute solitude of the landscape also has room for a family gathering of hundreds. The Sands harbor important cultural resources and have significant historical tales to tell and yet offer unique recreational opportunities. They are home to plants and animals specially adapted to this environment. They allow for the ravages of a Hollywood movie set and seemingly heal overnight with a freshening wind. They seem as dry and lifeless as a desert, but a few inches of digging will bring water to the surface. They can seem otherworldly, and then overhead will appear the latest in twenty-first-century aircraft. They are changeless and yet ever-changing. That dichotomy is worthy of a visit—come see for yourself.

PHOTOGRAPHS OF WHITE SANDS NATIONAL PARK

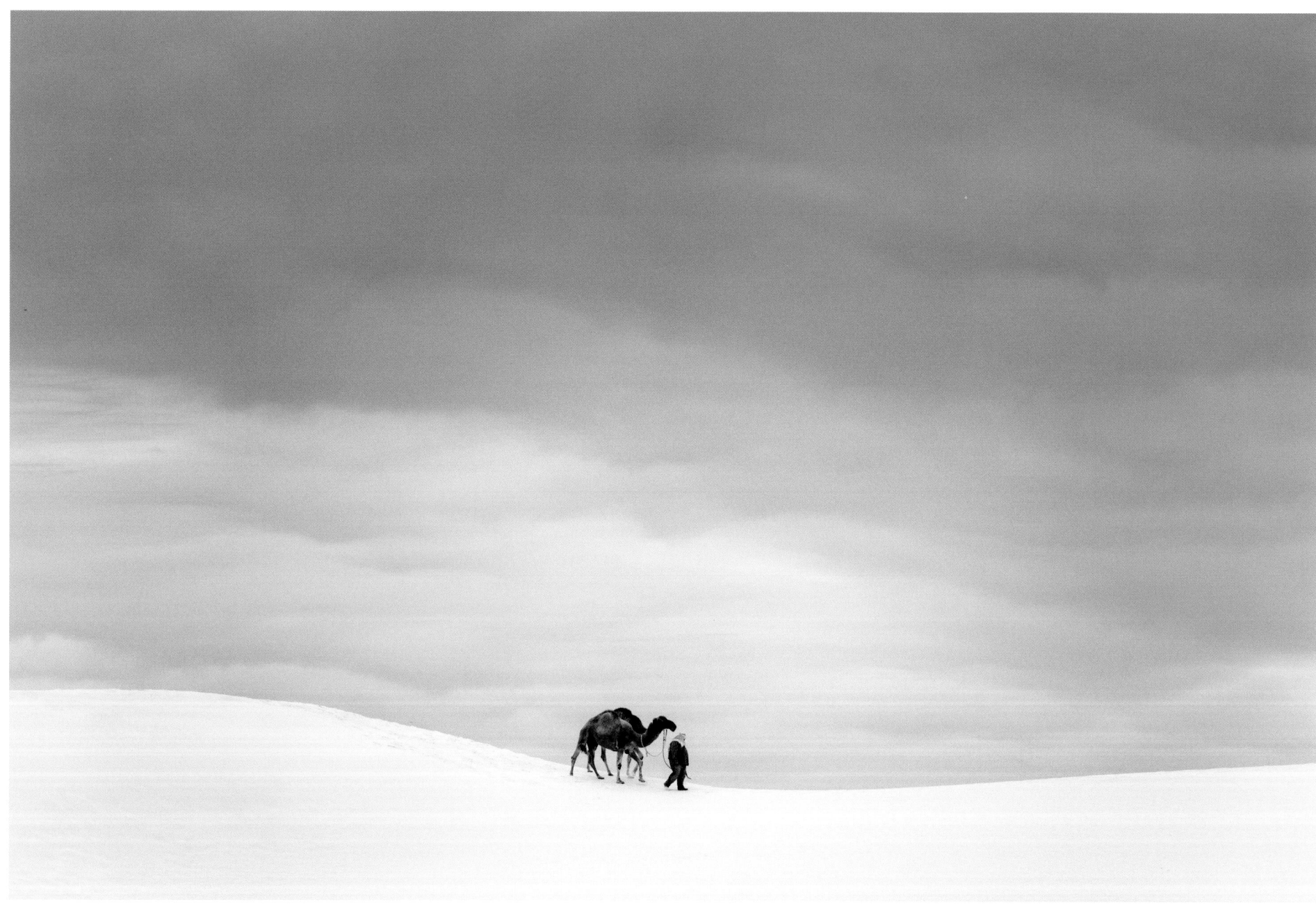

George Stone and his Camels, Winter.

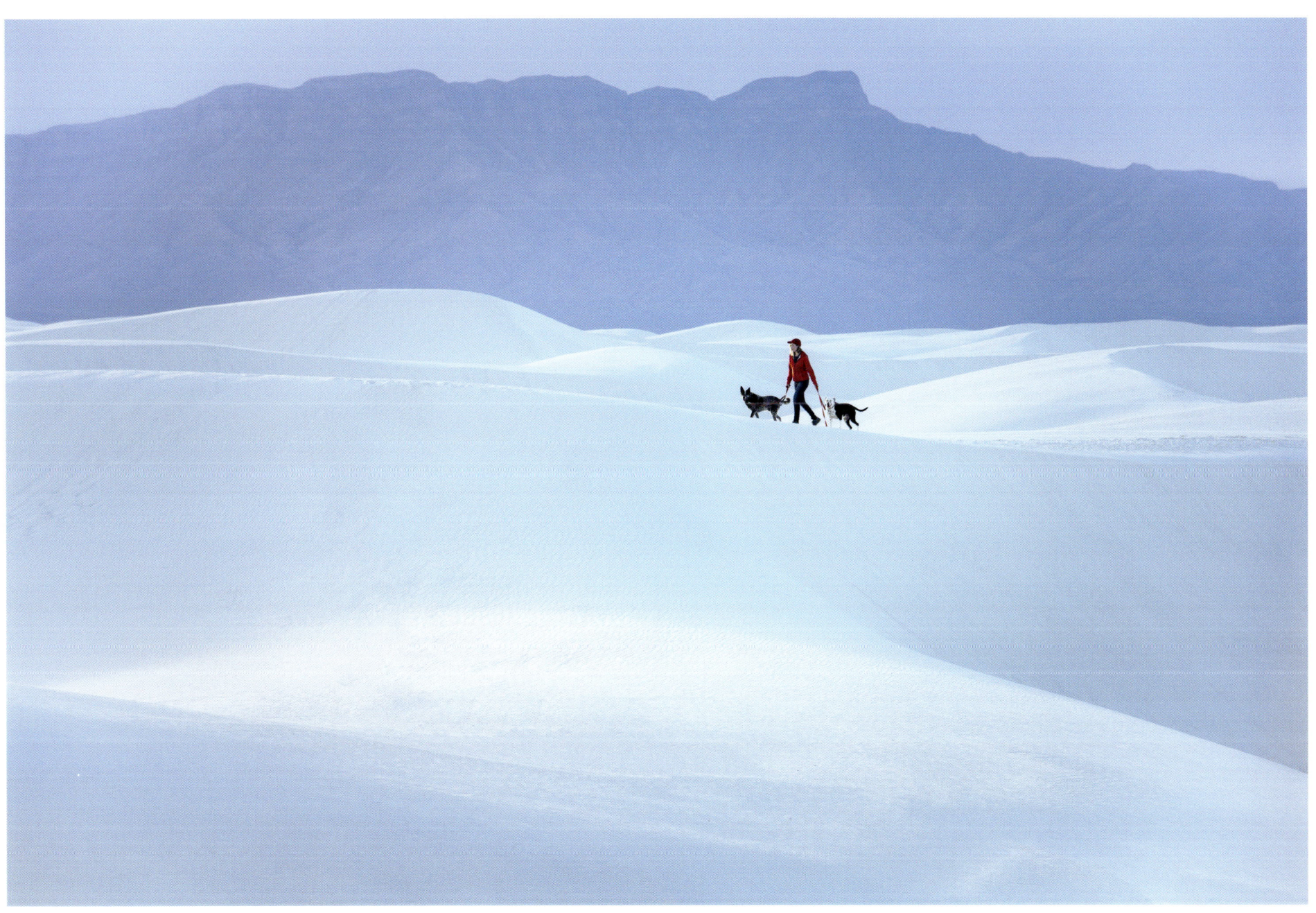

Walking Two Dogs, Winter. Dogs are welcome at White Sands and may be walked almost anywhere on leads.

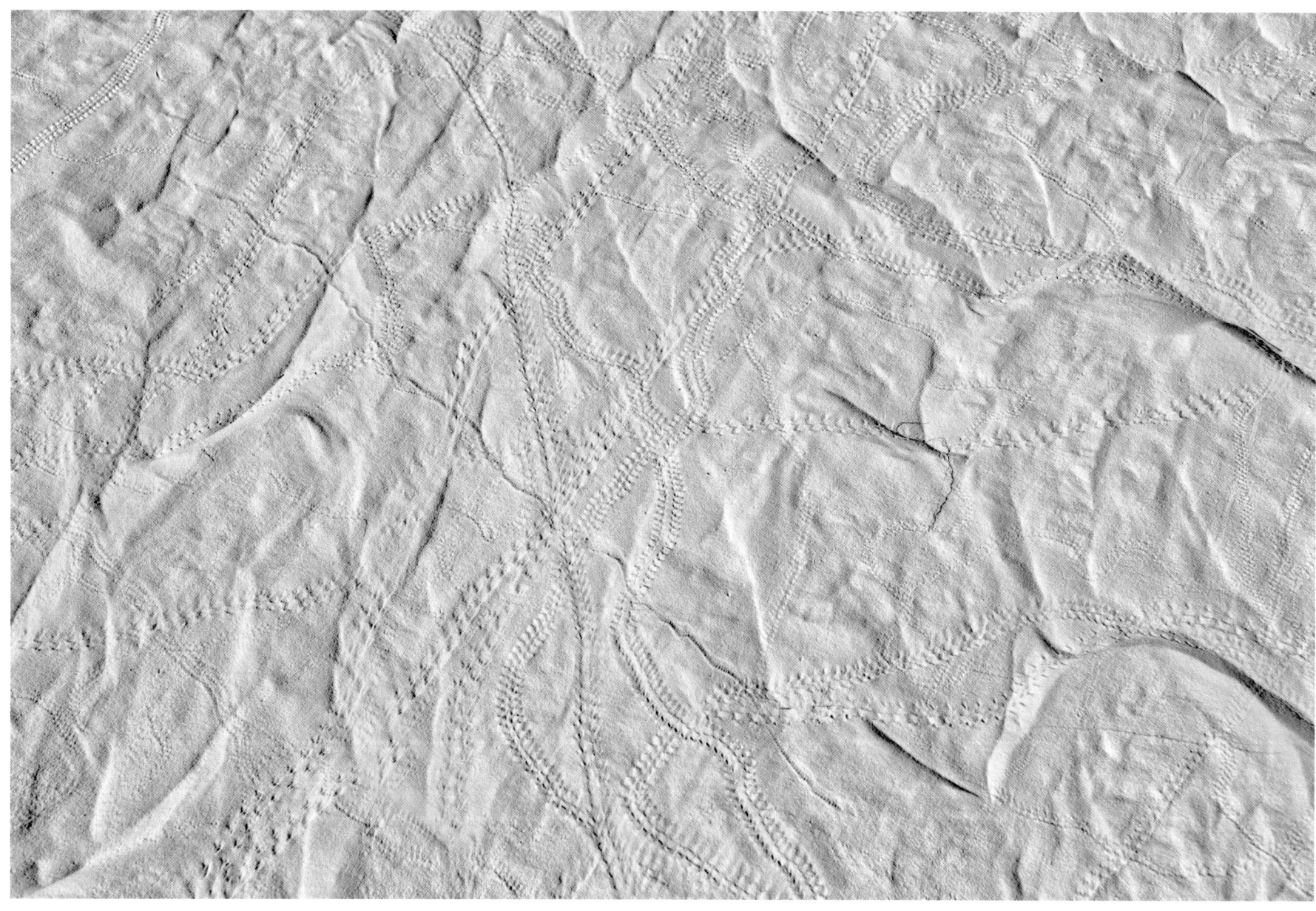

Darkling Beetle Tracks.

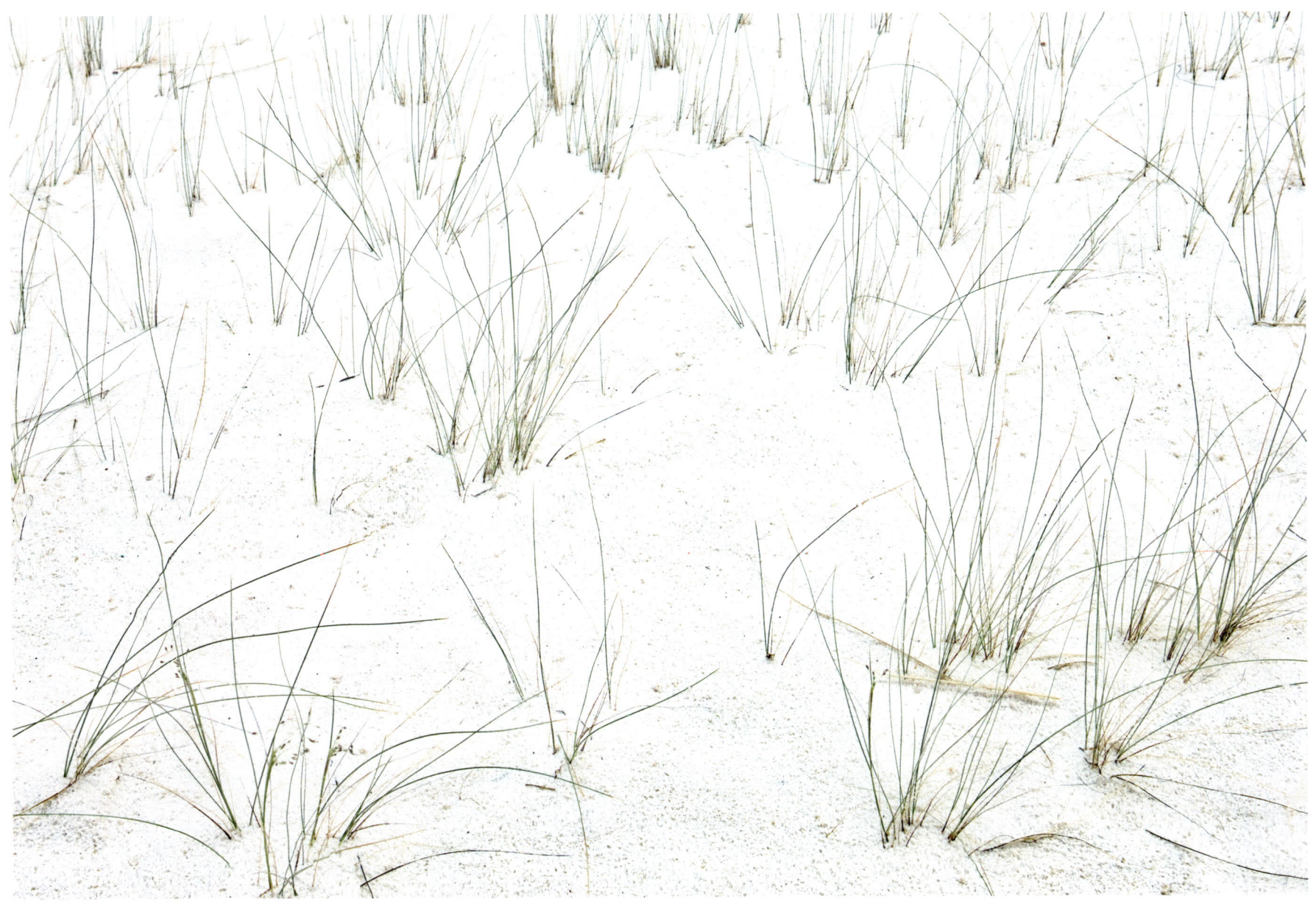

Indian Rice Grass, Early Spring.

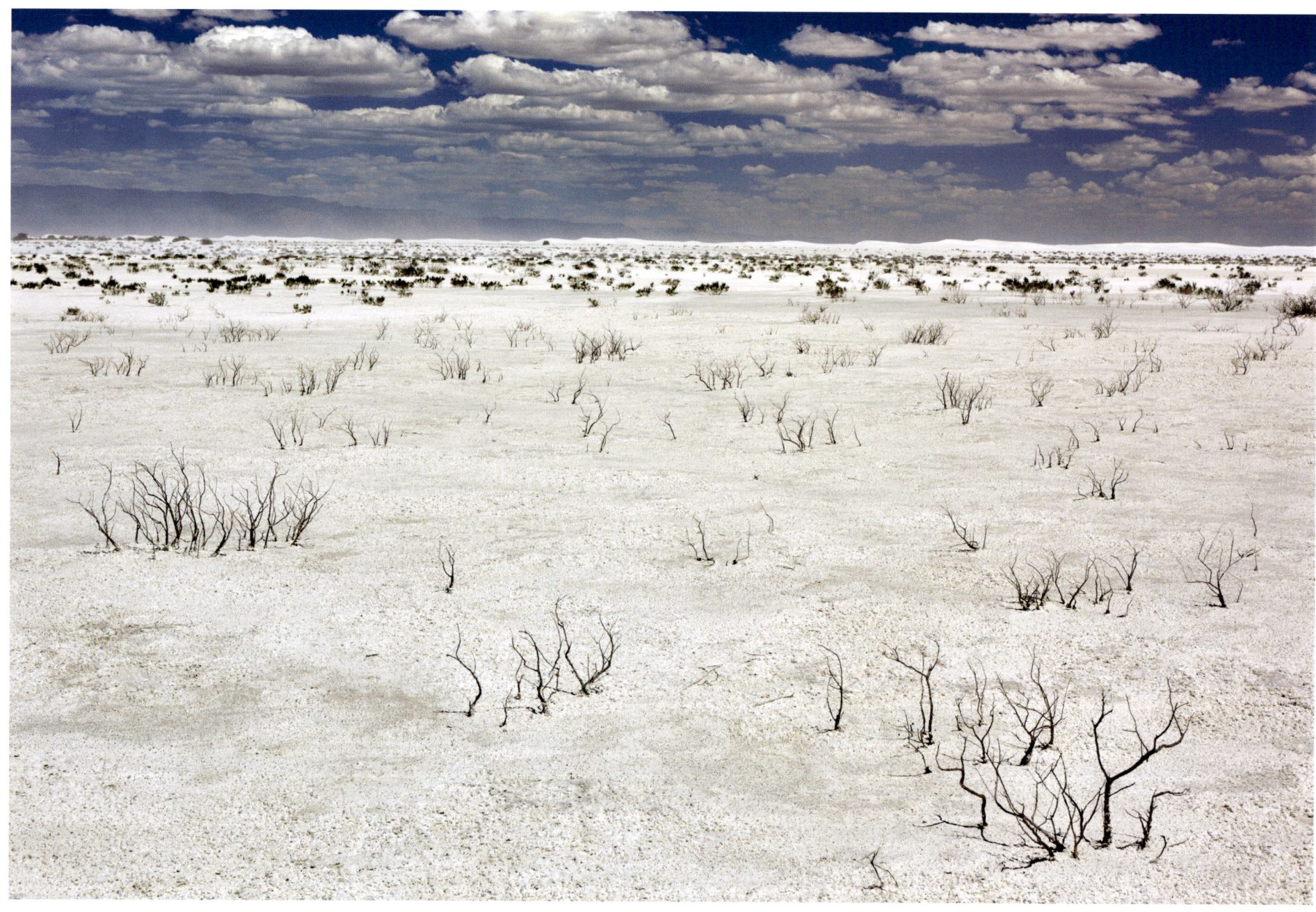

Iodine Bush on Alkali Flats Facing Dune Field, Summer.

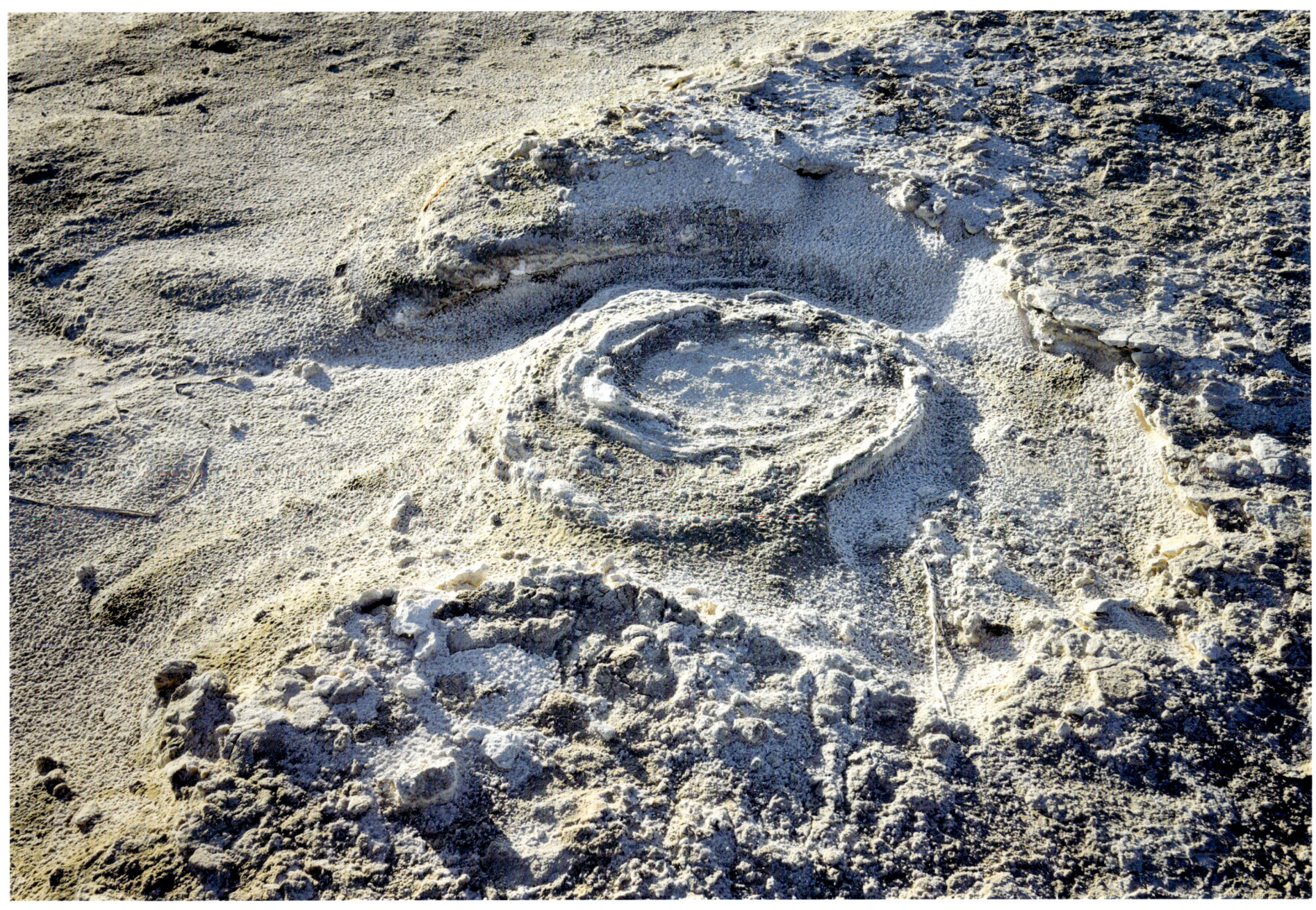

Mammoth Print, Edge of Lake Otero and Dune Field, Spring. This Mammoth print is nineteen thousand years old.

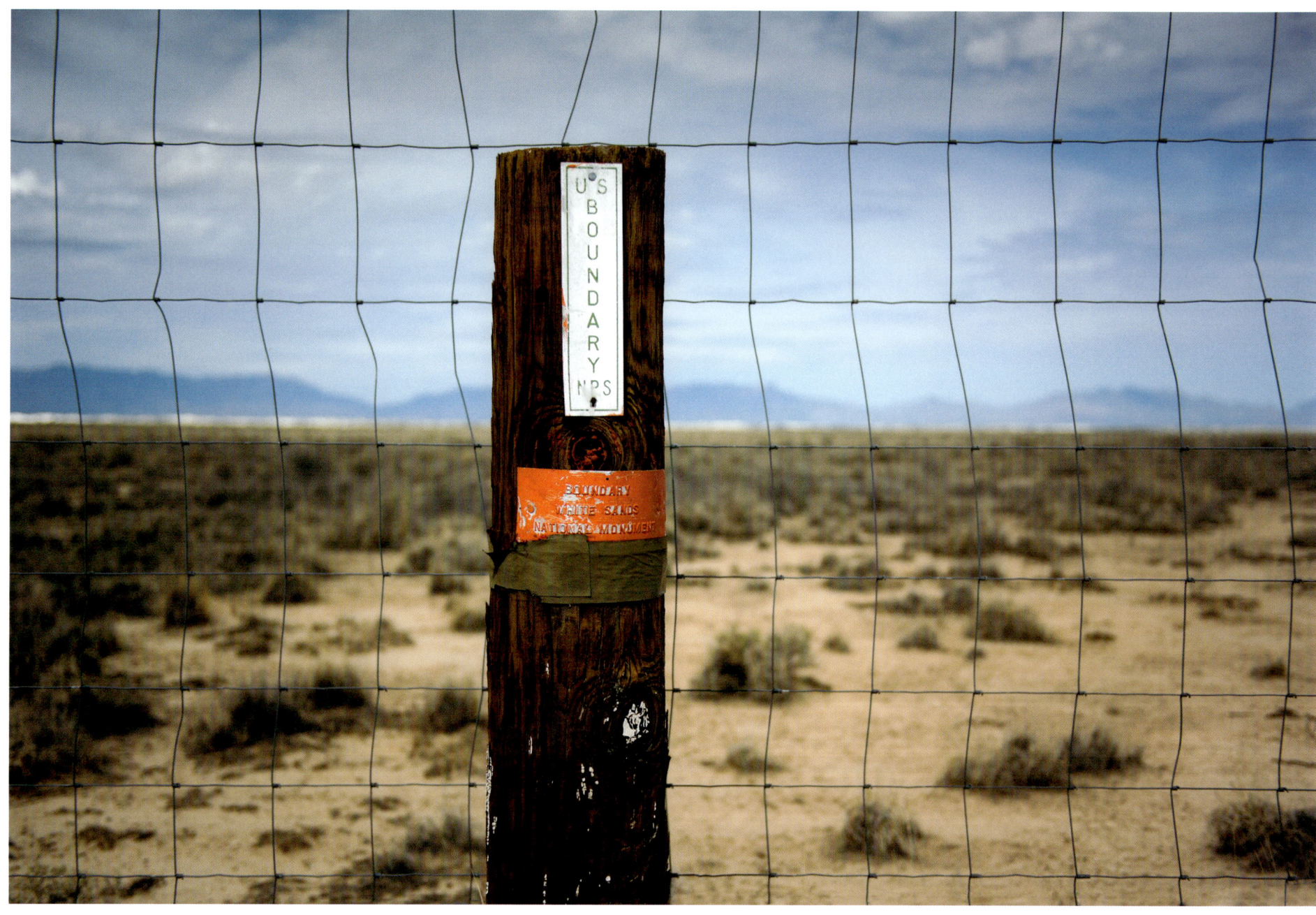

Eastern US Boundary Marker for White Sands National Park.

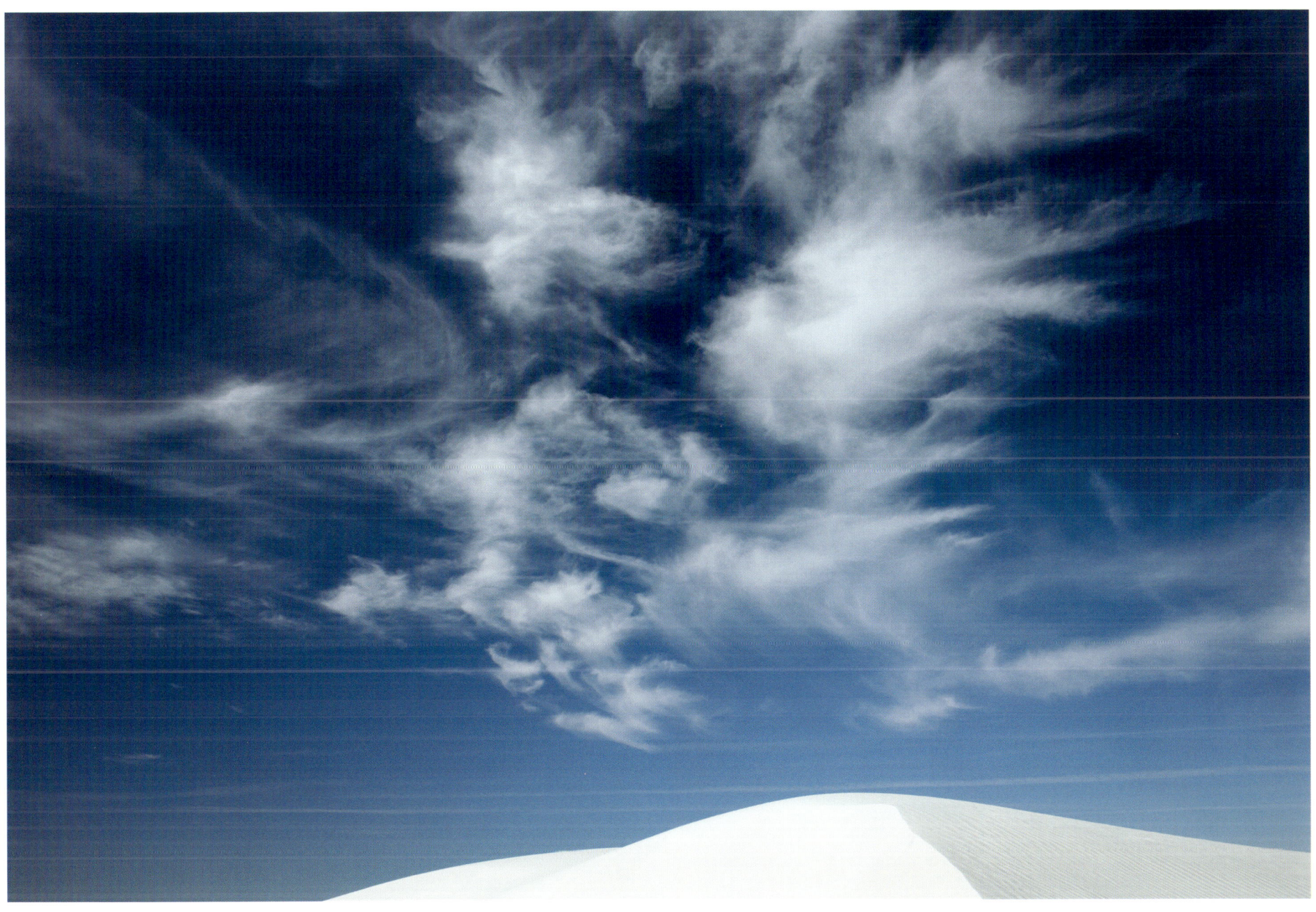

Cirrus Clouds over Dune, Spring.

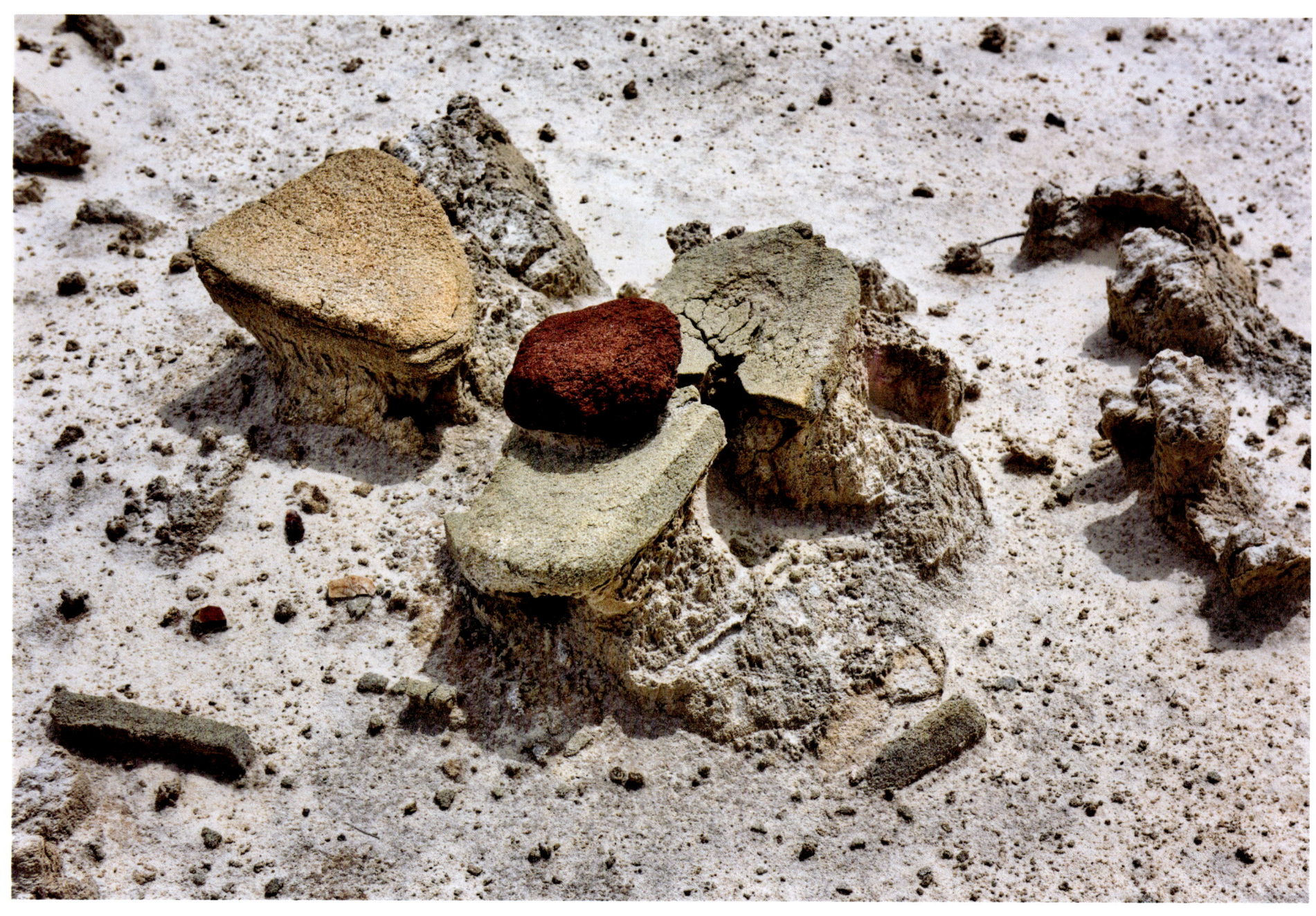

Native American Mano and Metate (Ground Stone and Mortar). Manos and Metates were used by Native American peoples (archaic period) to grind plant foods.

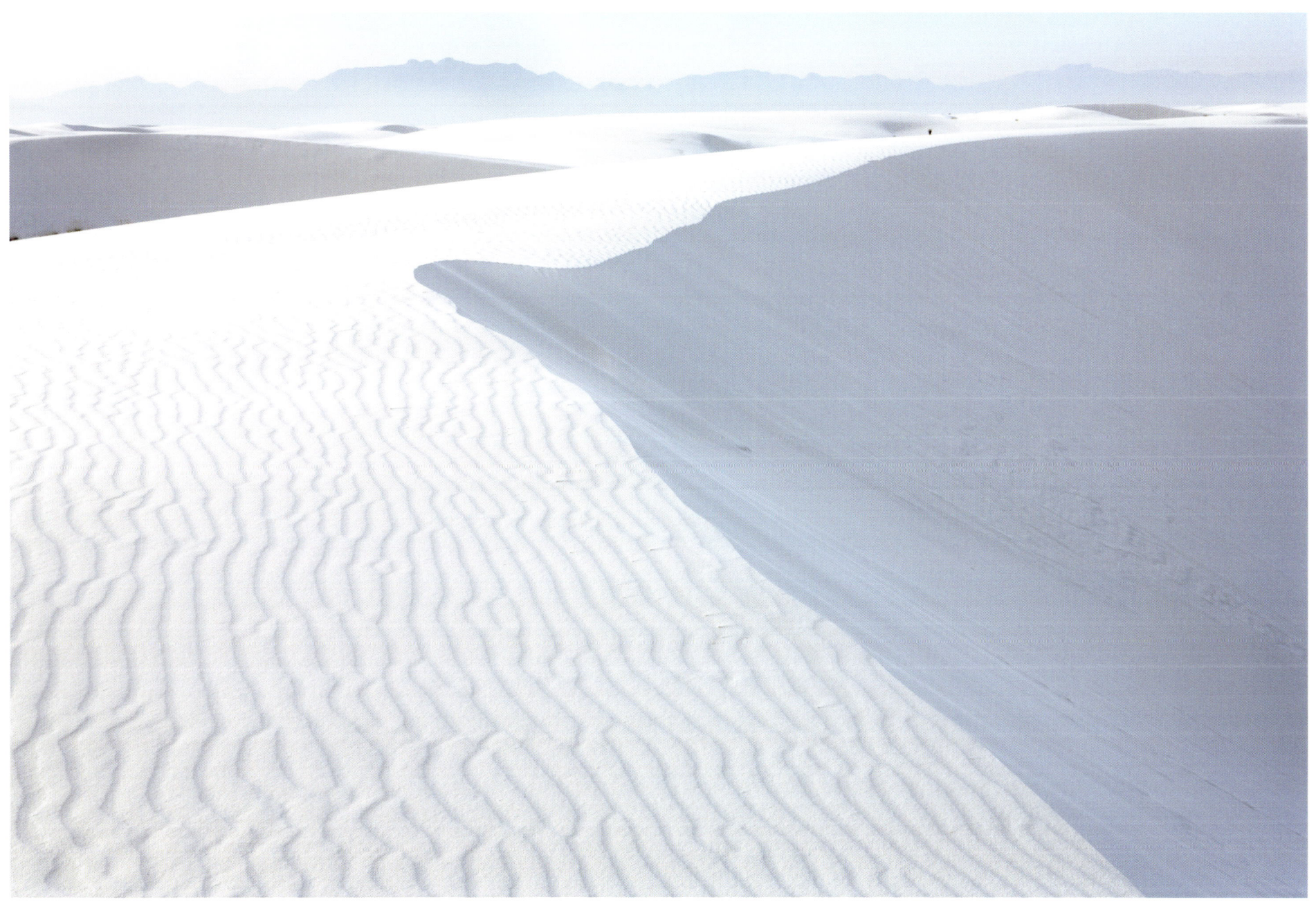

Pastel Sand Dune and Mountains, Spring.

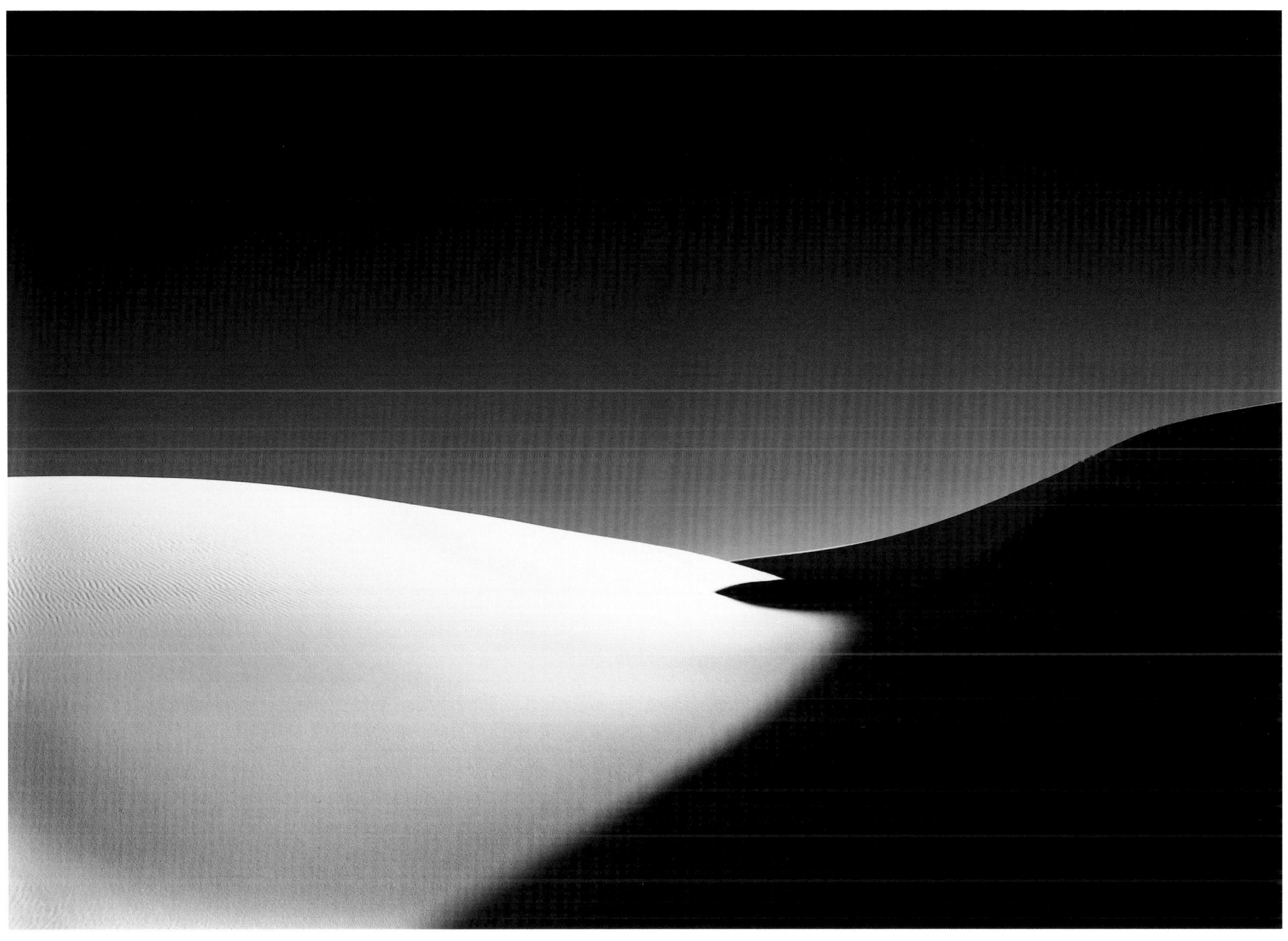

White Sands Study No. 1, Sunset.

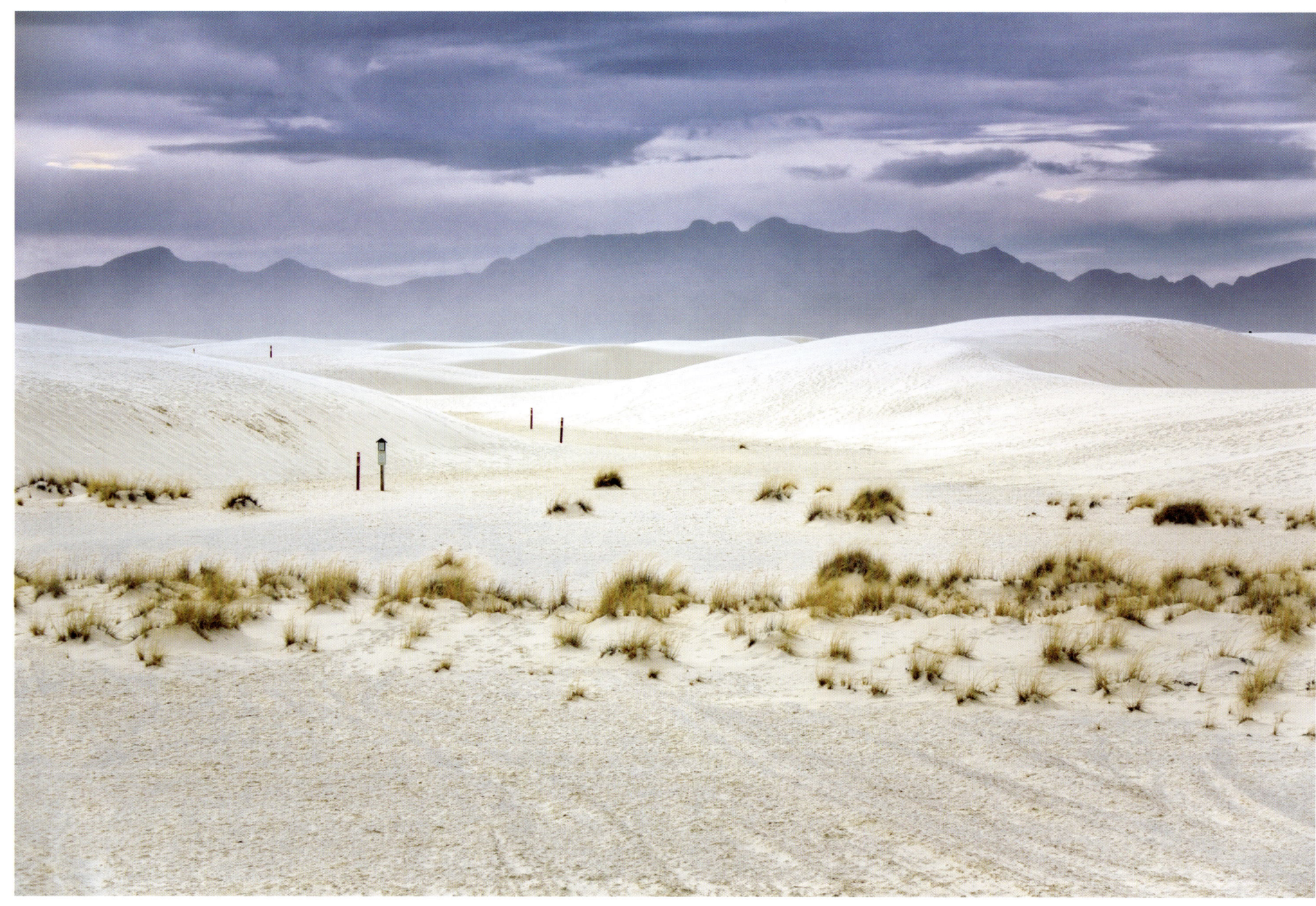

Alkali Flats Trail and Little Blue Stem Grass, Spring.

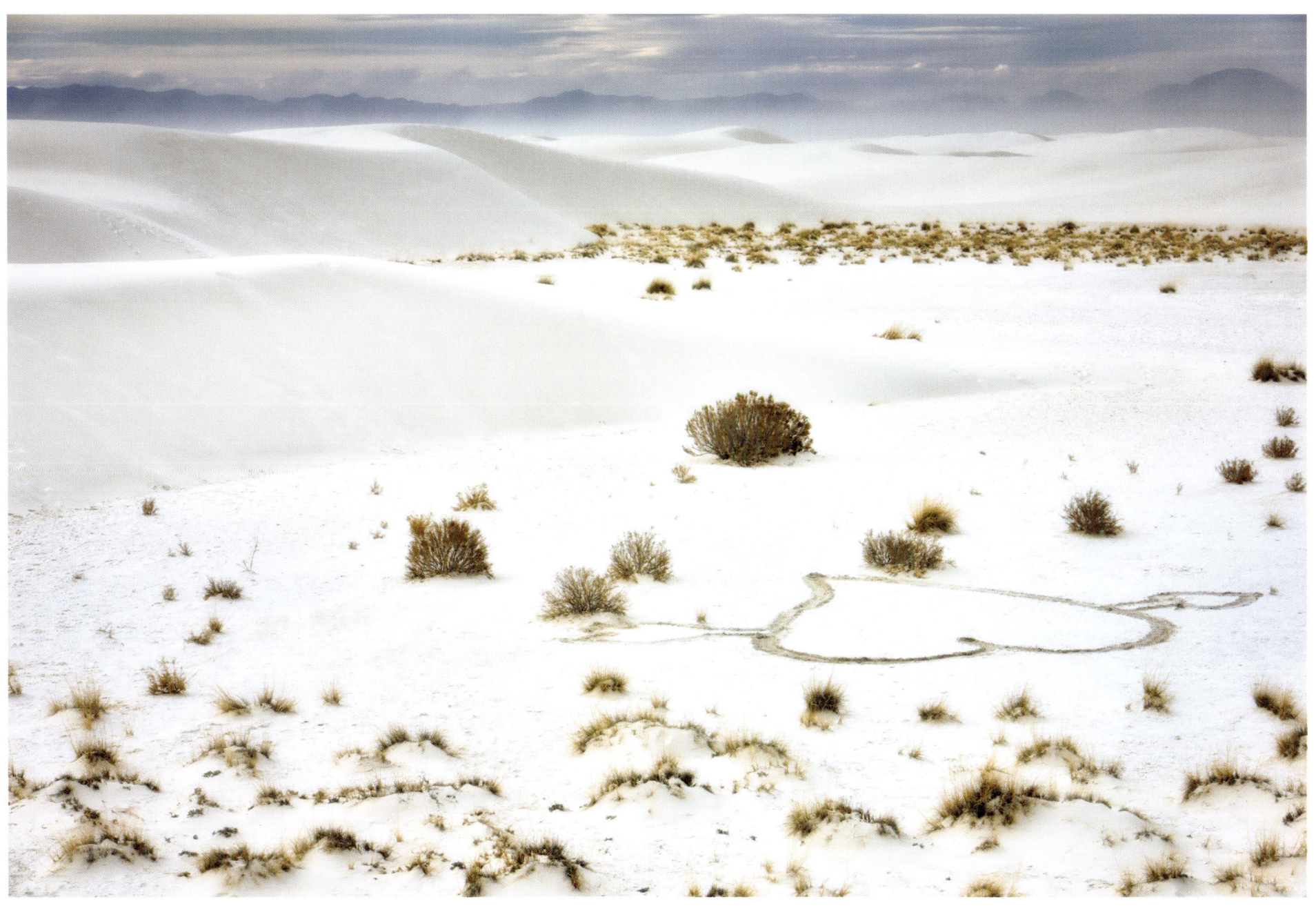

Heart of the Dunes and Spring Winds.

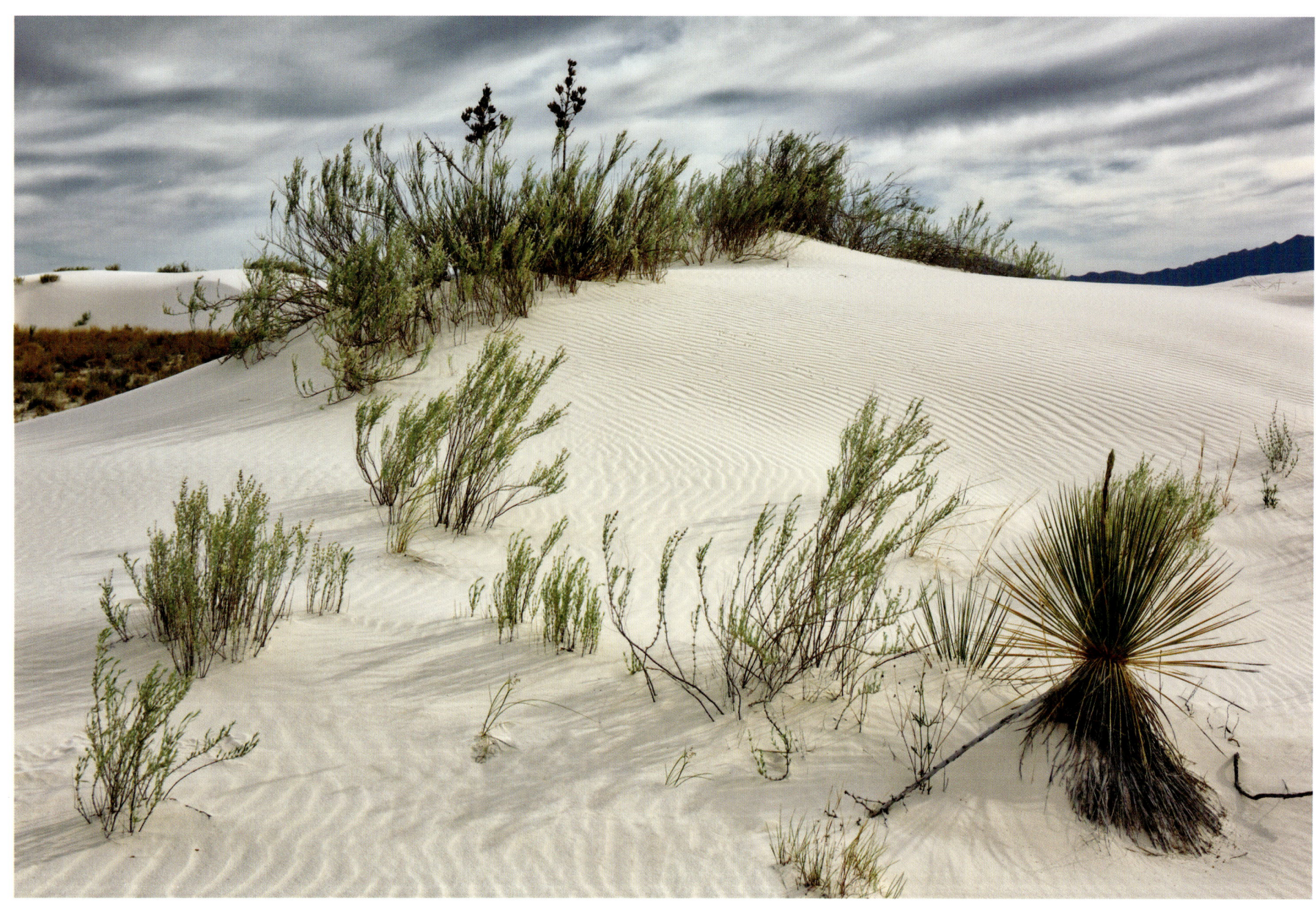

Rosemary Mint Sage with Old and New Growth Yucca, Spring.

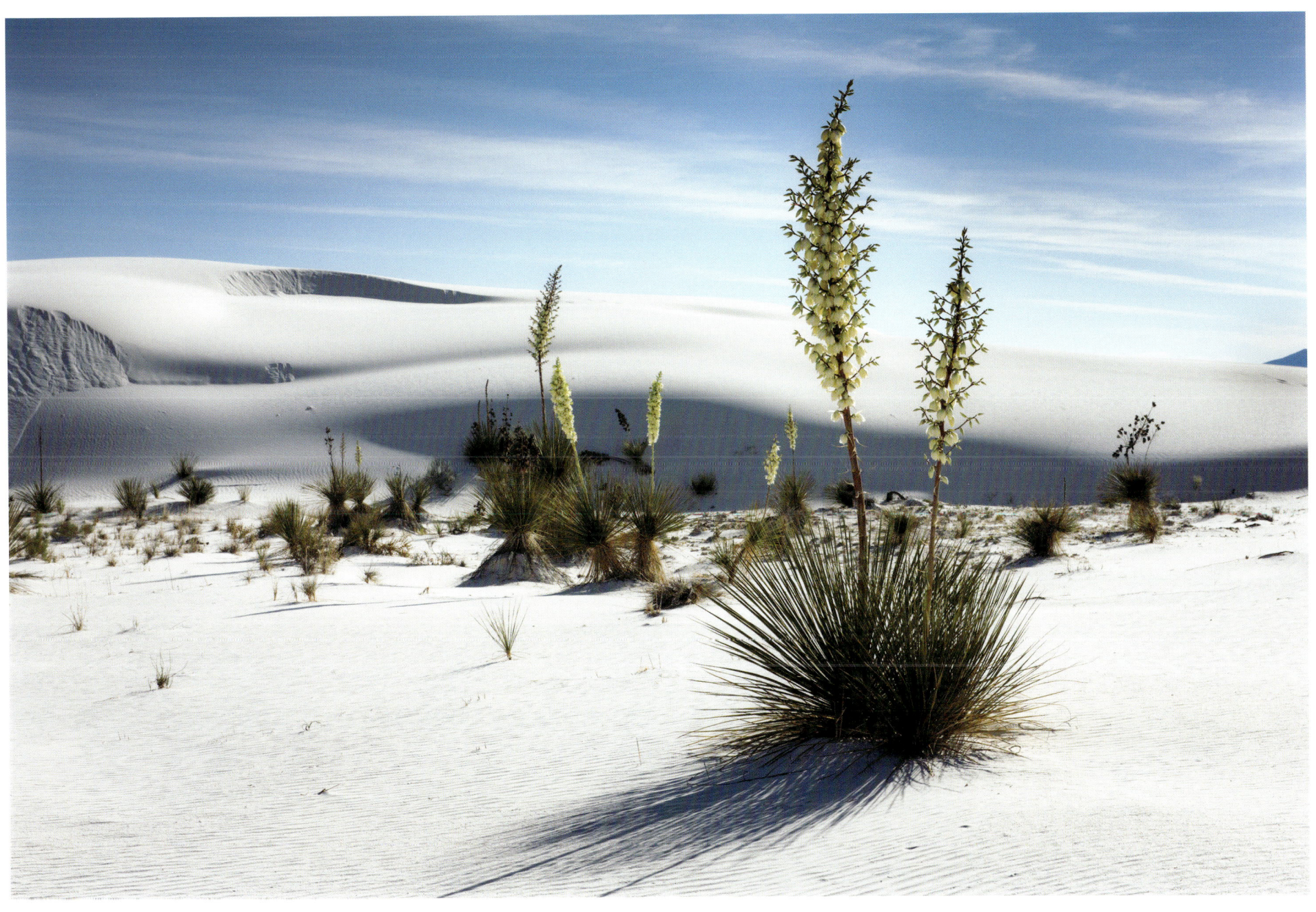

Soaptree Yucca Blooms and Dune, Spring.

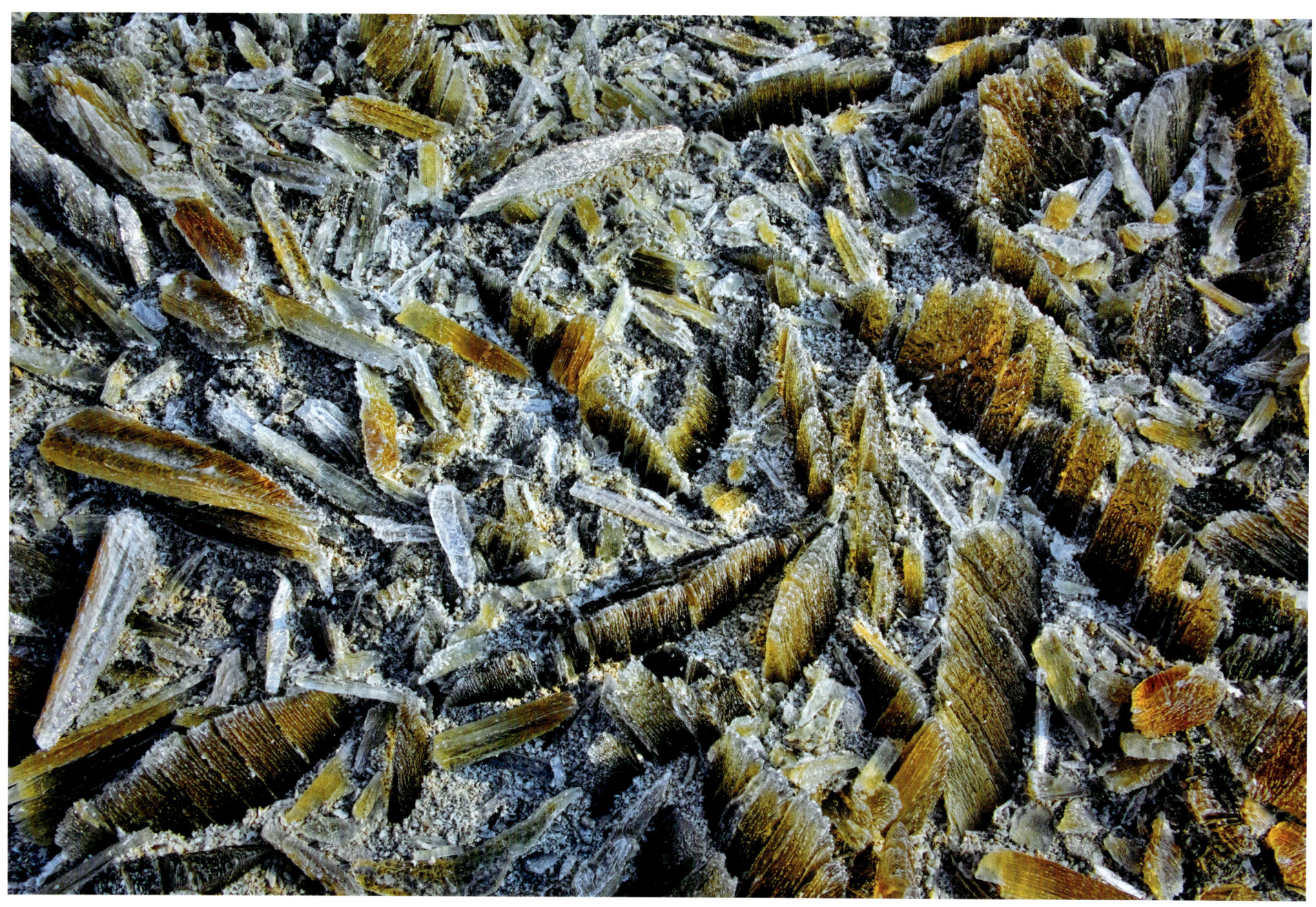

Amber Selenite Crystals and Salt Crust, Spring.

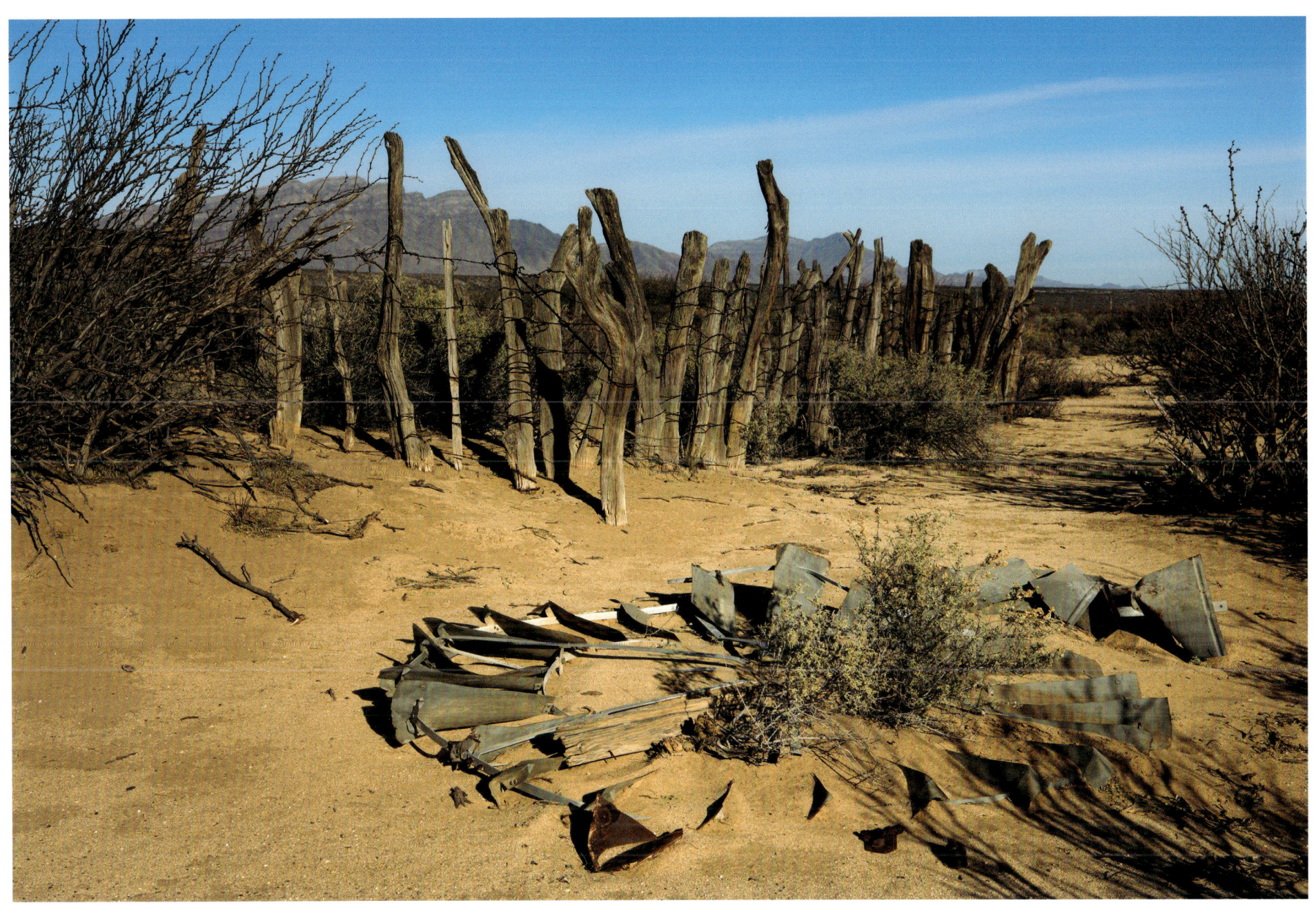

Fallen Windwheel at Lake Lucero Ranch Site, Sunrise, Winter. In 1897 Jose and Felipe Lucero began ranching on the south shore of the lake that bears their name. During special ranger-led tours, visitors to Lake Lucero can see stock pens, a well, a watering trough, and this fan from the fallen windmill at this historic ranch site.

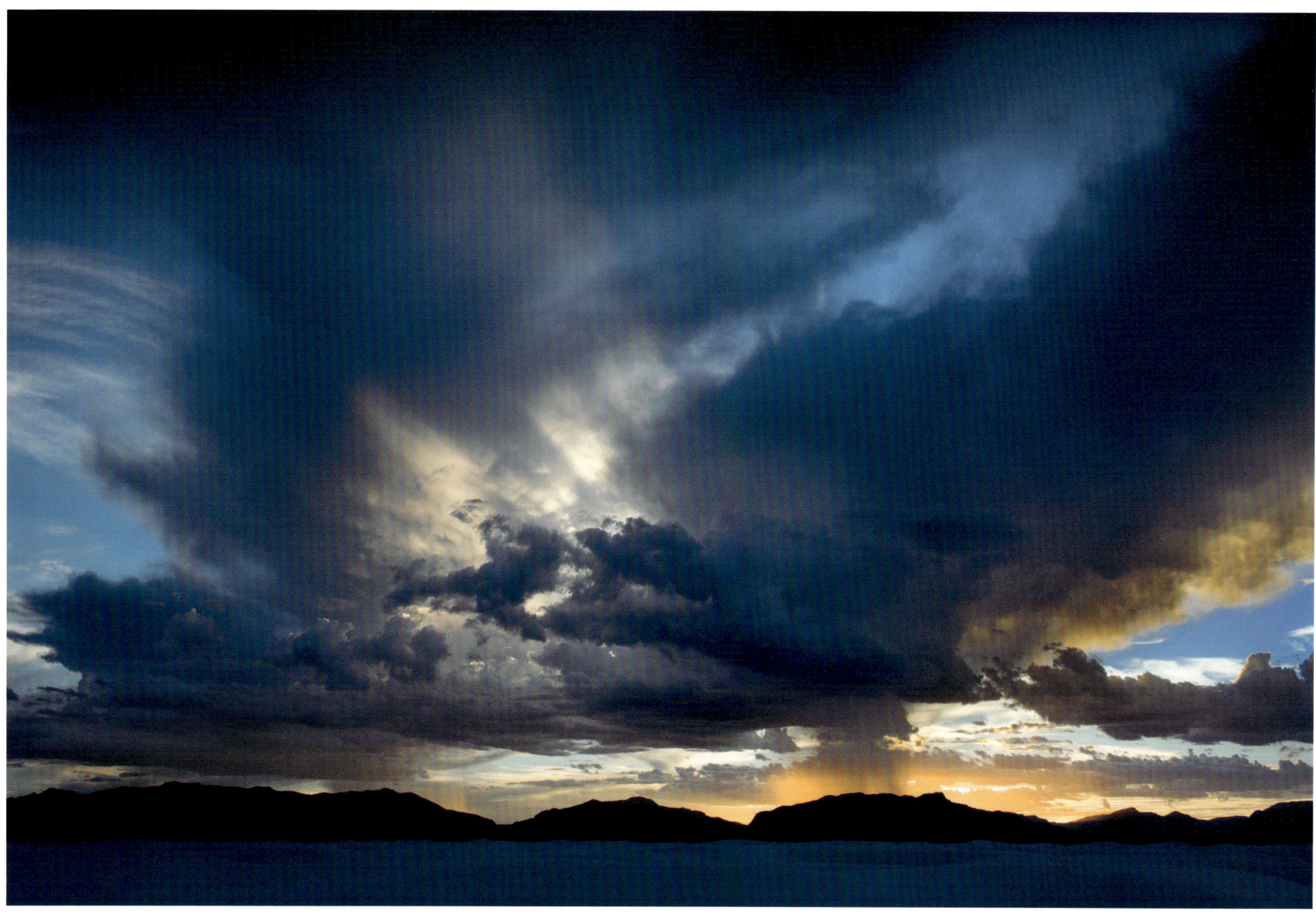

Sunset with Light Rays over San Andres Mountains.

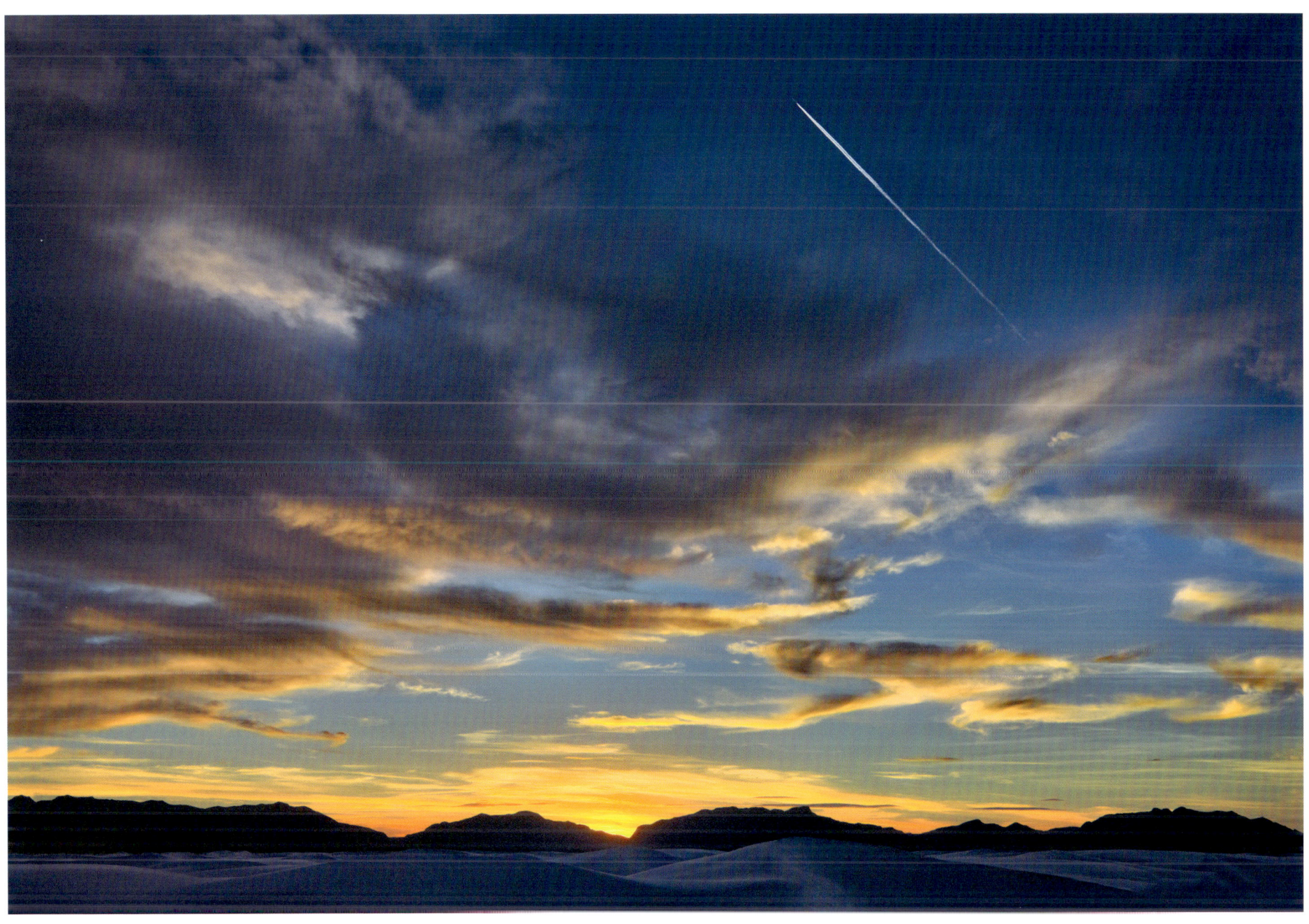

Sunset Clouds and Contrail, San Andres Mountains, Autumn. Visitors to the park will experience the local military presence as fighter jets on flight training pass over the dune field.

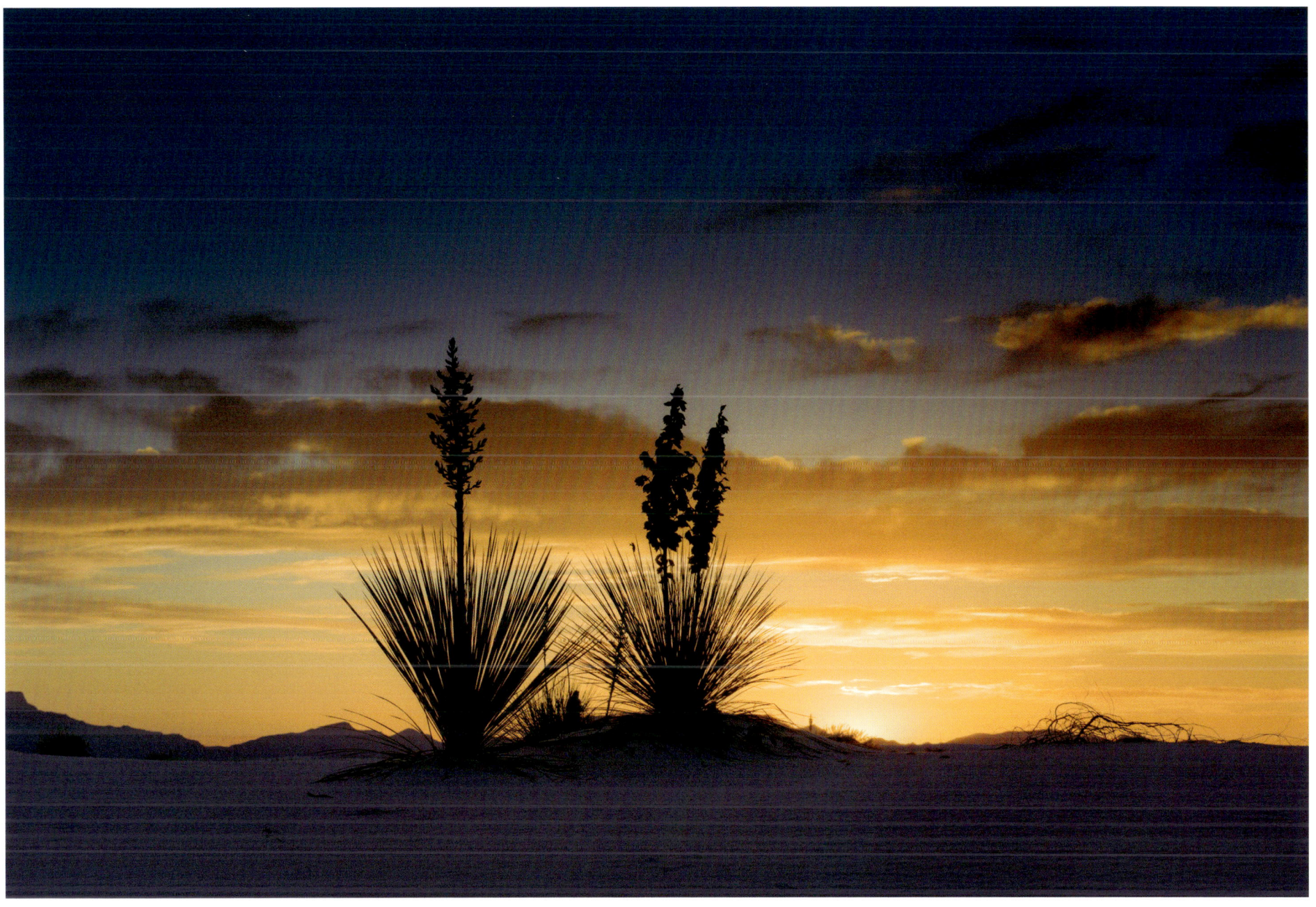

Yuccas at Sunset, Autumn.

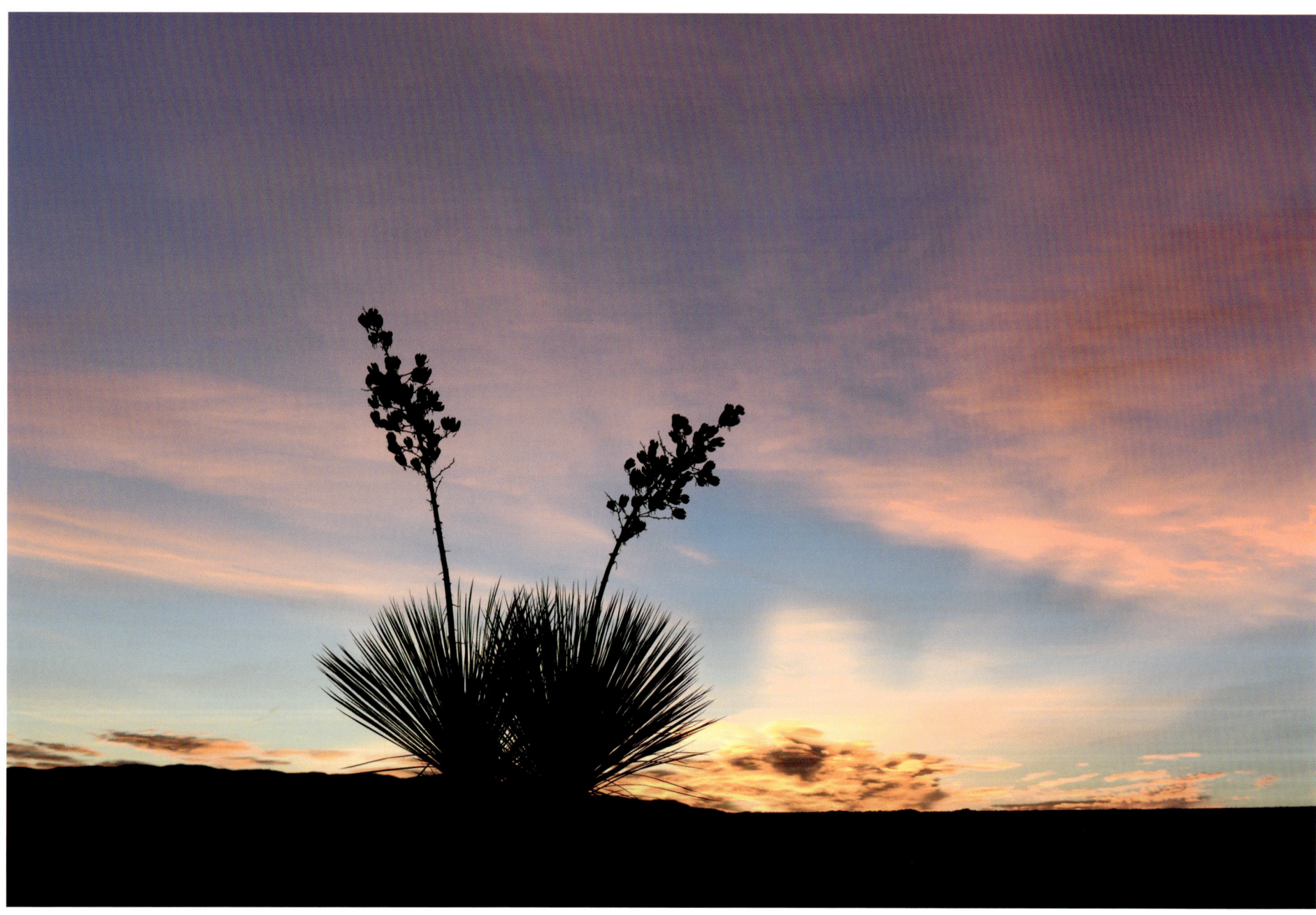

Yuccas at Sunrise, Autumn.

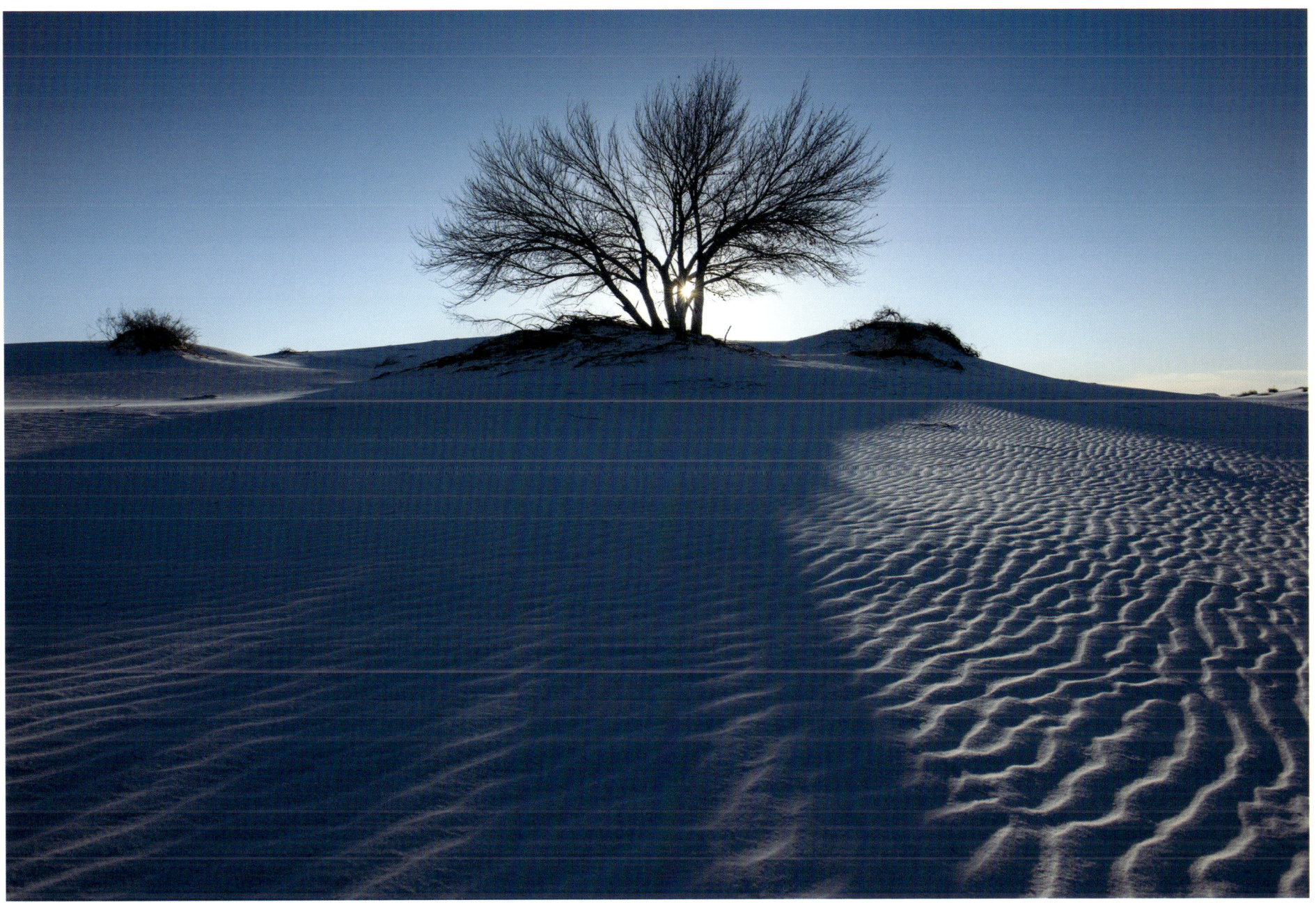

Cottonwood Tree at Sunrise, Winter.

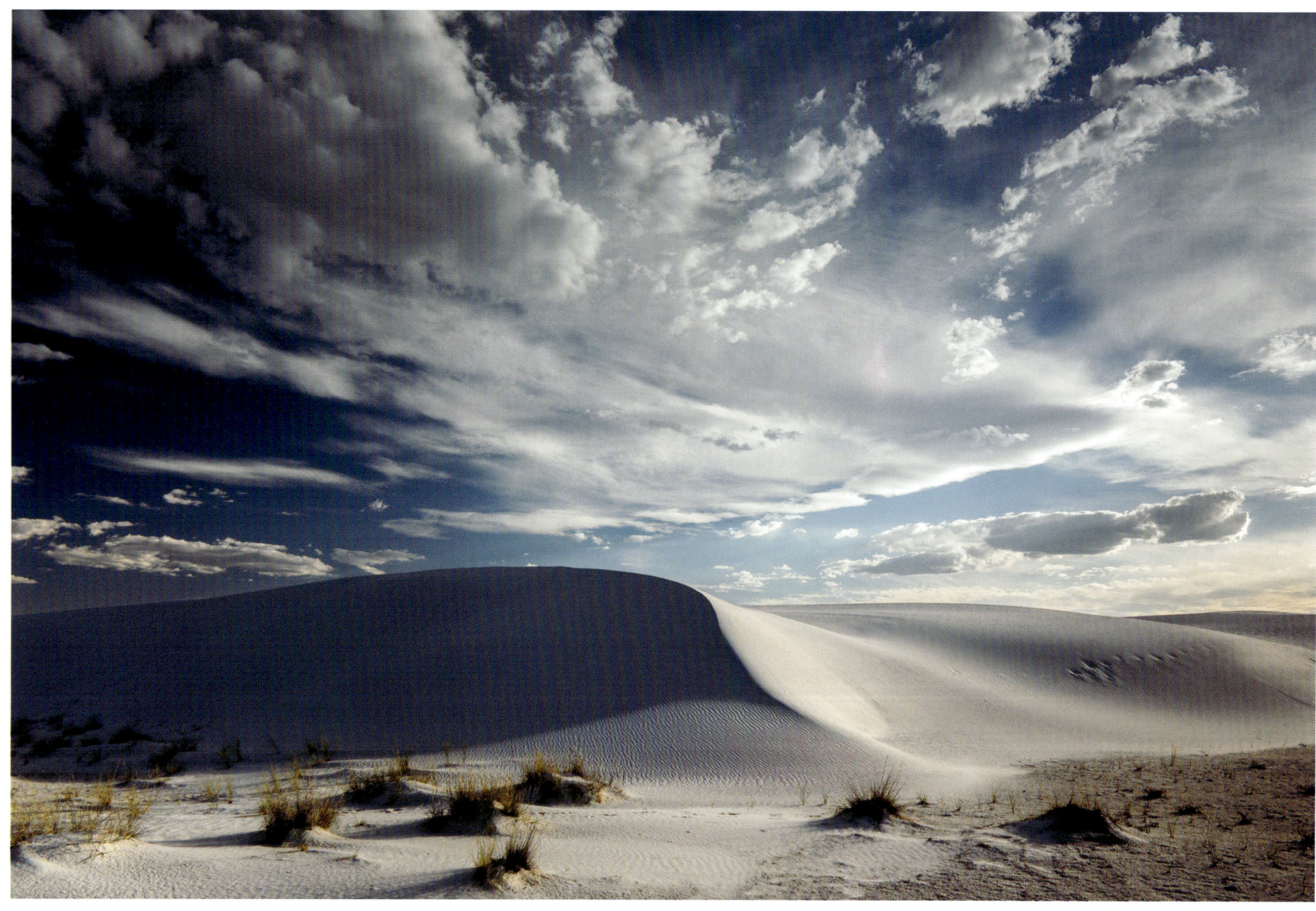

Storm Clouds over Dunes, Spring.

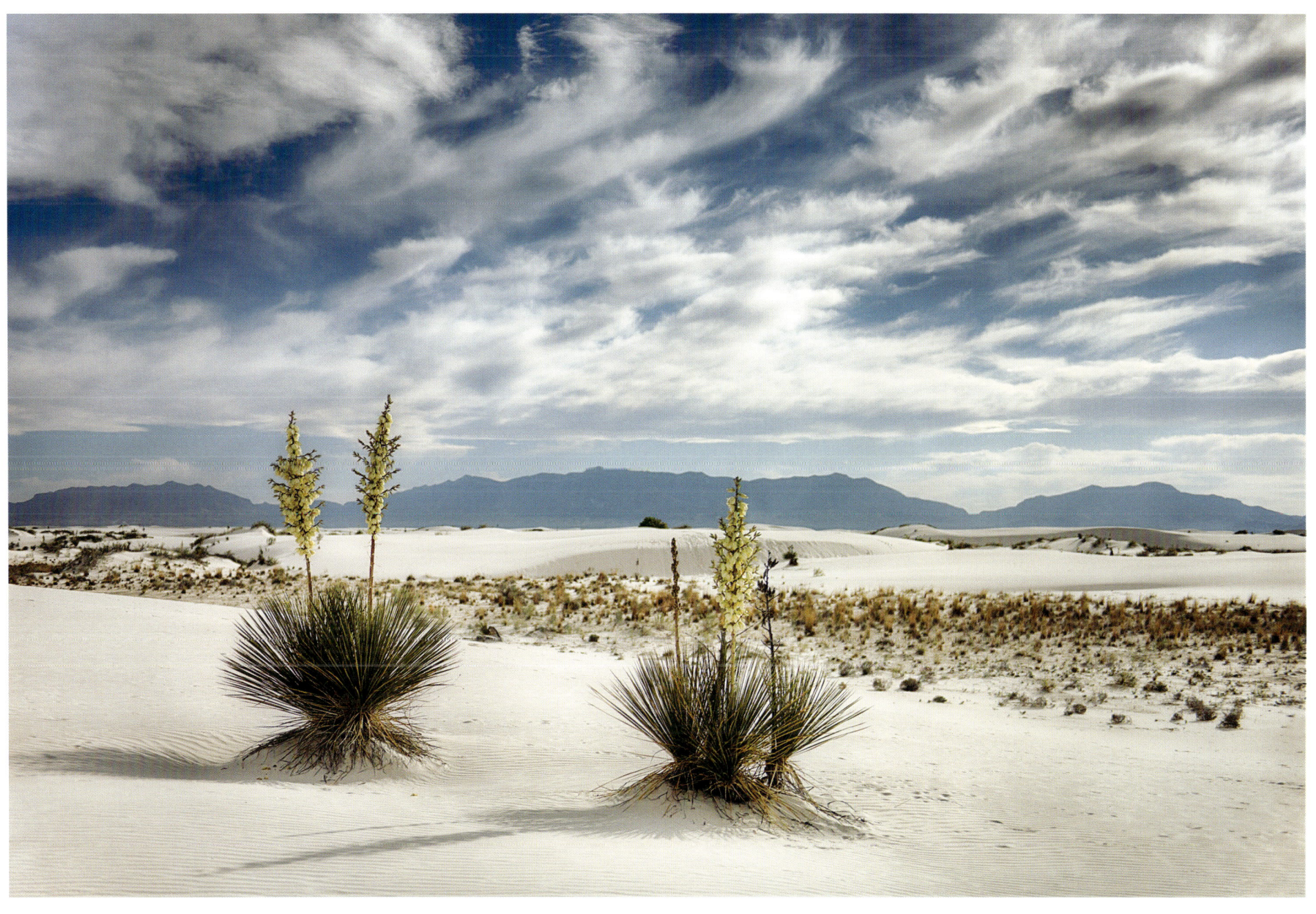

Soaptree Yuccas and Clouds, Late Afternoon, Spring.

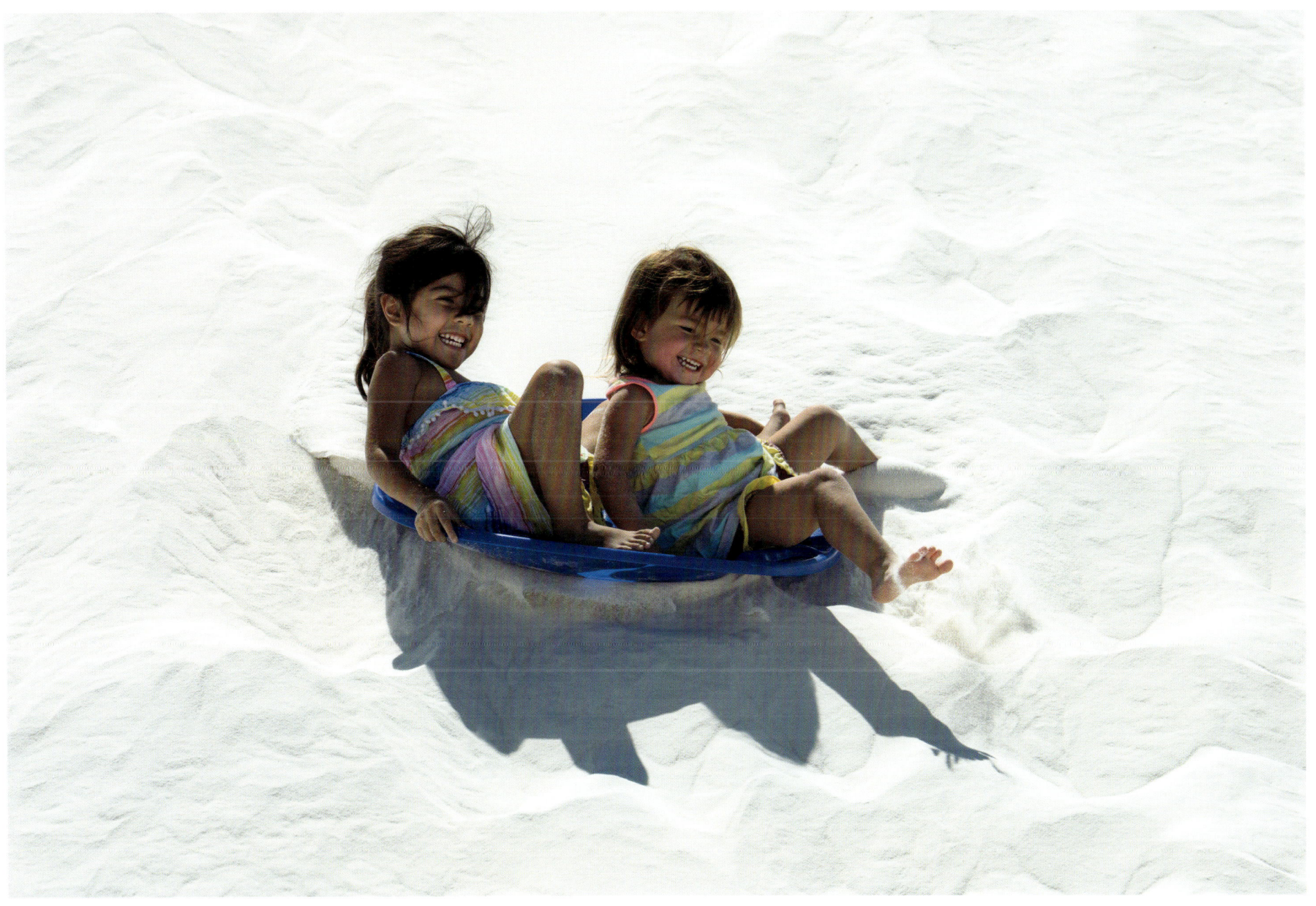

Children Sliding Down the Dunes, Spring.

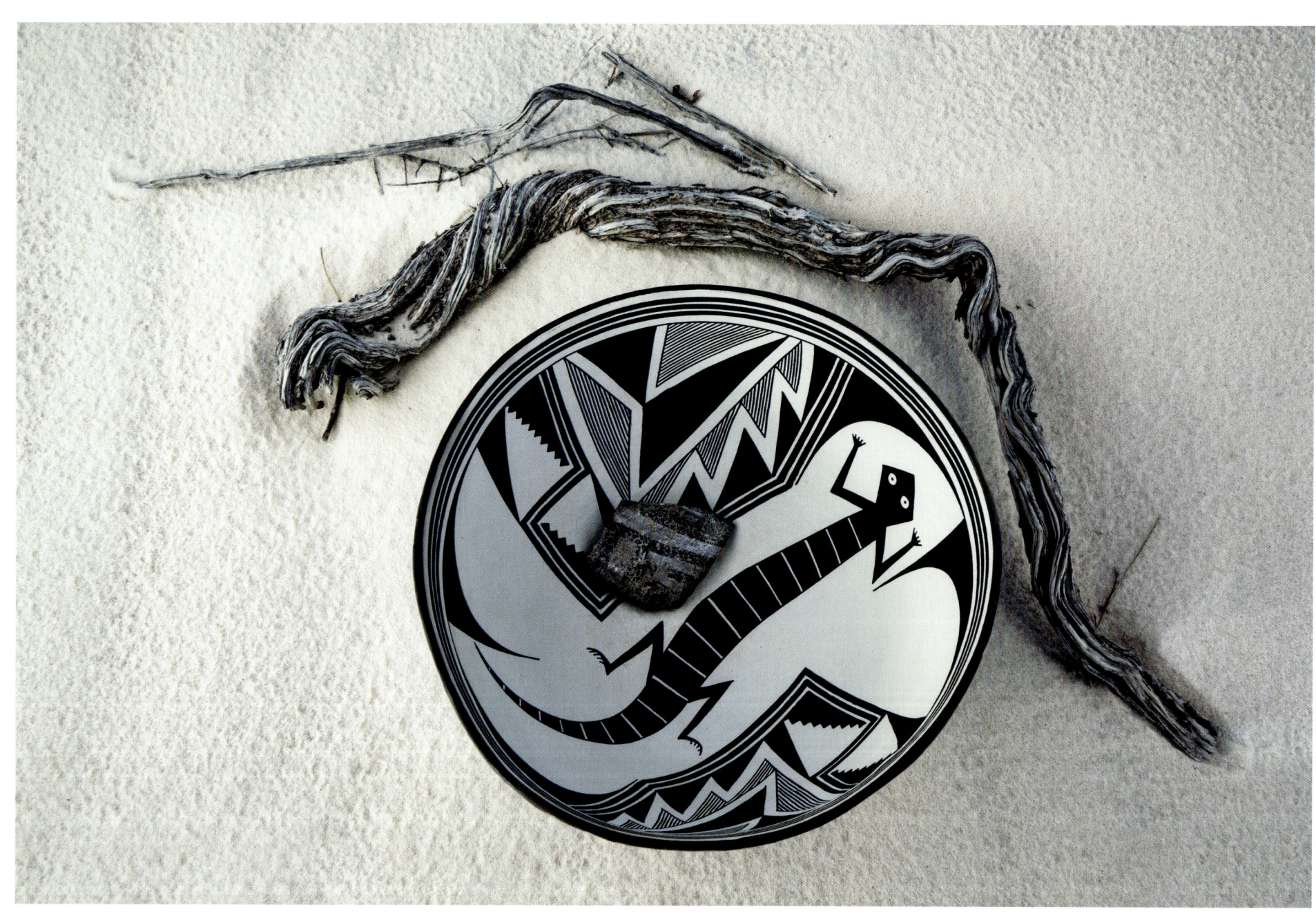

Reproduction Mimbres Black-on-White Bowl with Authentic Potsherd Found at White Sands, Spring.
Replica Mimbres Bowl was made by Paul & Laurel Thornburg of Sonita, Arizona.

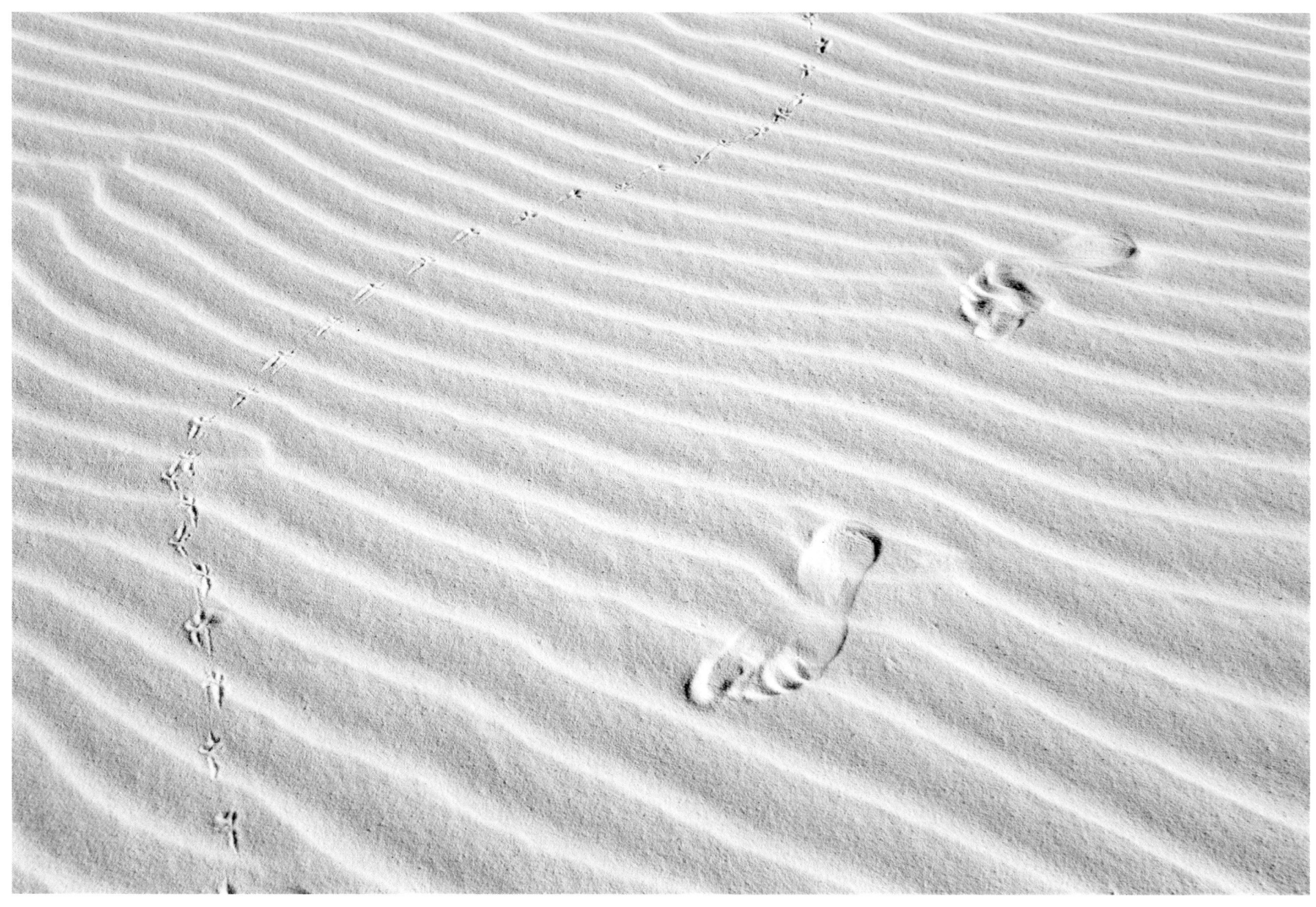

Footprints and Ripples, Spring.

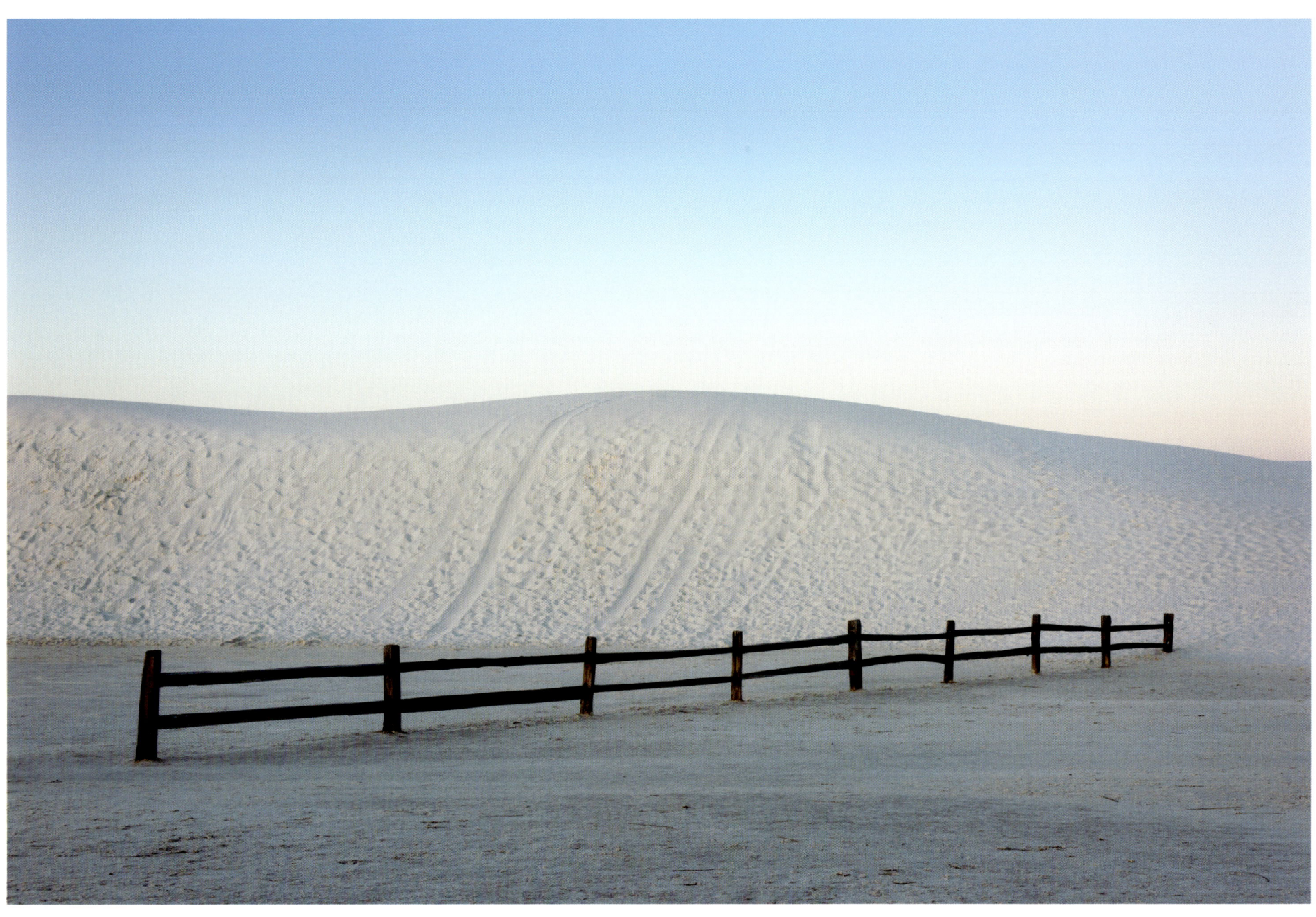

Dune and Fence, Alkali Flats Trail, Sunrise, Autumn.

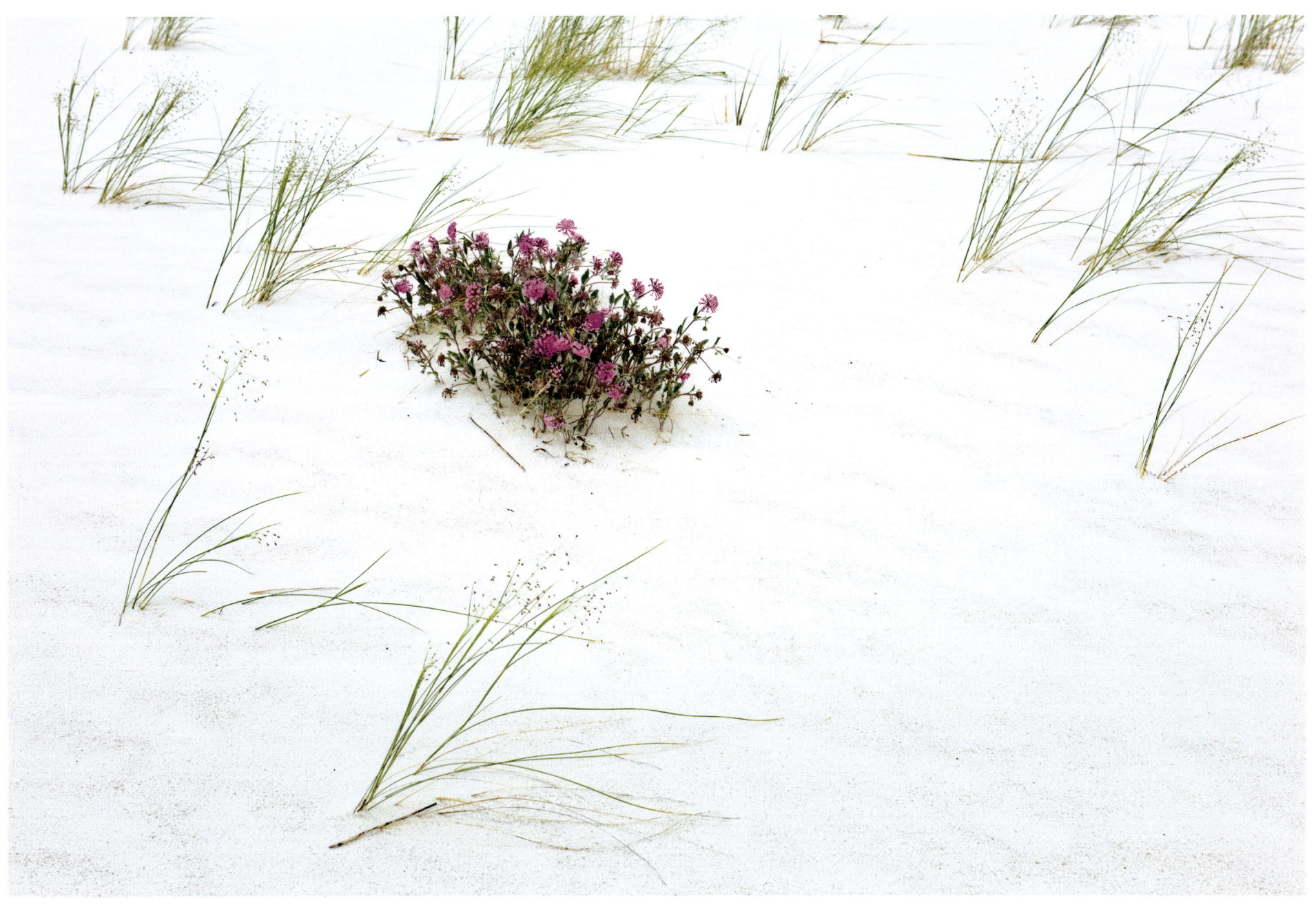

Sand Verbena and Indian Rice Grass, Spring.

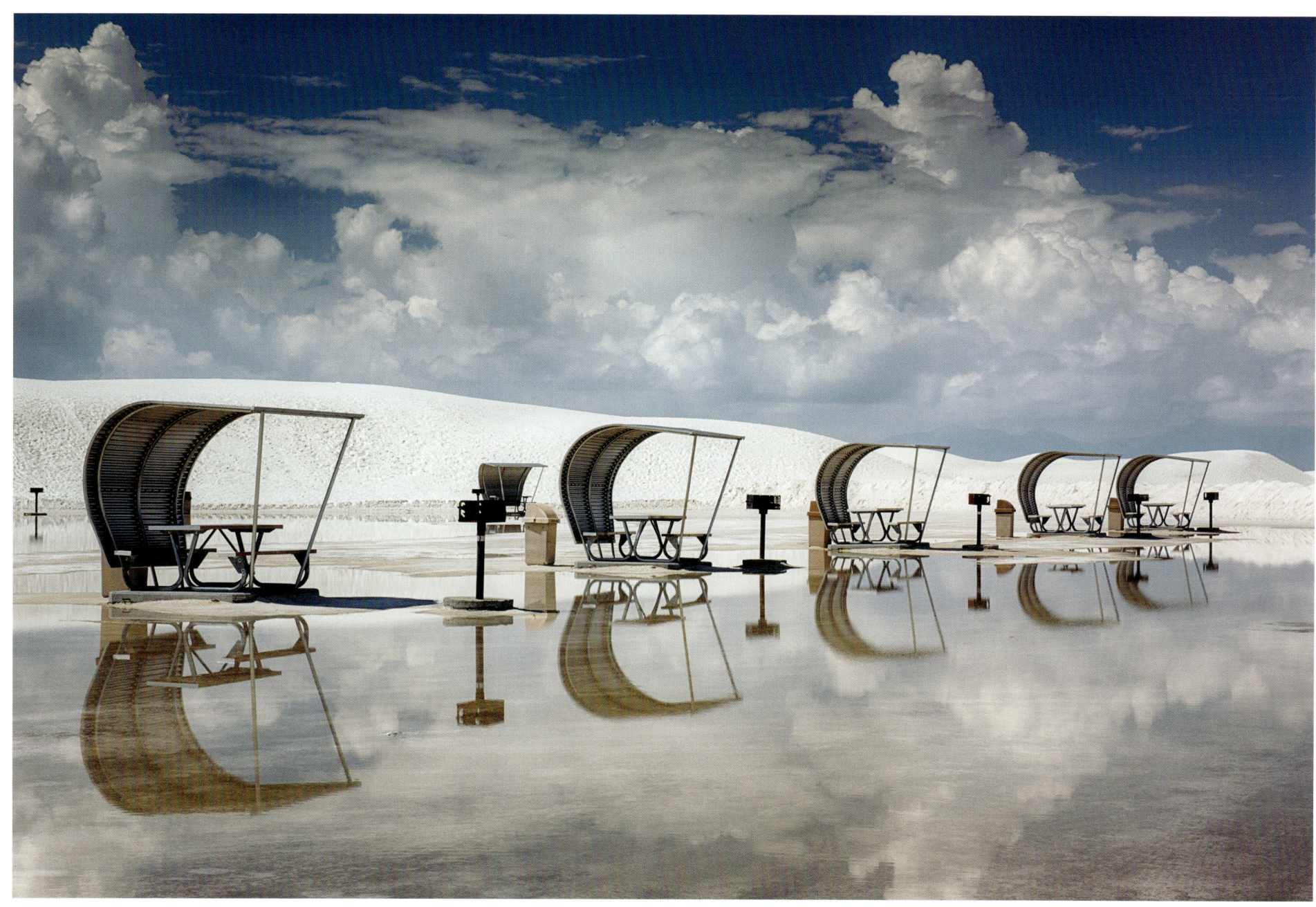

Picnic Tables after Rainstorm, Autumn.

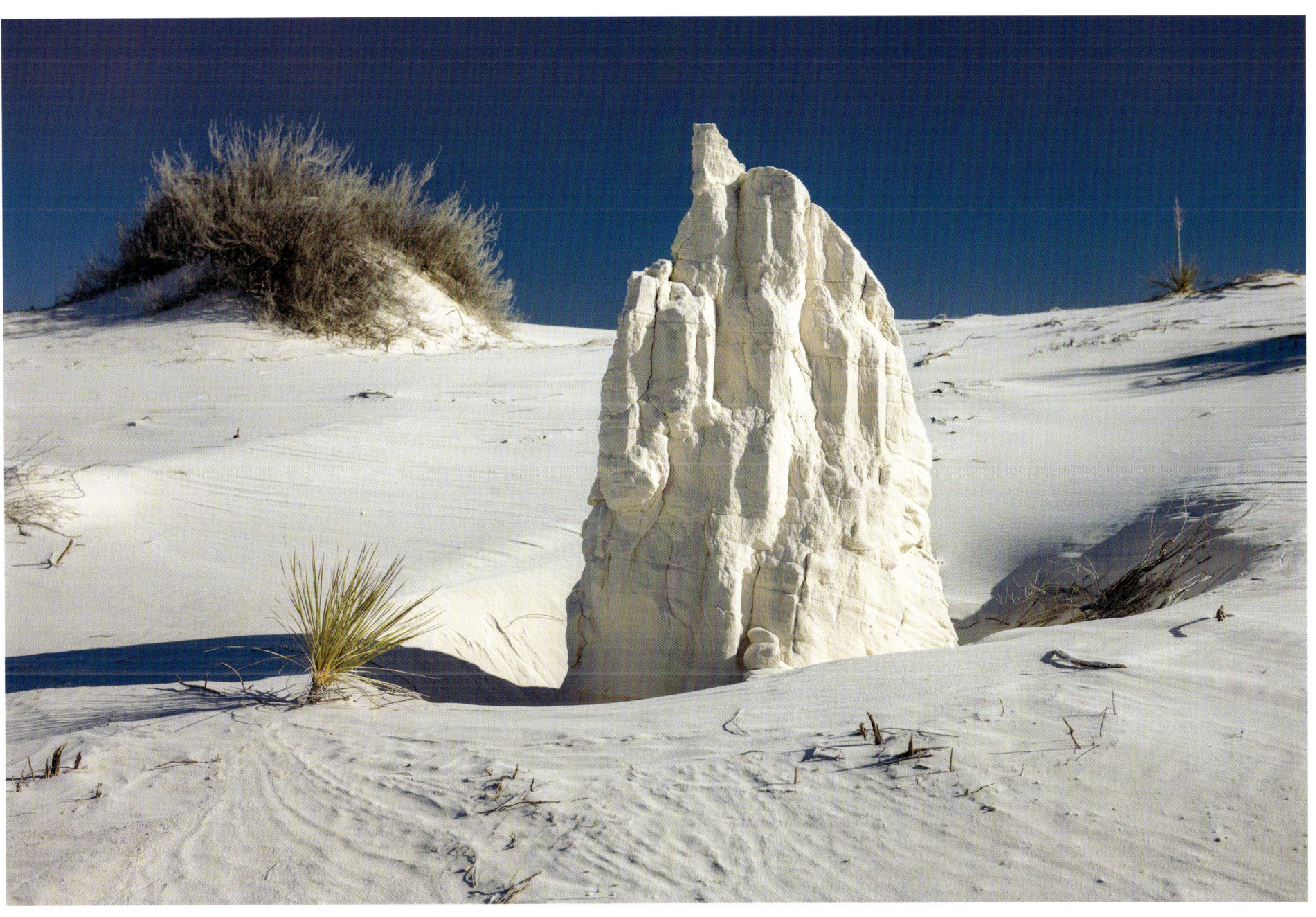

Yardang and Pedestal, Early Spring. A yardang is a sharp, irregular ridge of compact sand lying in the direction of the prevailing wind in exposed desert regions, formed by the wind erosion of adjacent material that is less resistant. Yardangs at White Sands seem to emerge from large dunes after they migrate.

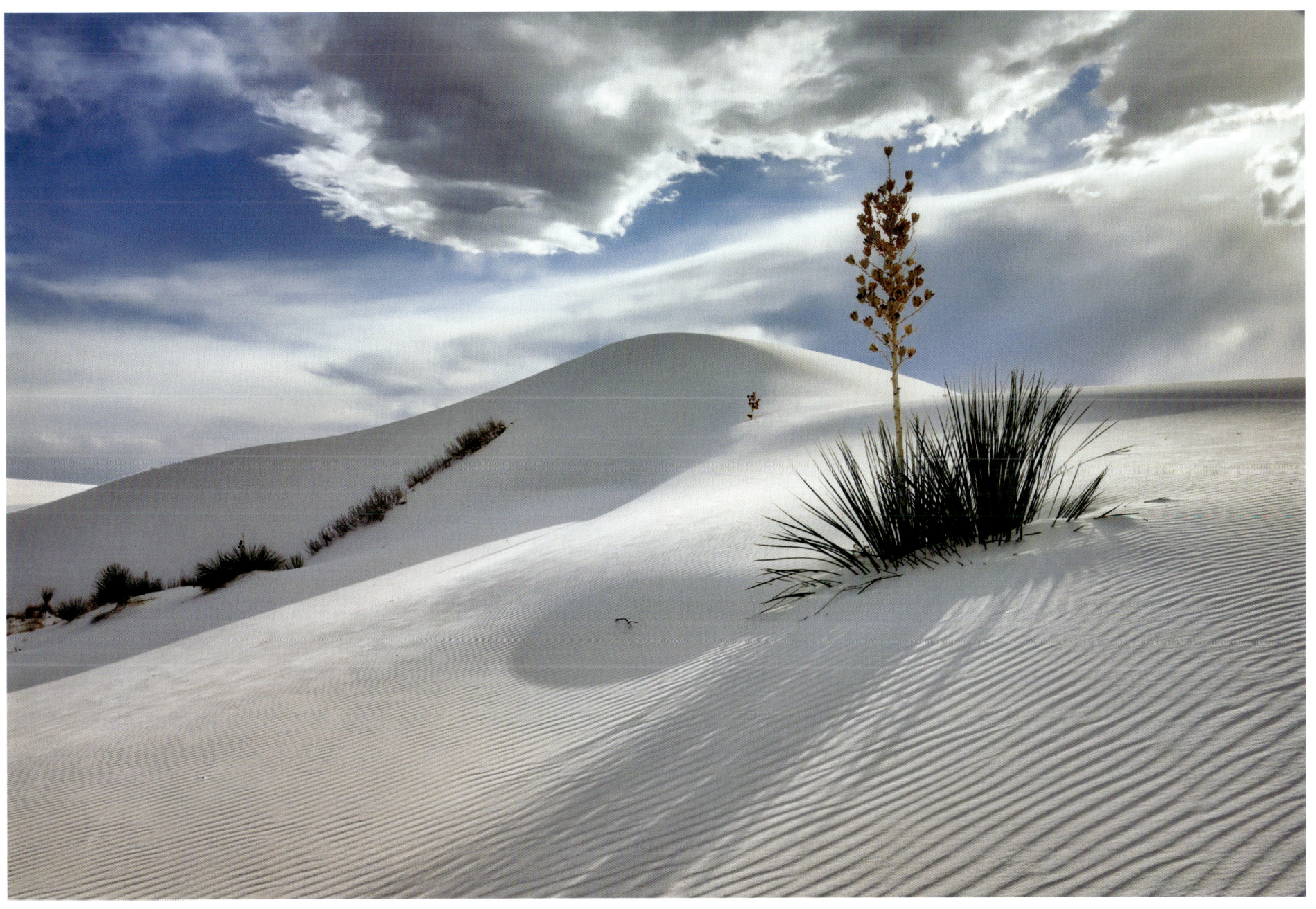

Yucca on Dune and Approaching Storm Clouds.

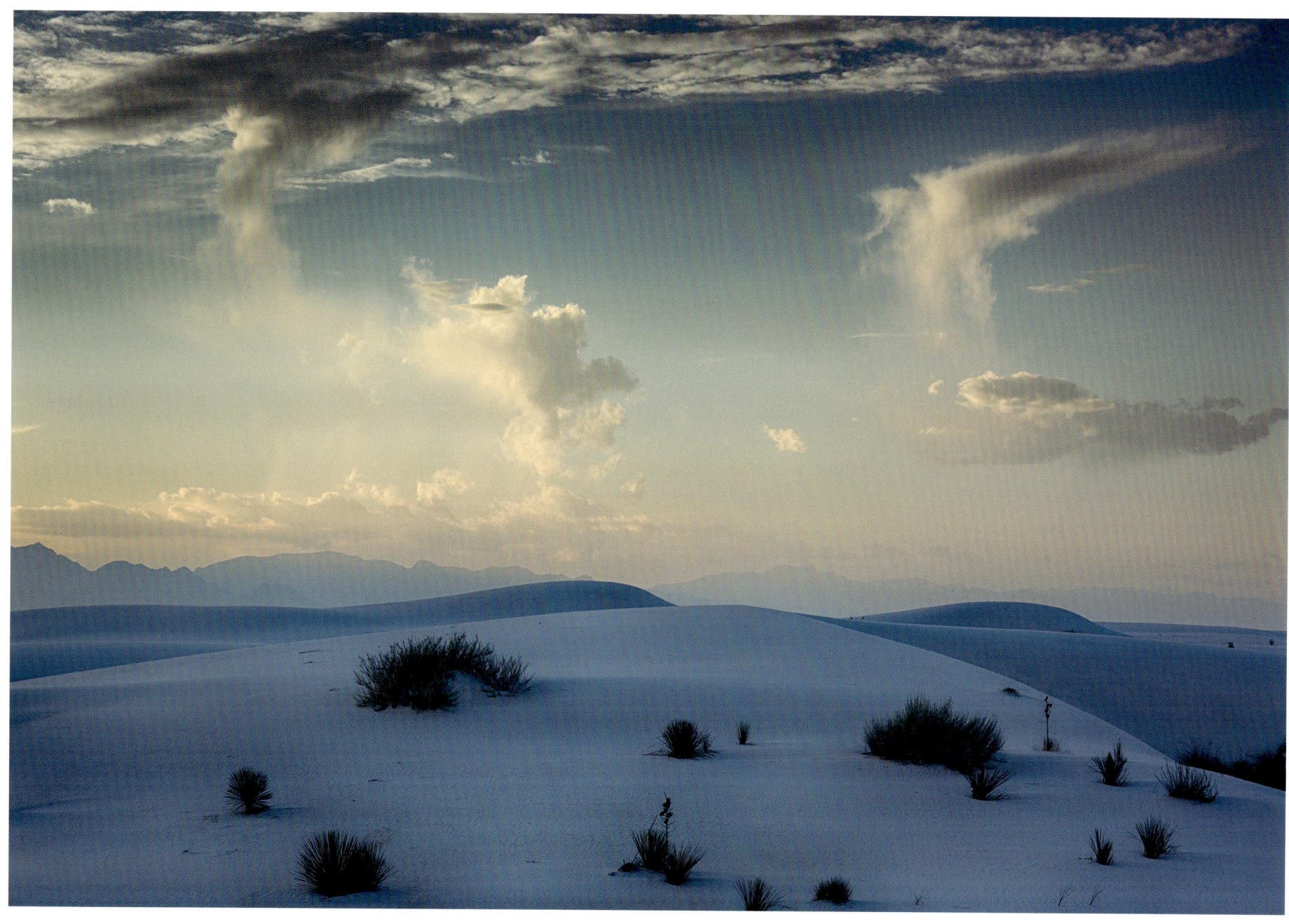

Rising Clouds over Dunes, Sunset, Autumn.

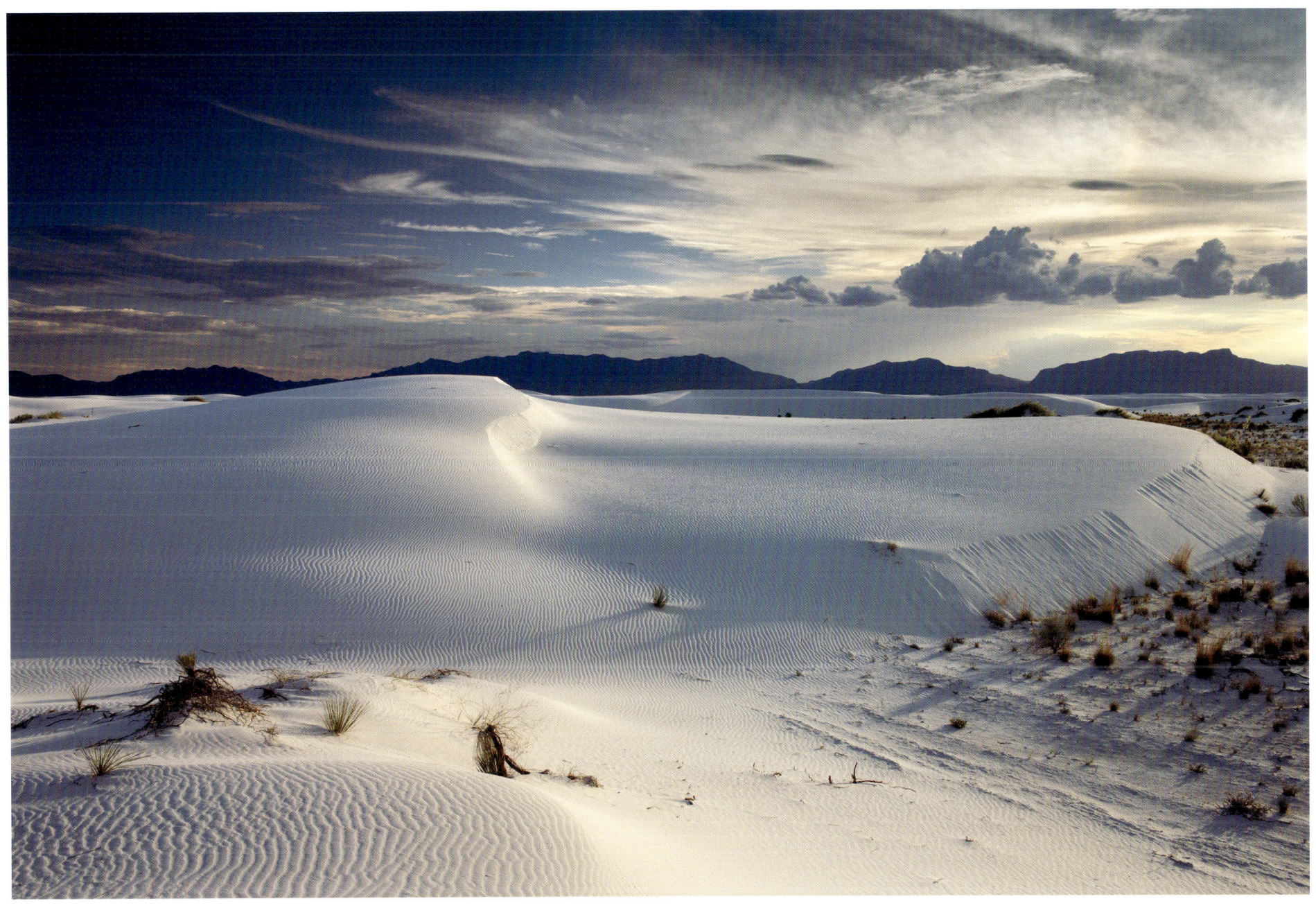

Dune Transition to Grassland Vegetation, Interdune Area, Autumn.

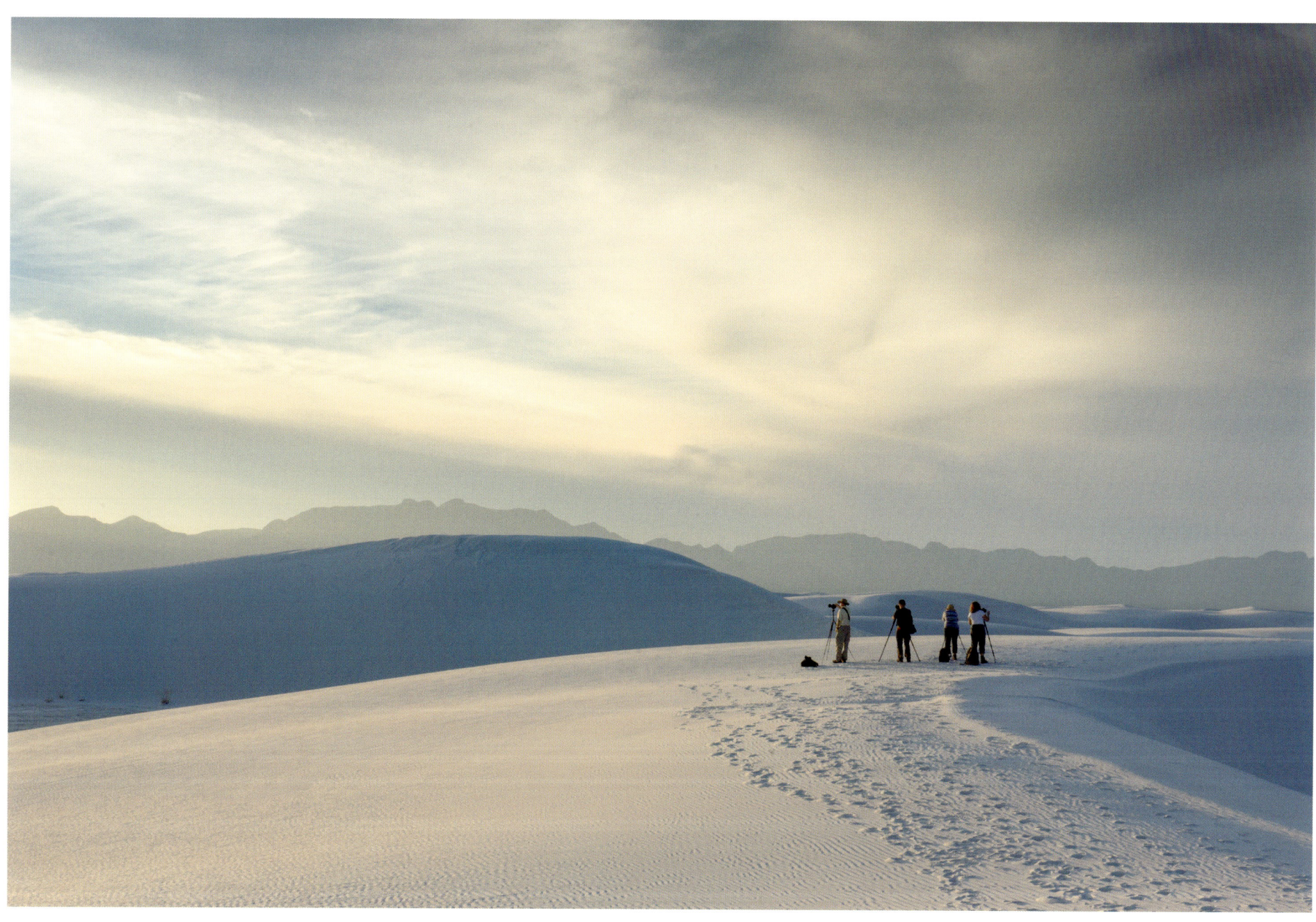

Photography Workshop on the Dunes. Photography workshops often visit White Sands
to experience and learn how to photograph the extraordinary dunes.

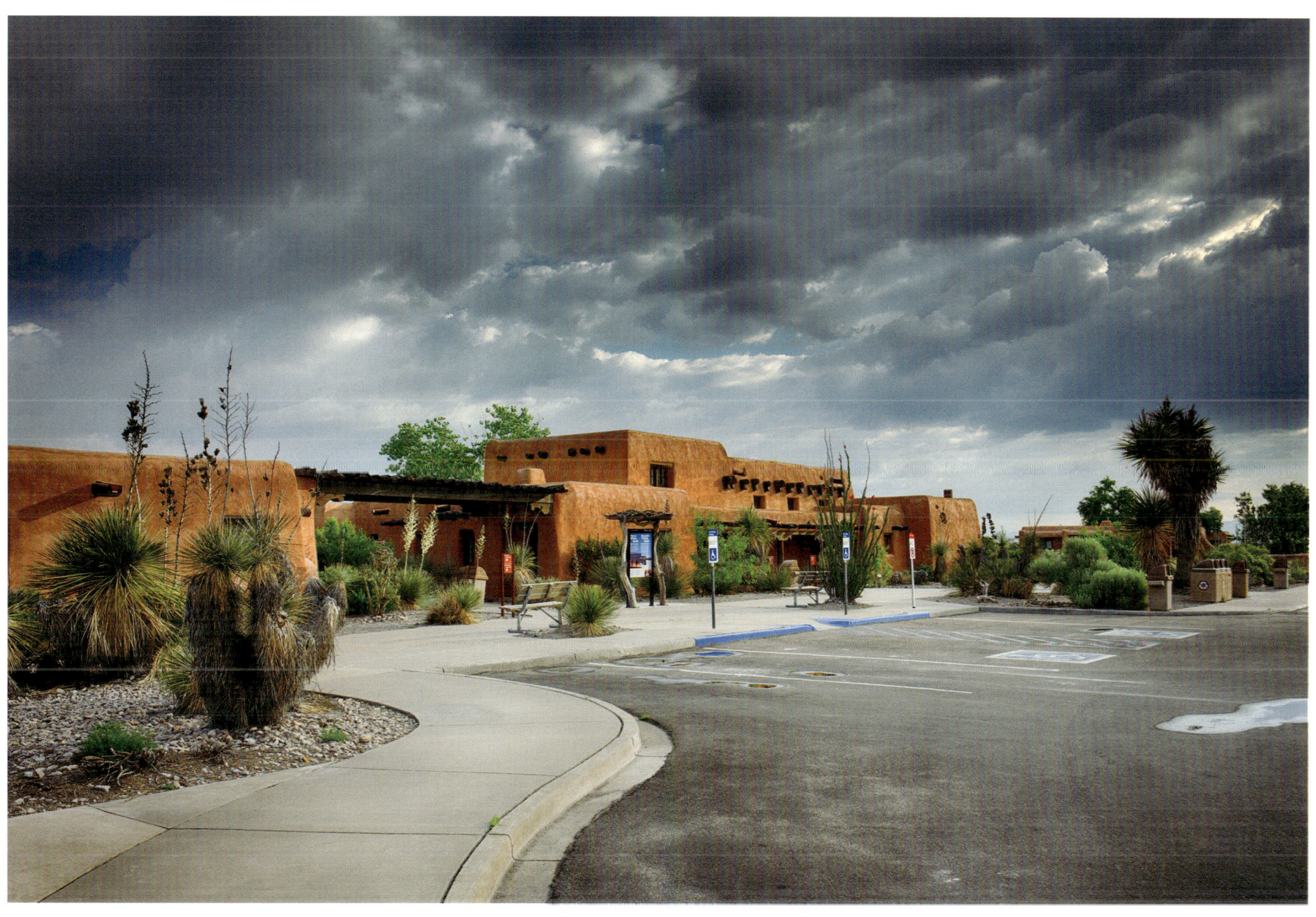

Historic Adobe Visitor Center and Approaching Storm, Spring. The Pueblo Revival–styled Visitor Center, designed by Lyle Bennett in the 1930s, was built with adobe bricks by several government agencies, including the Works Progress Administration, a prominent public works program created in the late 1930s by President Franklin Roosevelt.

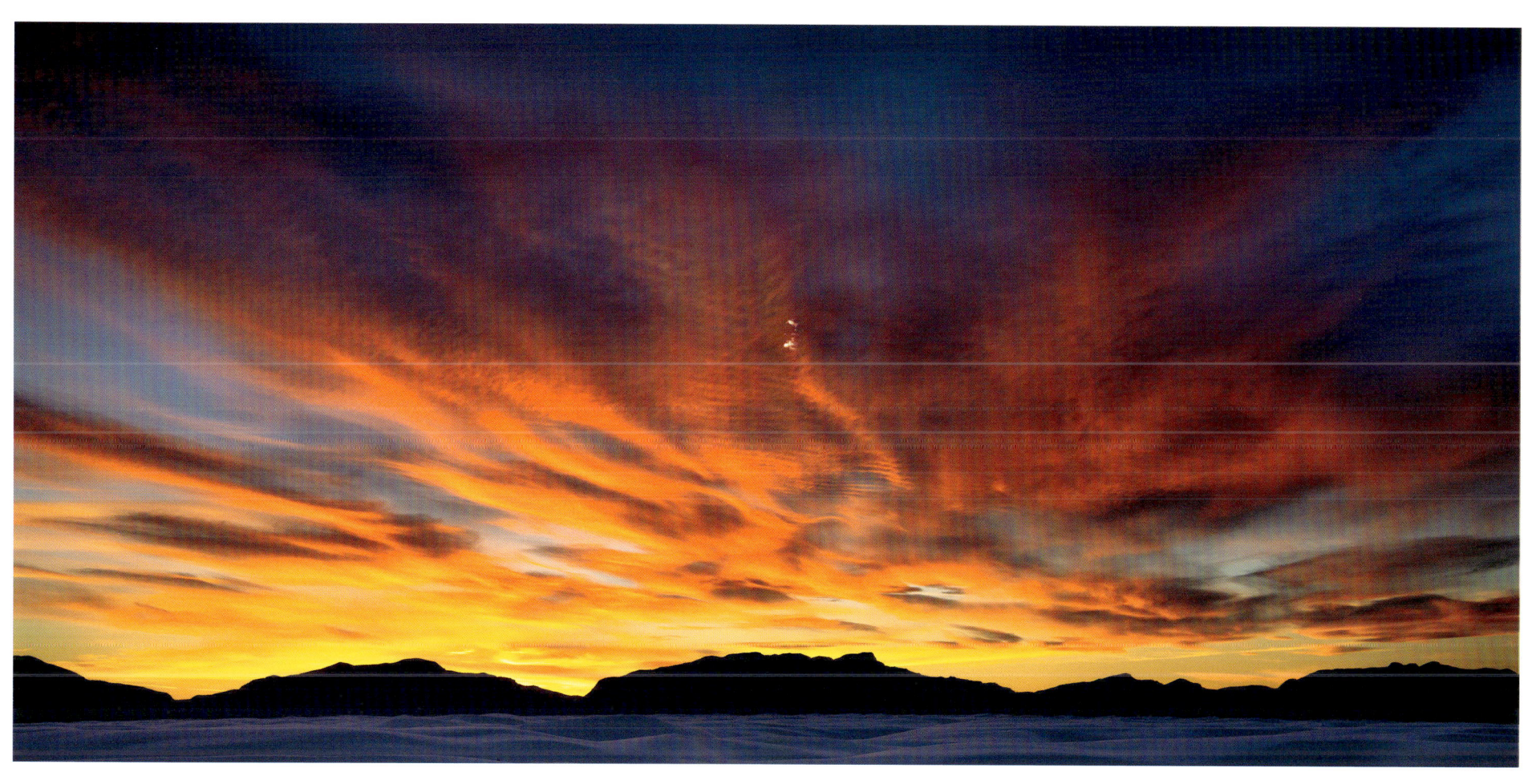

Farewell Sunset, Spring

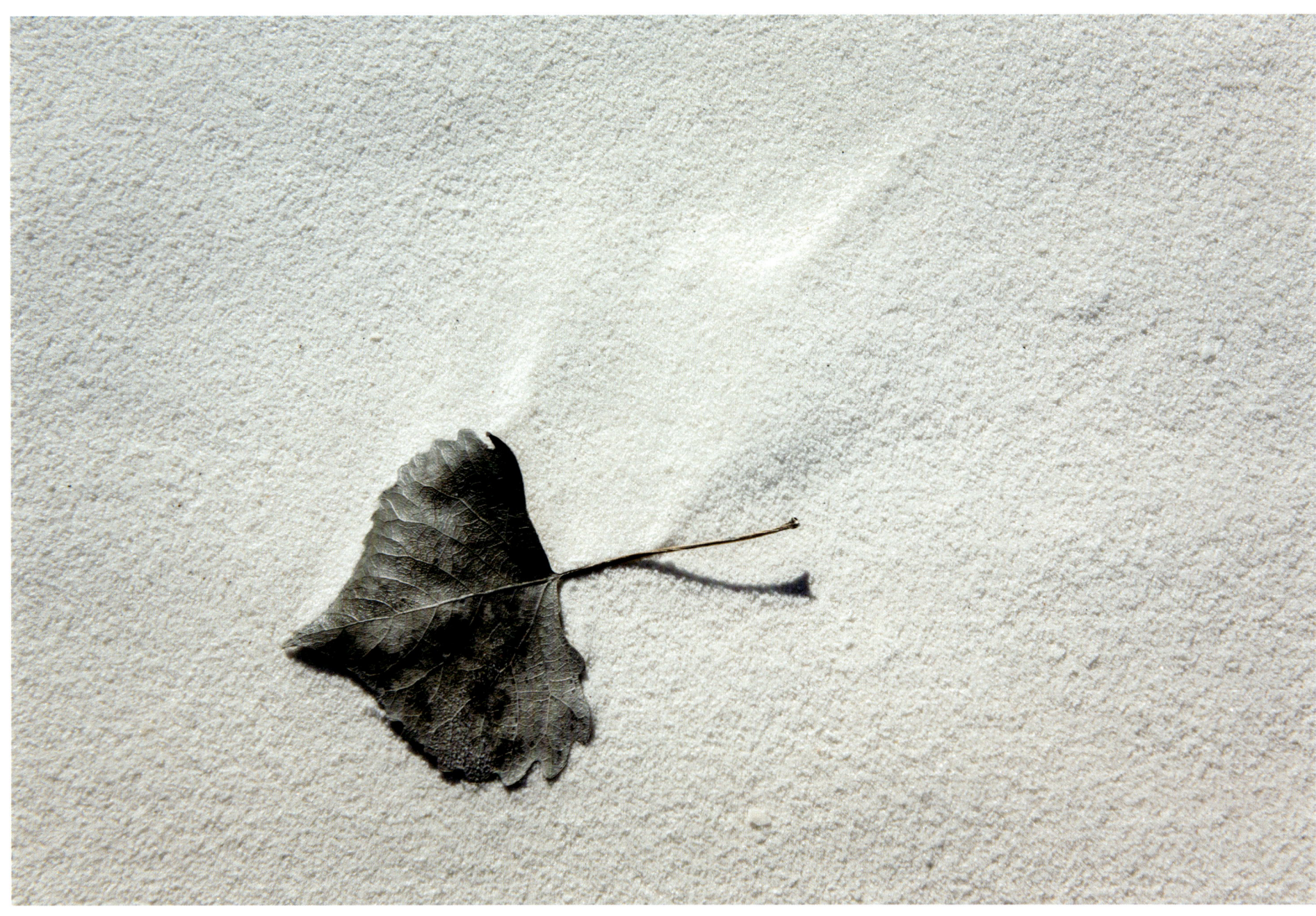

Cottonwood Leaf, Spring.

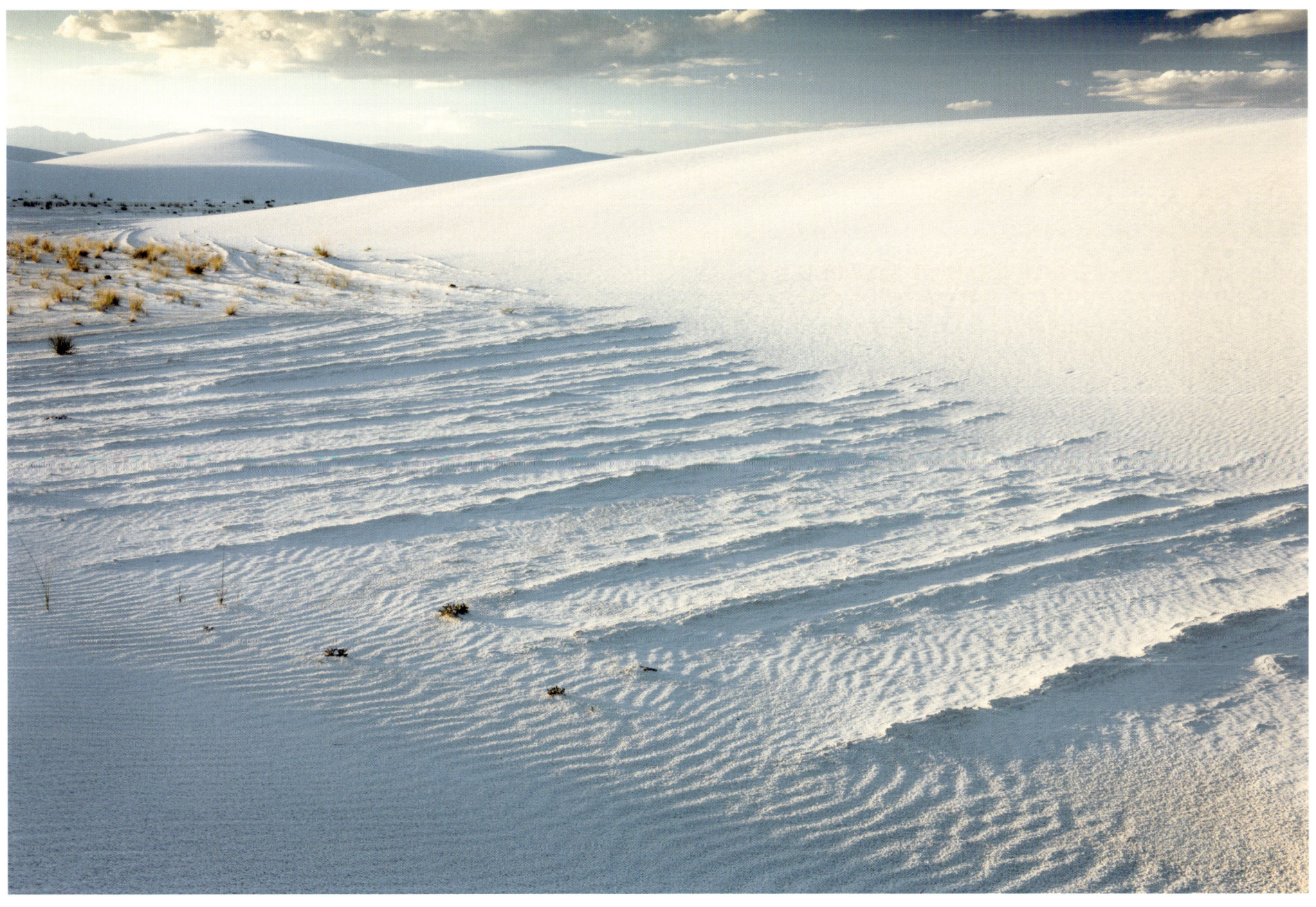

Footprints left by Moving Dunes, Autumn.

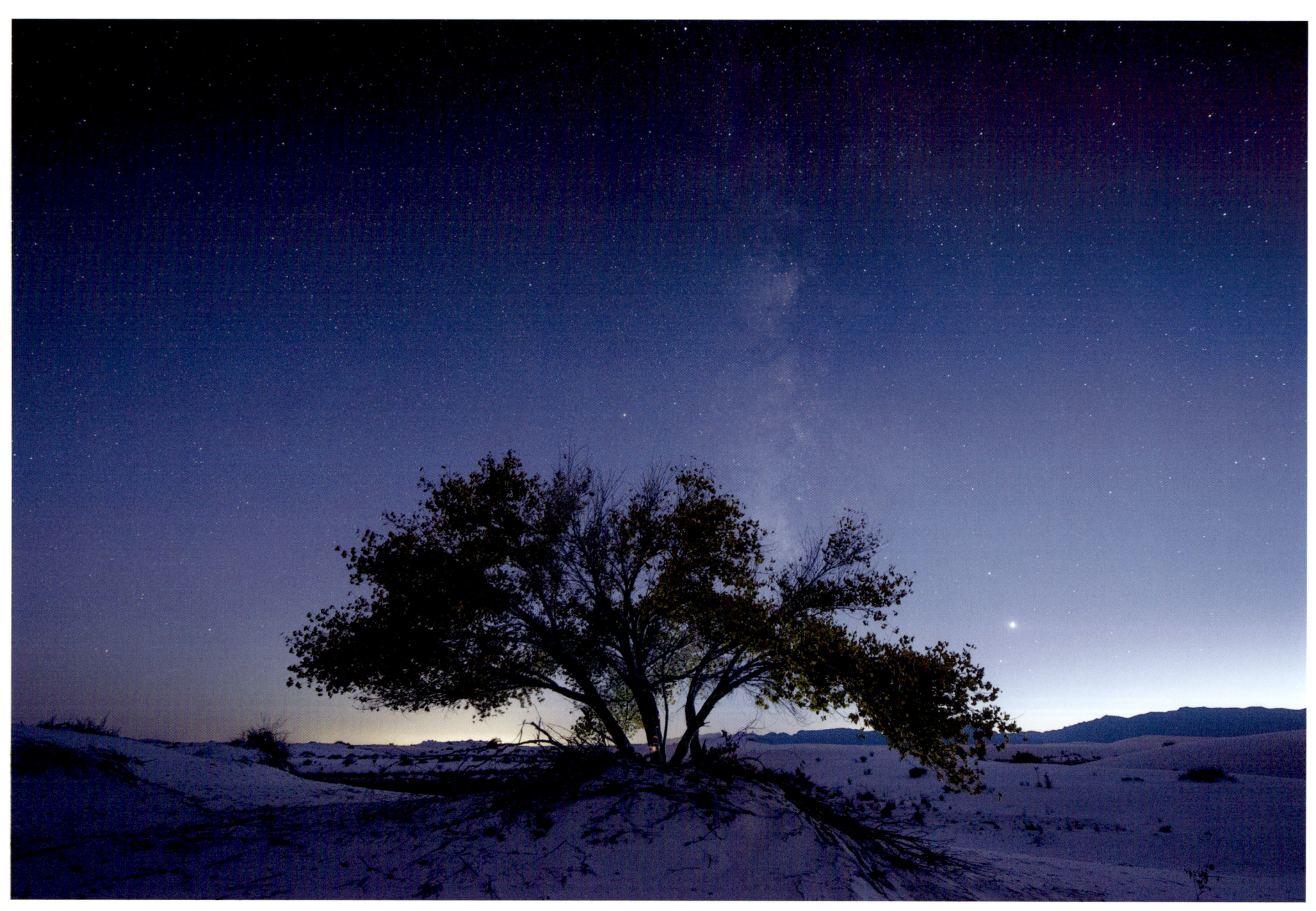

Cottonwood Tree and Milky Way, Blue Hour, Autumn. While the Milky Way is visible from March to October in the Northern Hemisphere, the best time to view and photograph it is from late April to late July because the galactic center is visible for a longer time during the night.

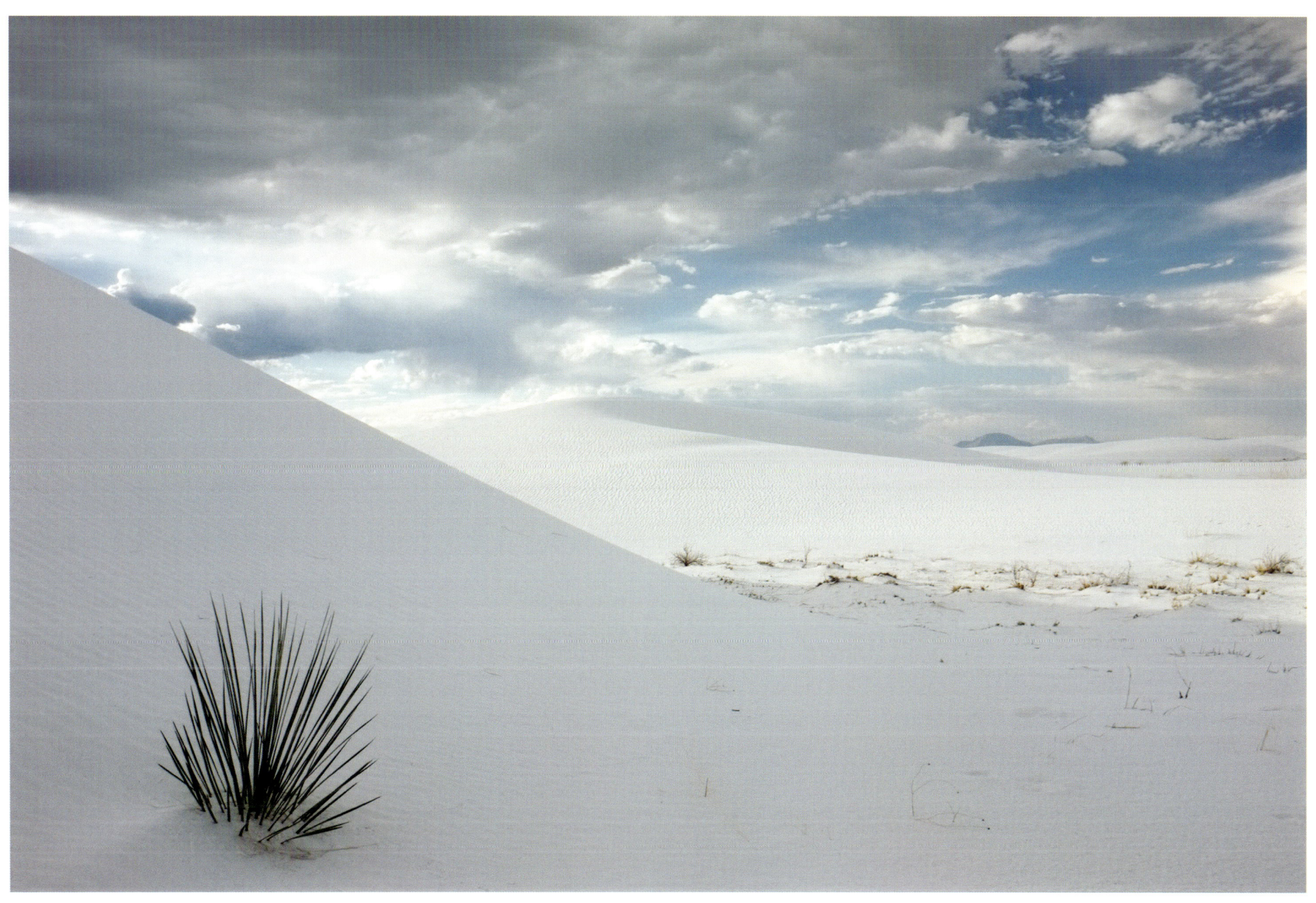

Barchan Dune and Soaptree Yucca, Heart of the Dunes, Summer.

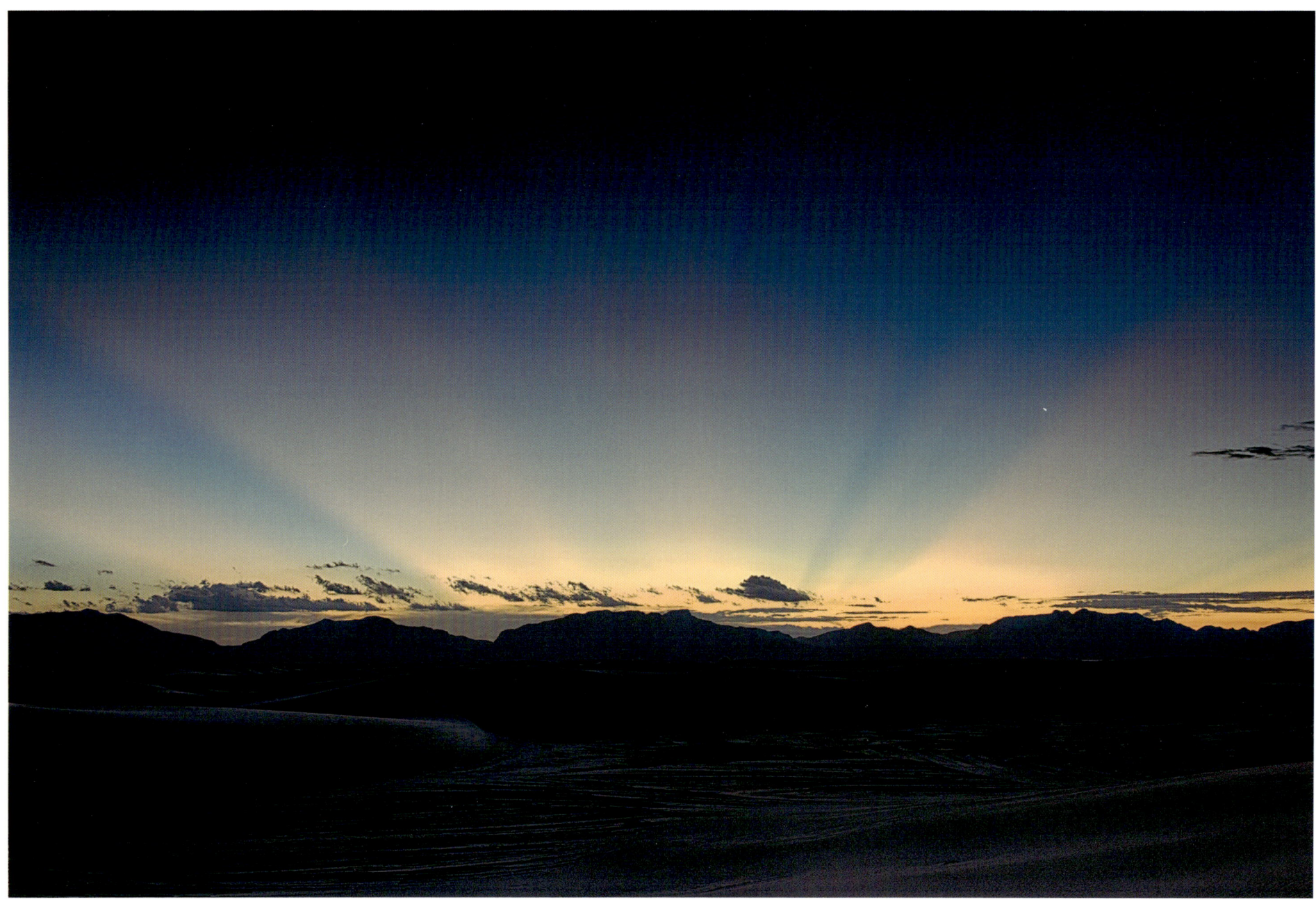

Sunset Streaks over San Andres Mountains, Autumn.

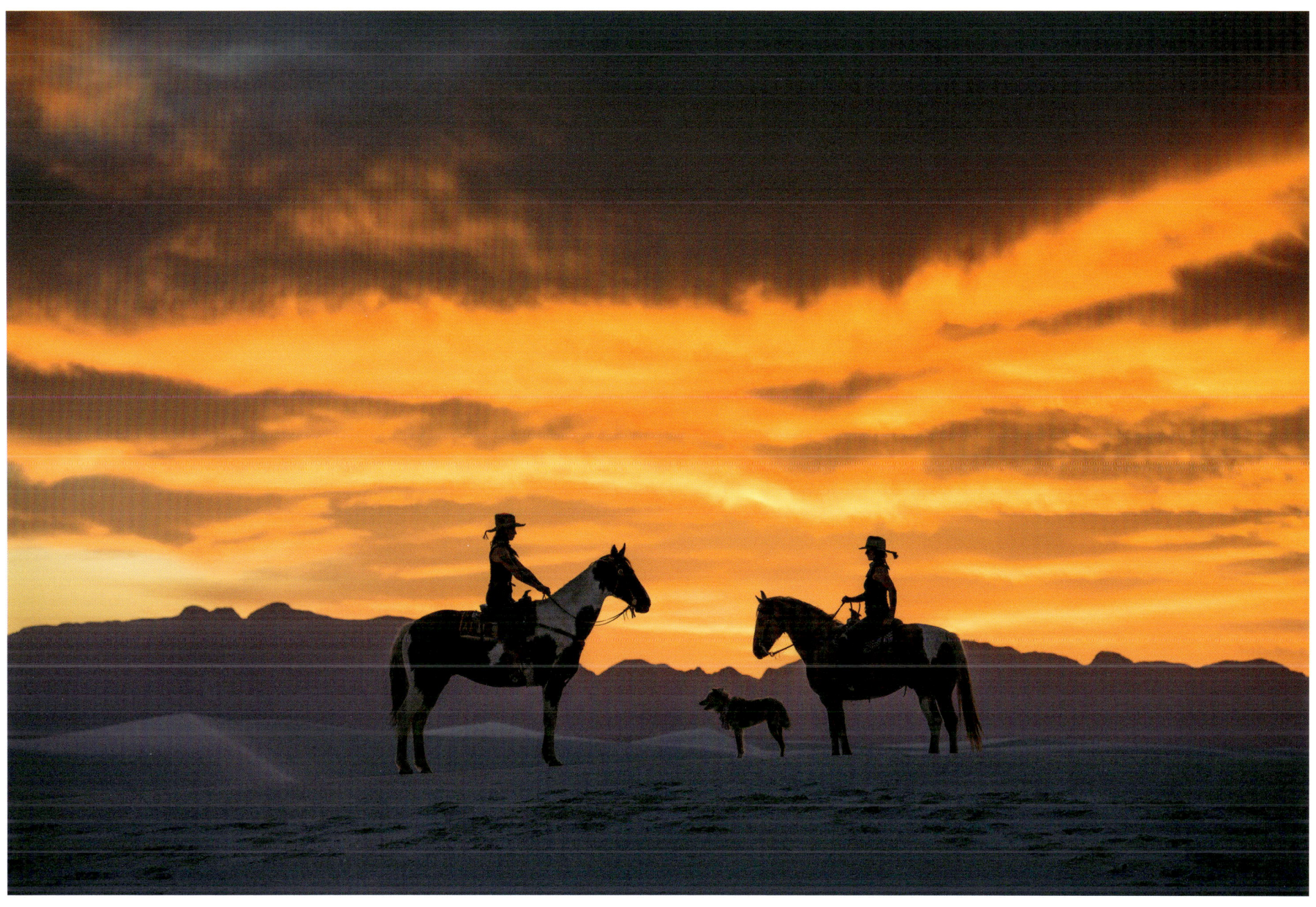

Horses at Sunset, Late Summer.

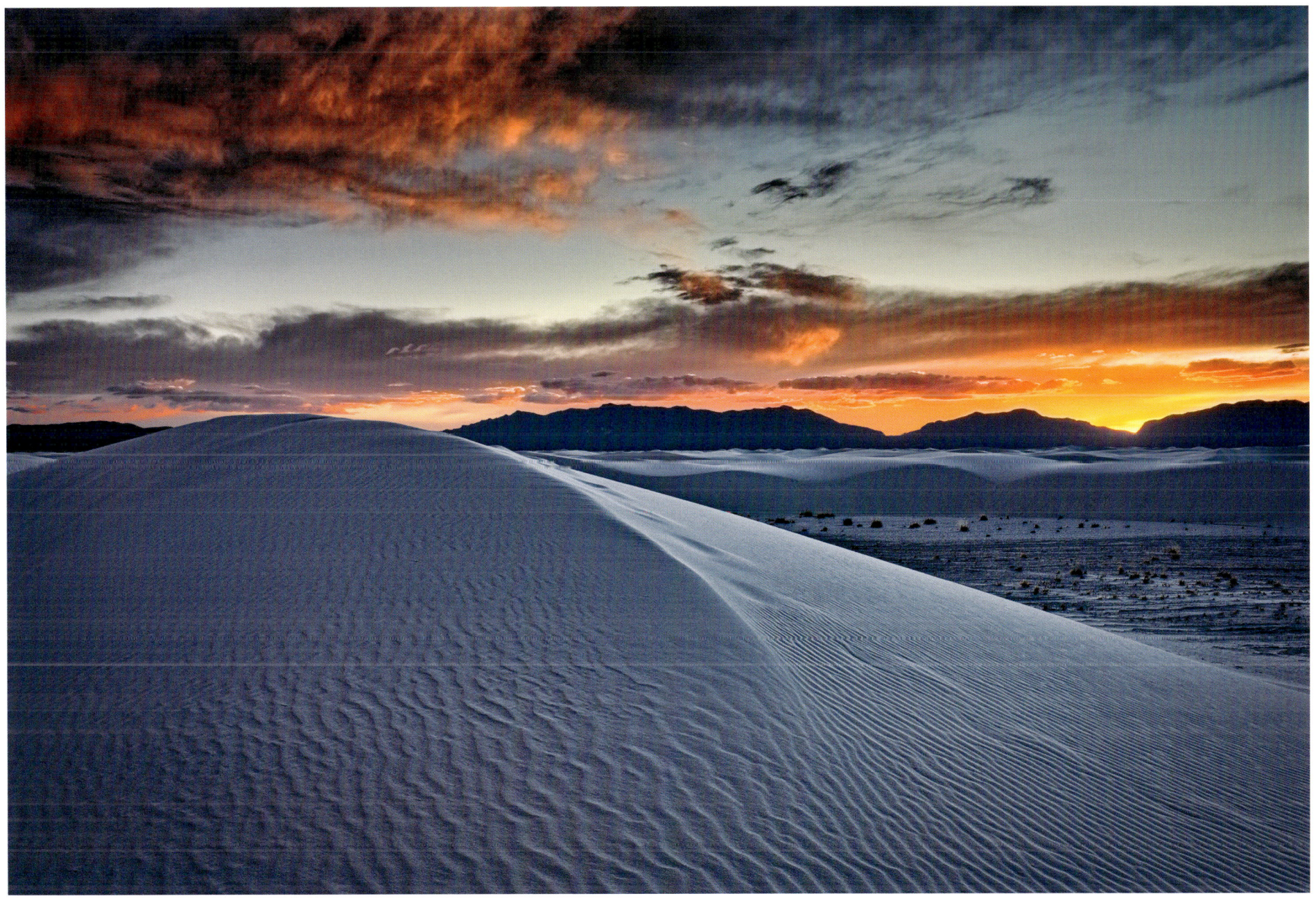

Red Sky and Dunes at Sunset, Autumn.

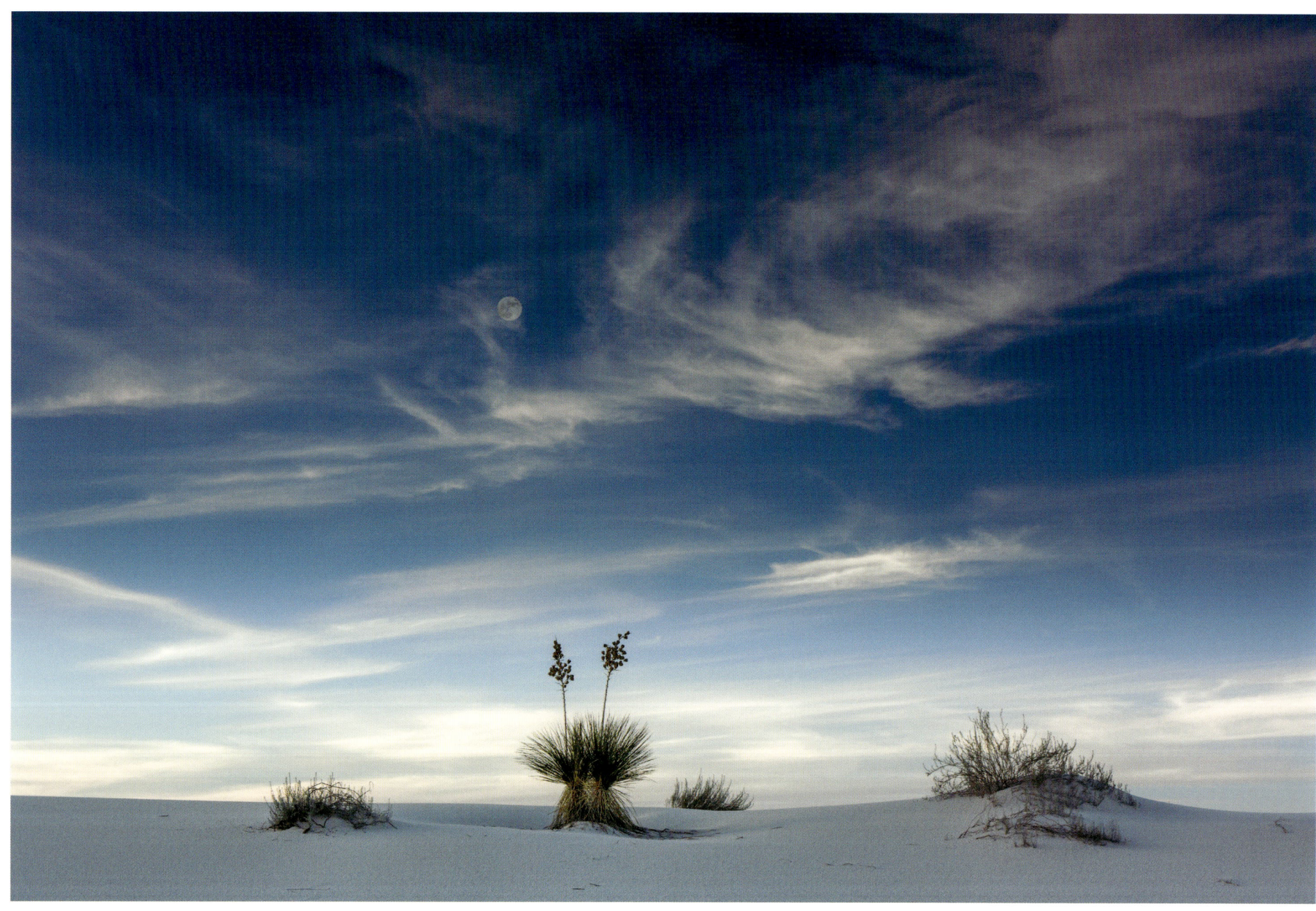

Moon over Yuccas, Autumn.

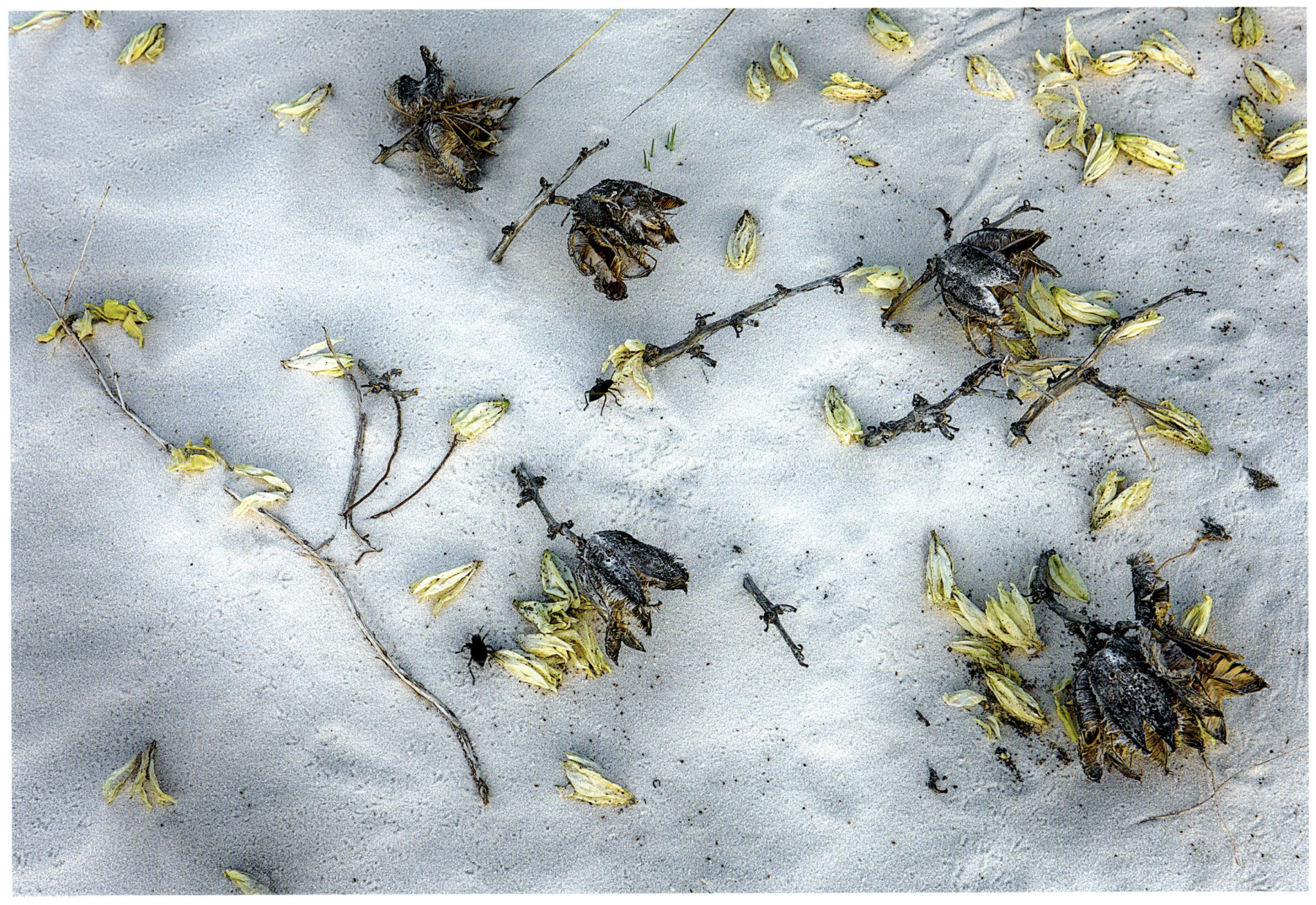

Fallen Yucca Blossoms with Beetles, Spring.

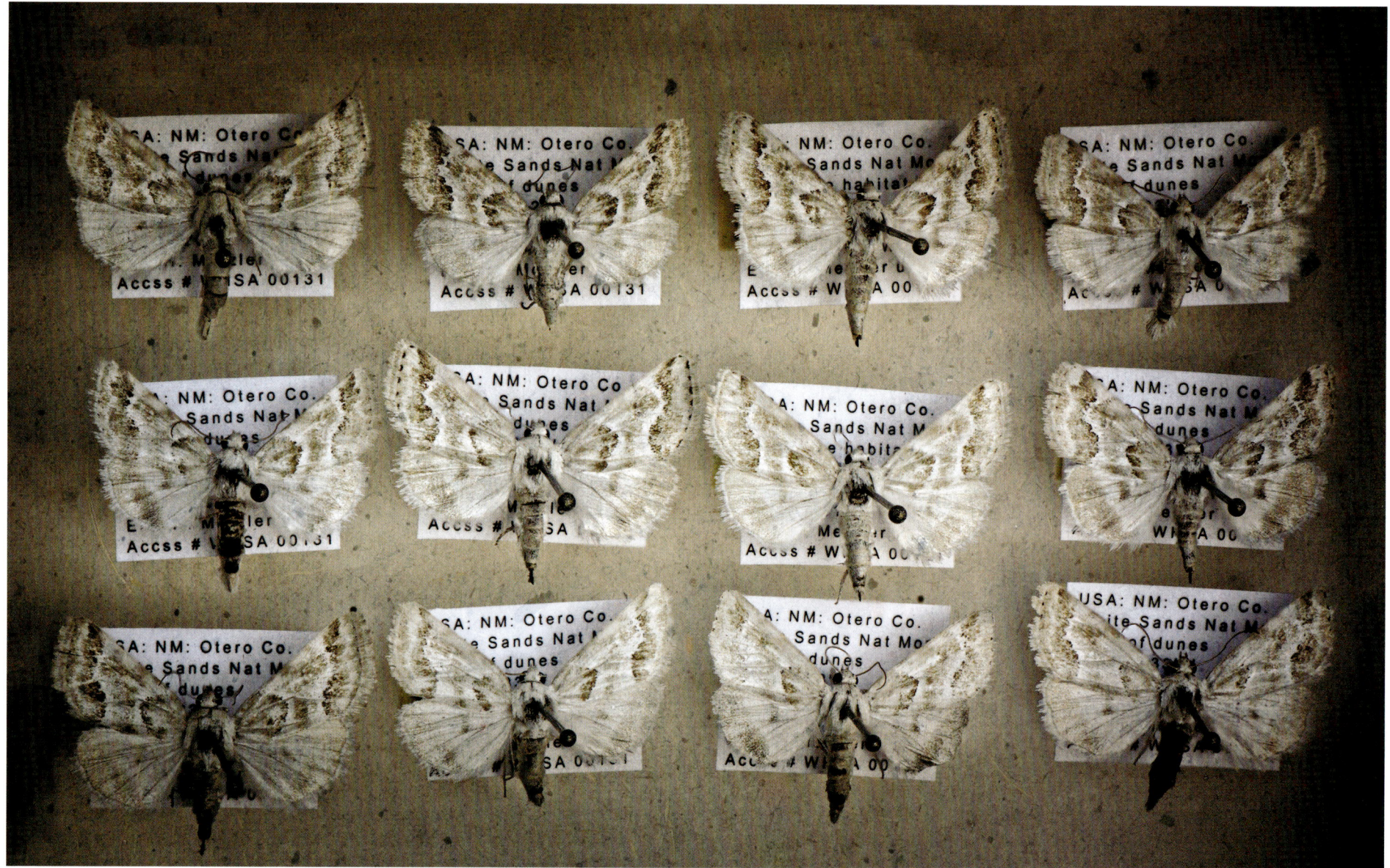

White Sands Schinia Moth. Schinia poguei is a new species of moth discovered at White Sands by Eric H. Metzler.

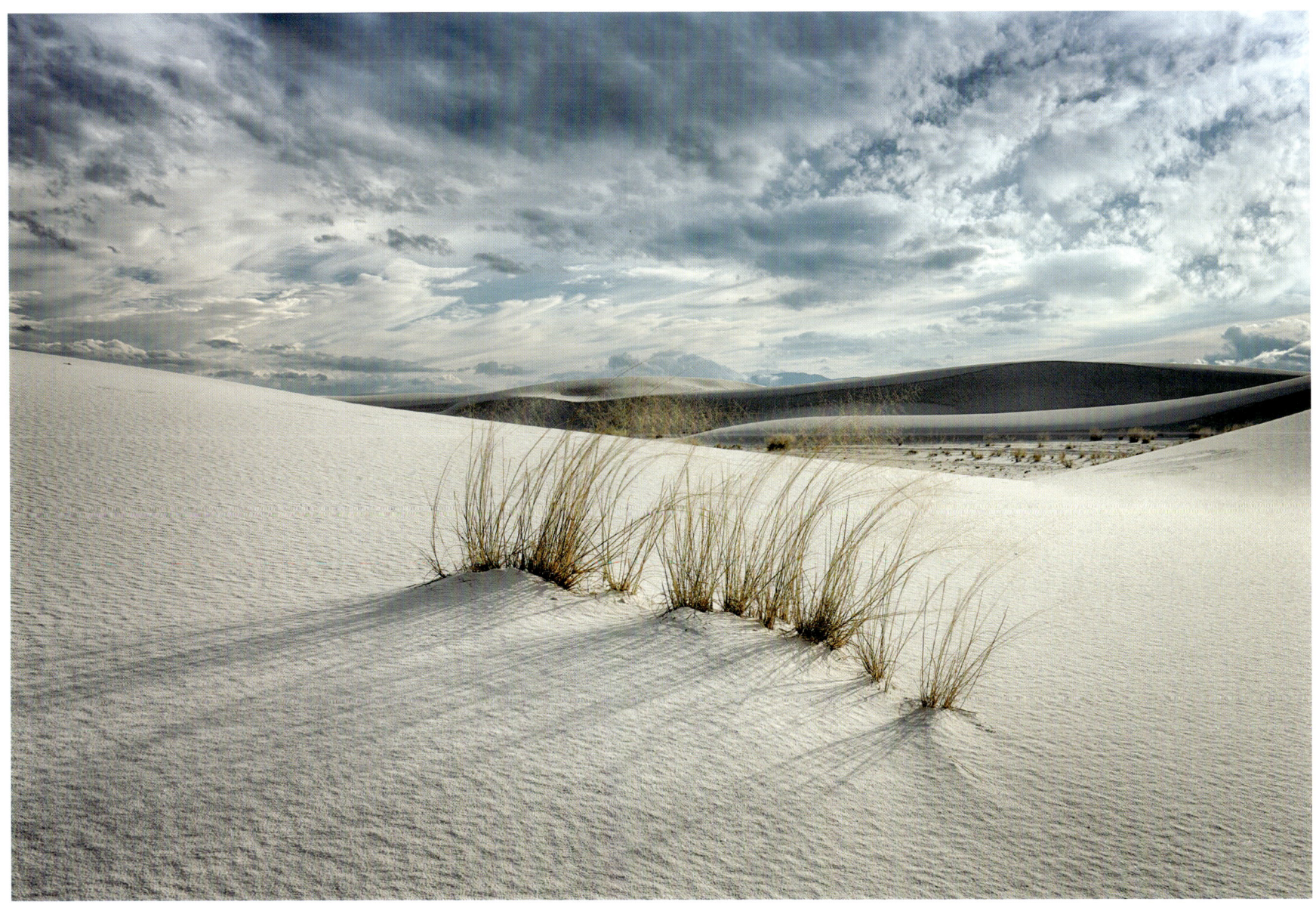

Alkali Sacaton Grass on Dunes, Winter.

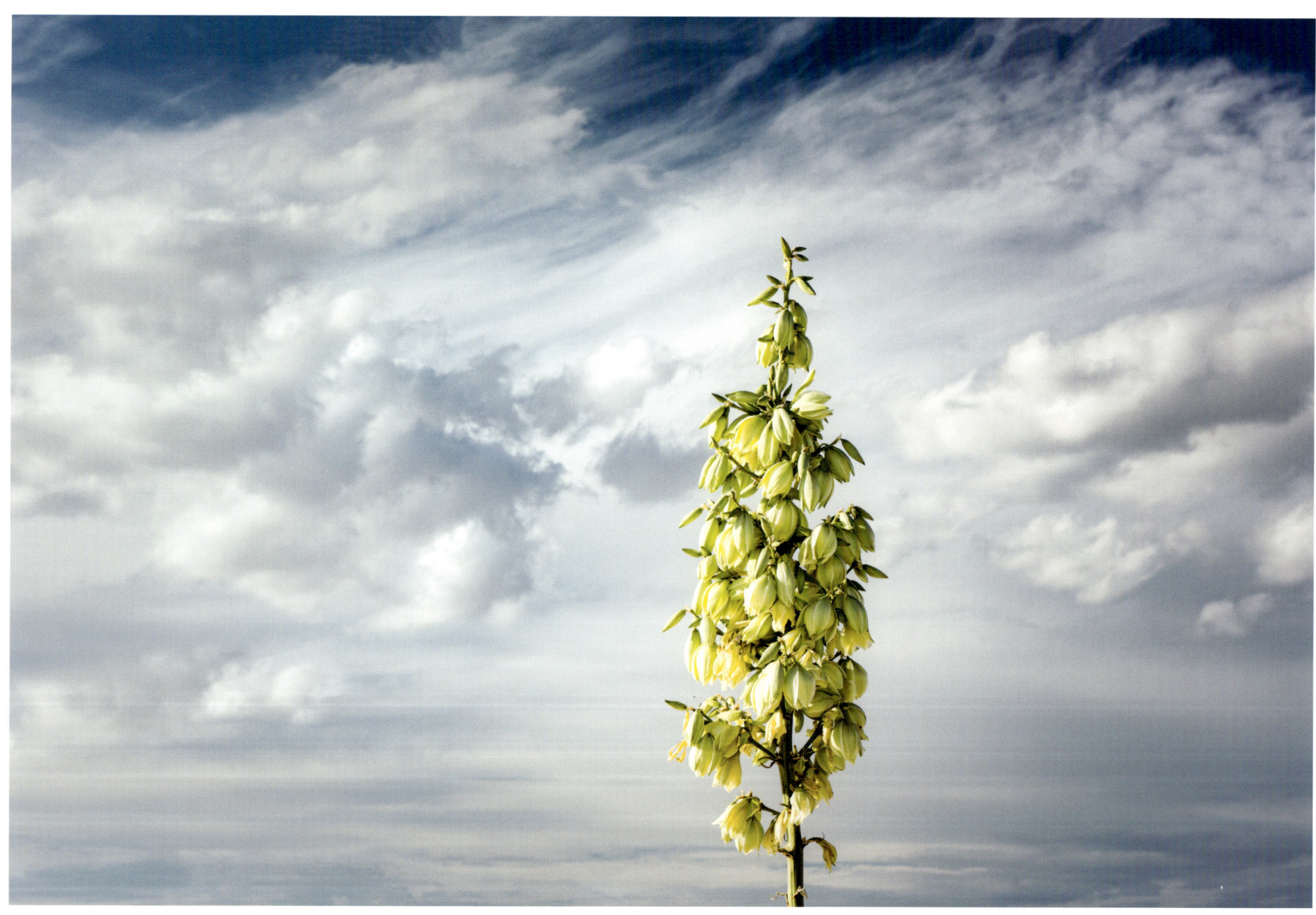

New Bloom Yucca and Sky, Spring.

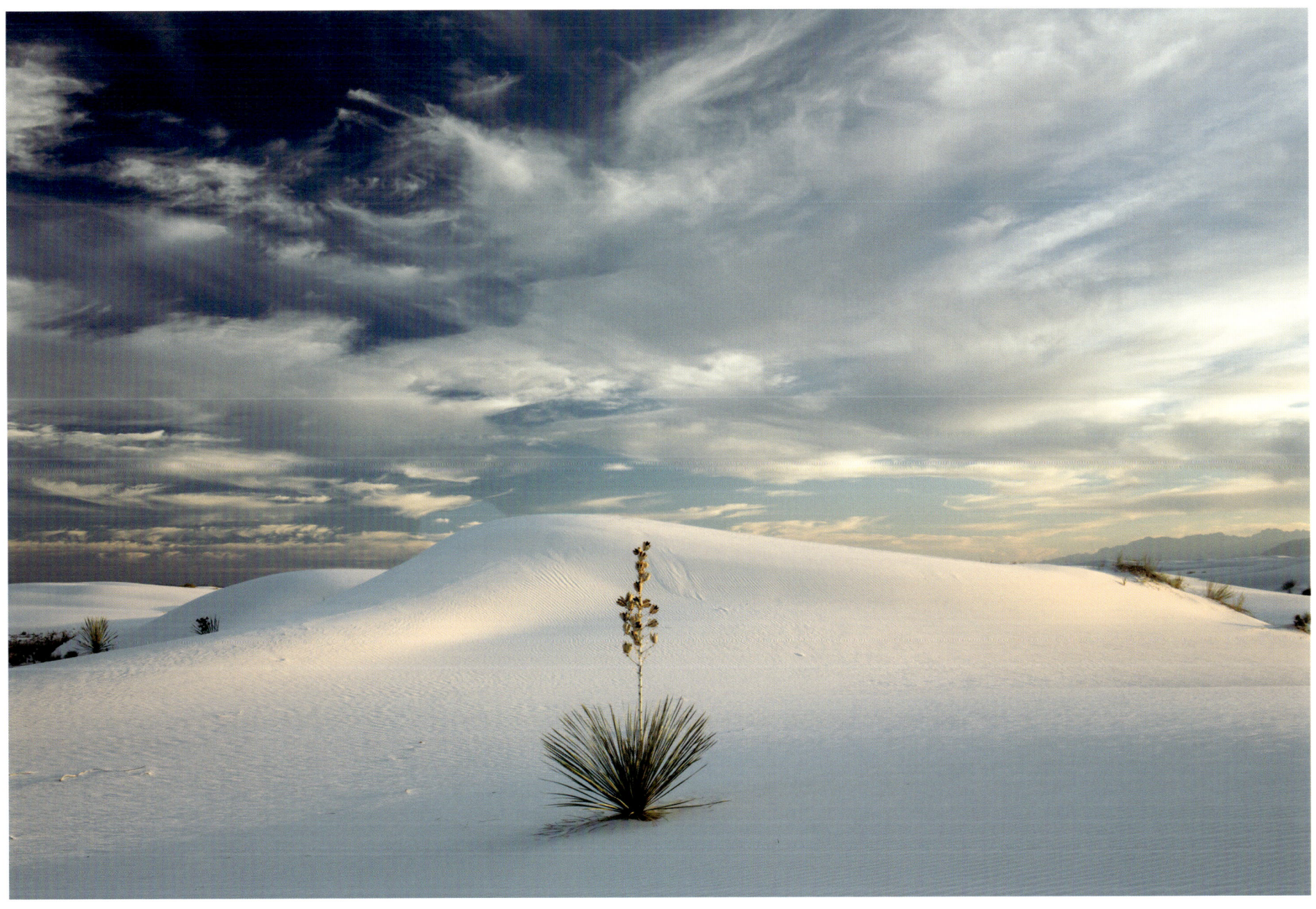

Single Yucca at Sunset, Autumn.

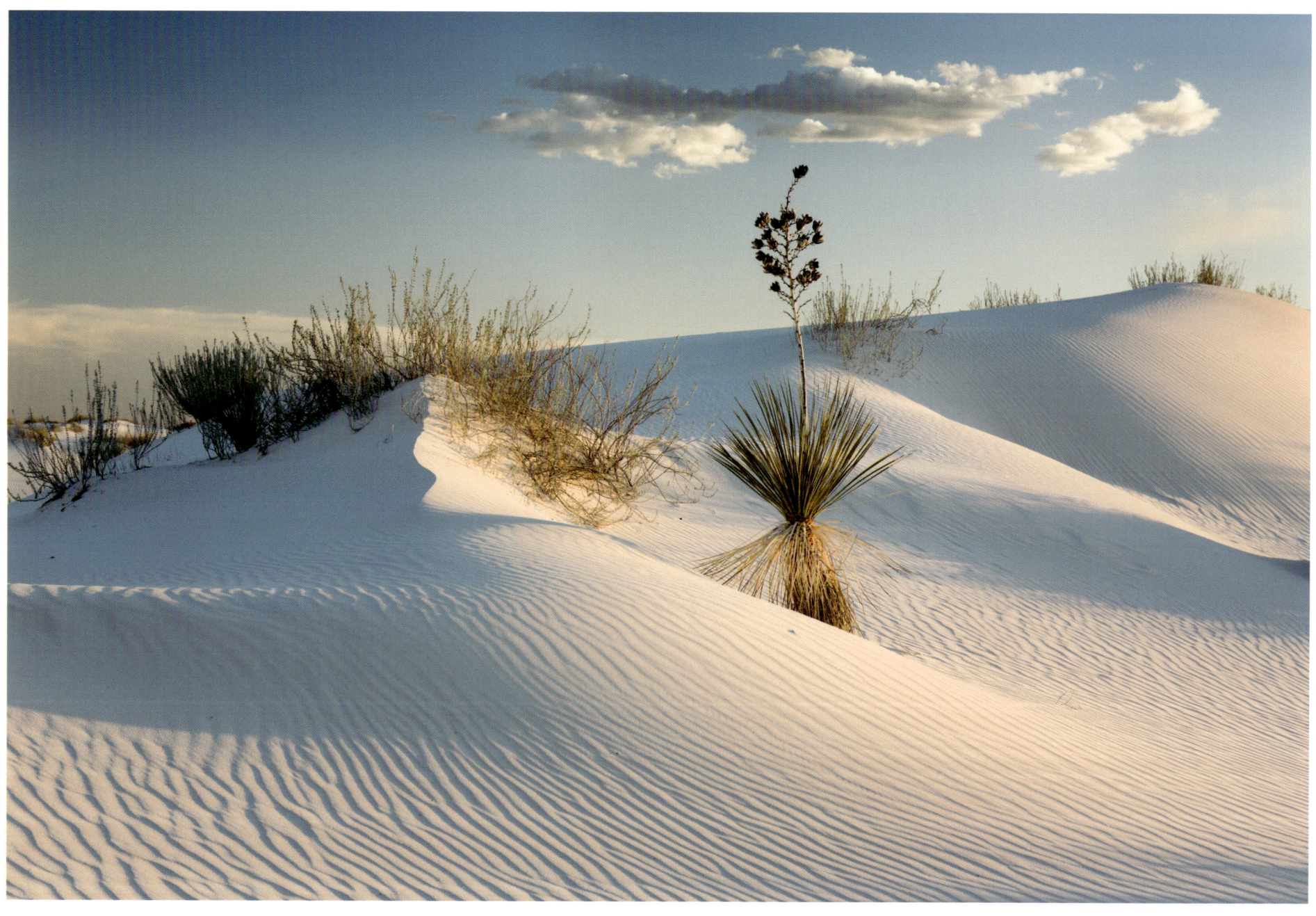

Yucca at Sunset, Autumn.

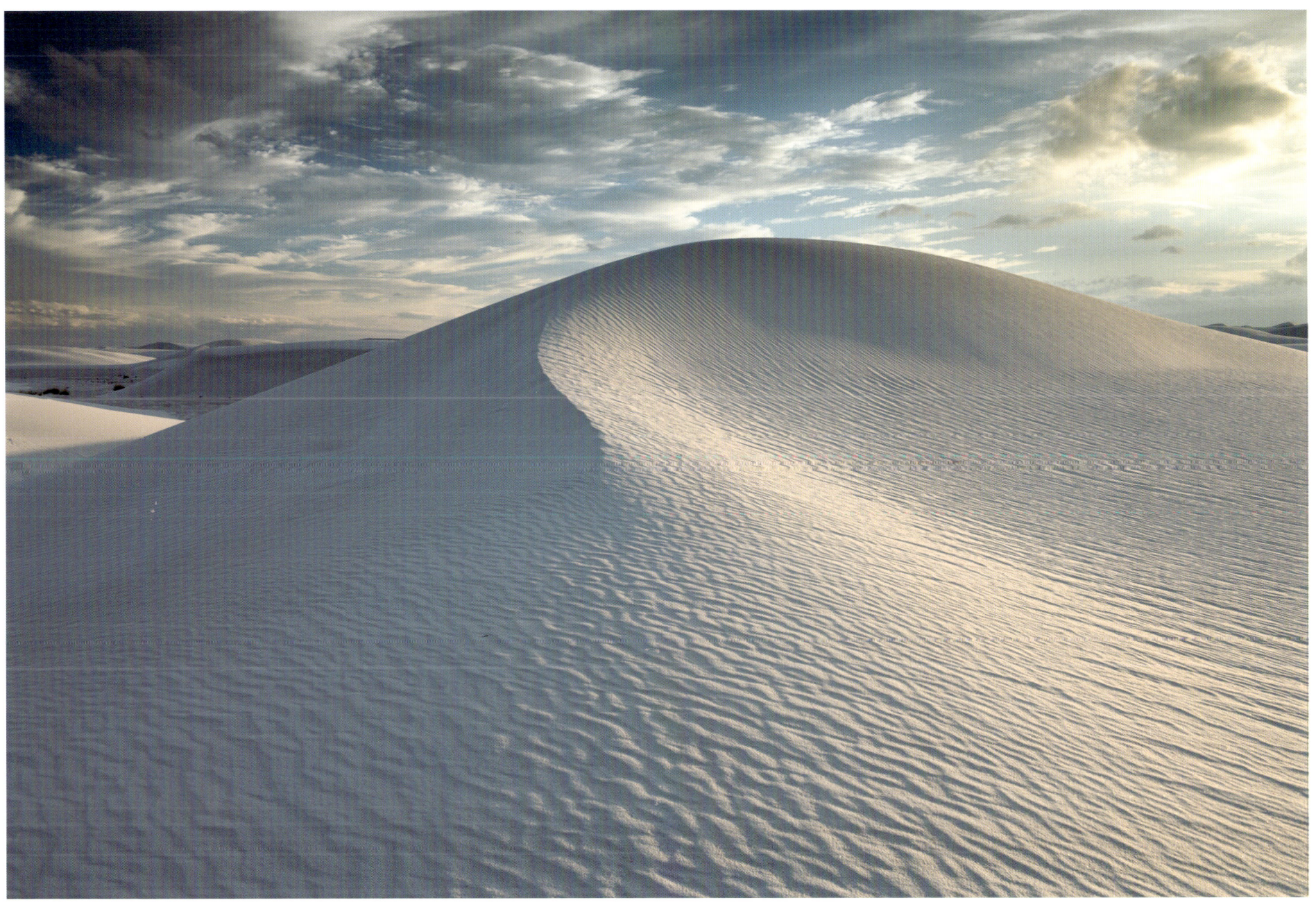

Barcan Dune after Windstorm, Sunset, Autumn.

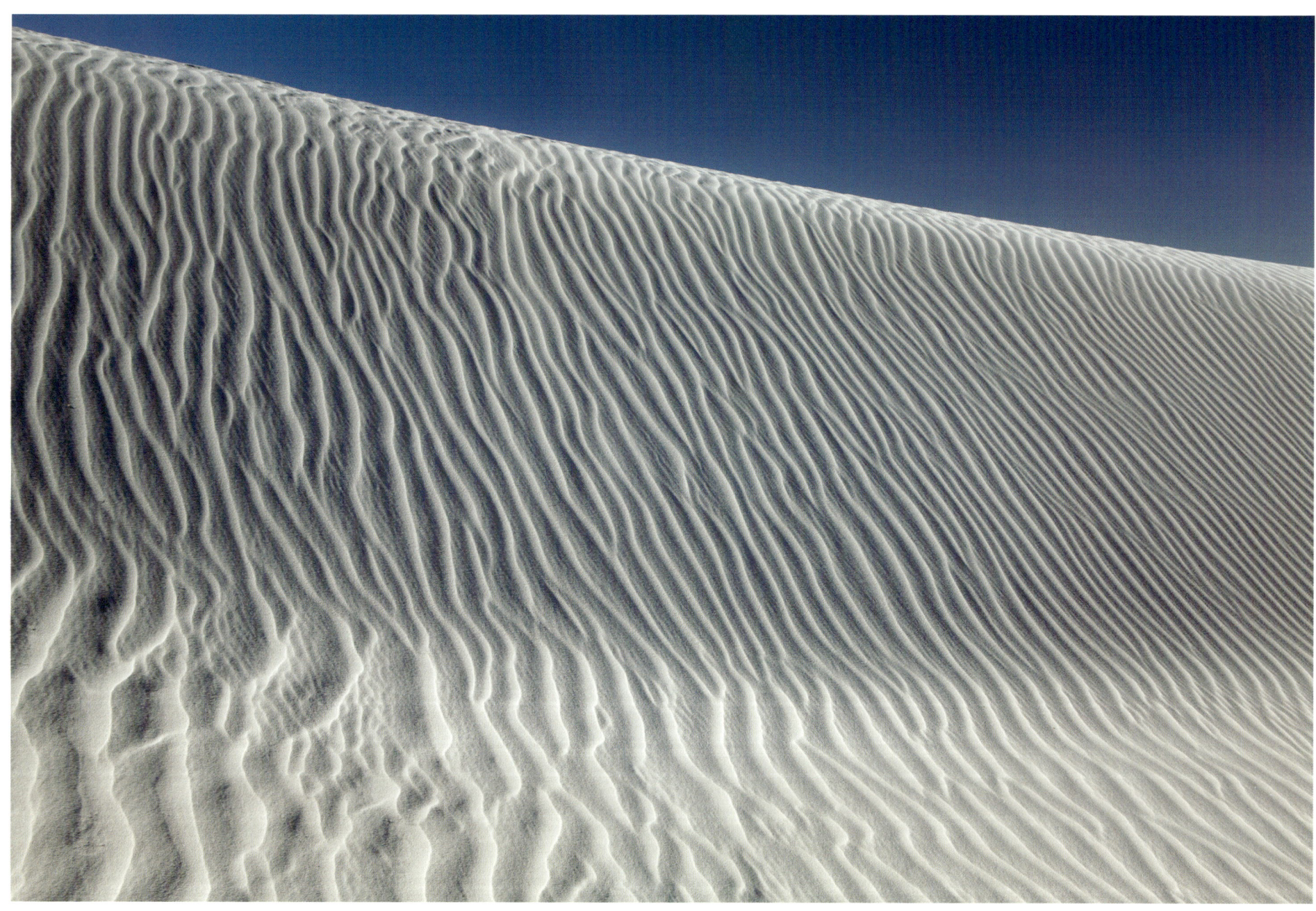

Slipface of Dune with Ripples, Spring.

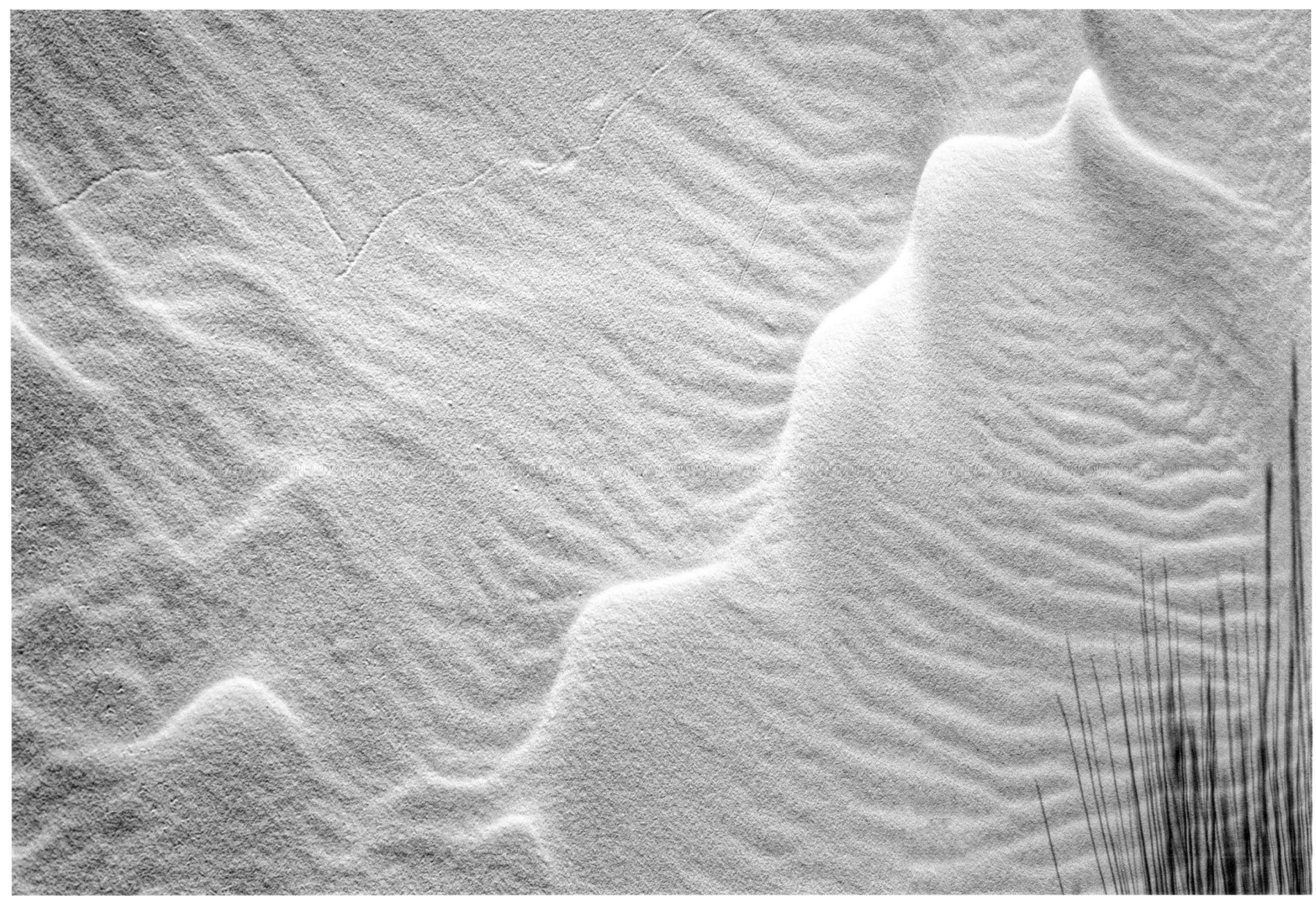

Avalanching Sand Pattern.

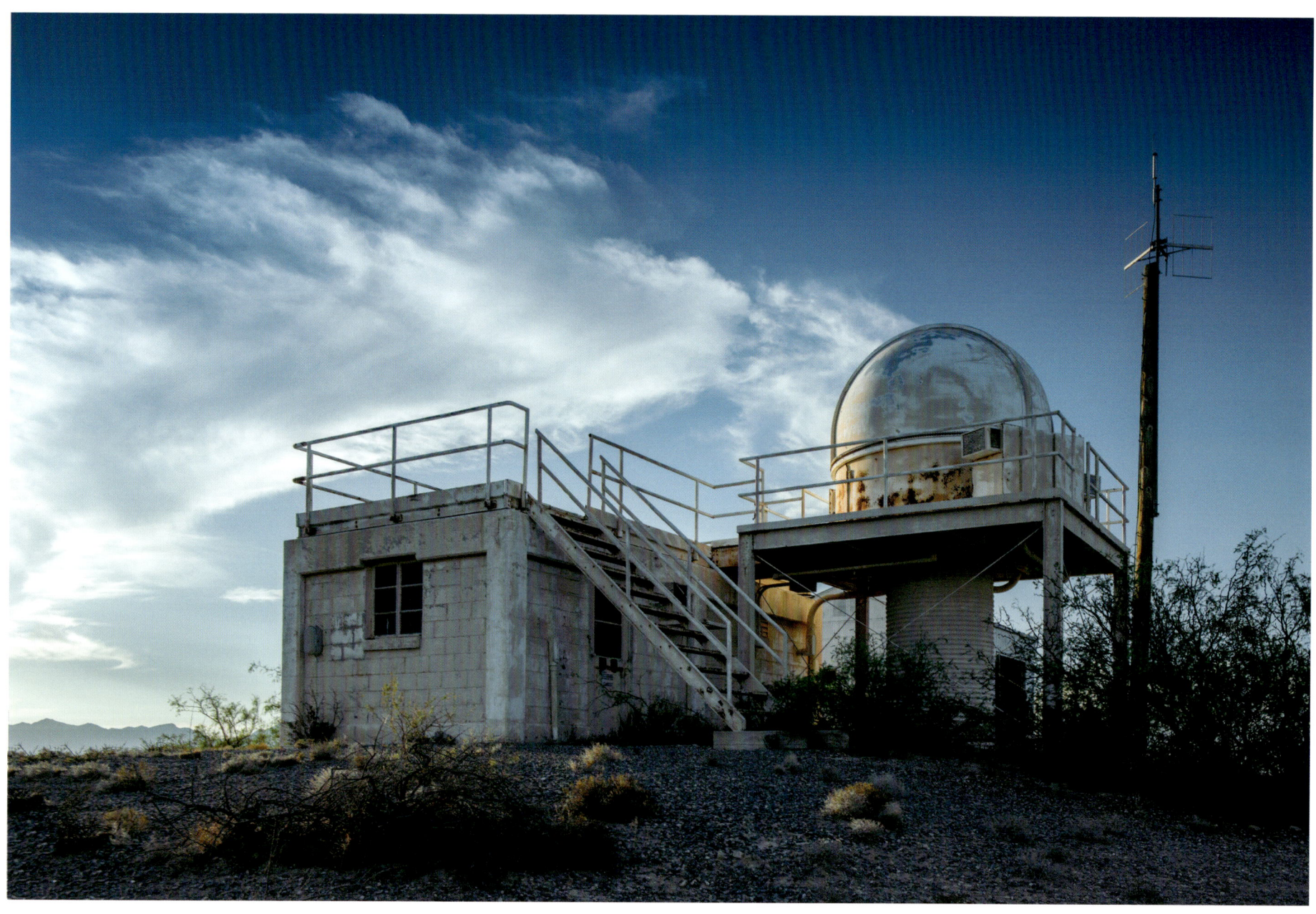

Northeast 30 Cold War–Era Camera Site and Cloud, Early Autumn, Sunset. Two generations of missile range optical instruments were housed in these structures during the Cold War at NE 30 located in the park. When the White Sands Missile Range was first established a number of impact areas were defined and named based on their distance from the launch complexes south of US Highway 70. These impact areas were rectangles with instrumentation sites on or near the corners. This one is near the northeast corner of the thirty-mile impact area located on a joint use area between the Missile Range and the National Park. This camera site was constructed in 1953.

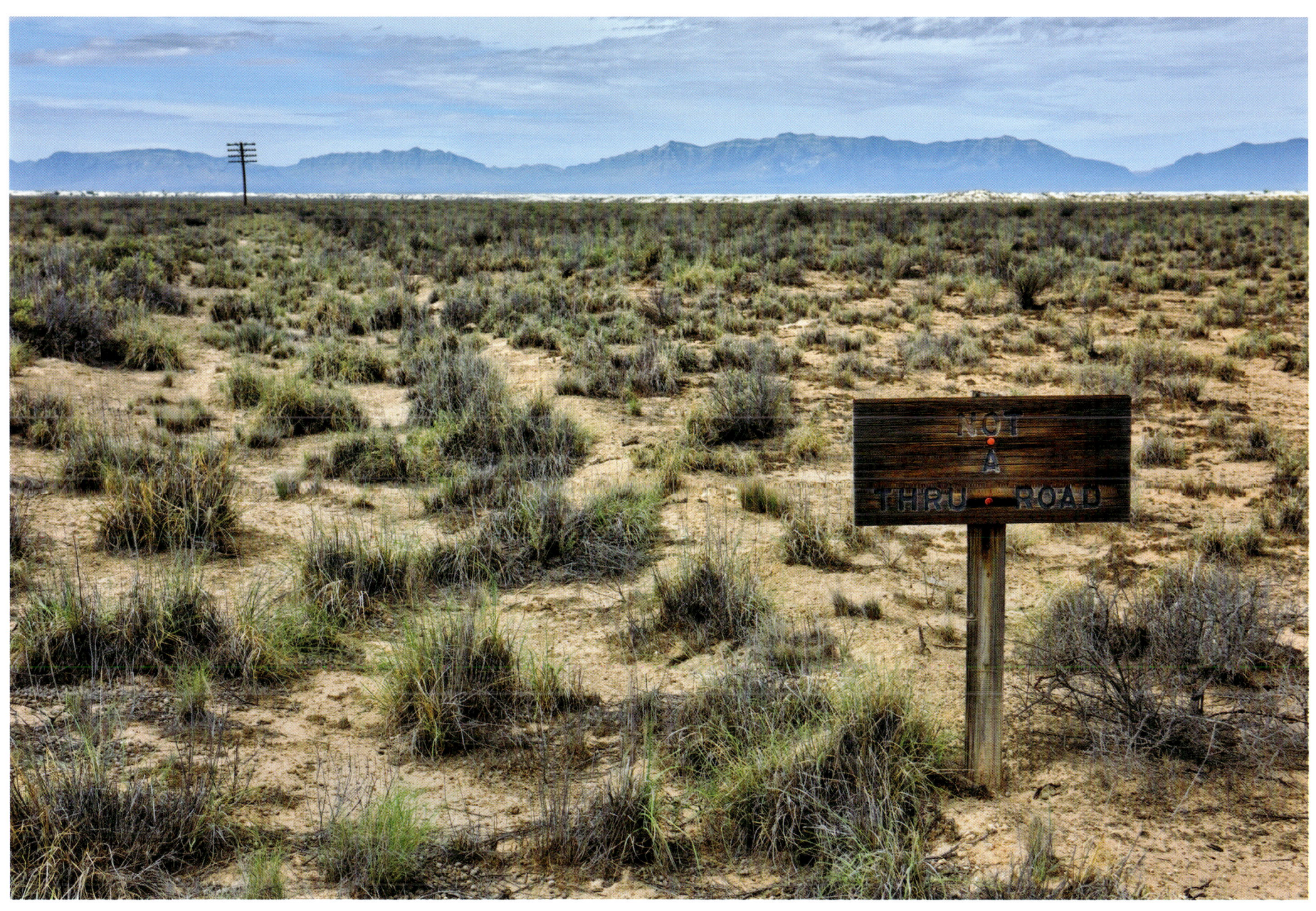

Not a Thru Road, WWII Army Access Road, Autumn. During World War II, the US Military established a permanent presence in the Tularosa Basin around White Sands National Park, creating the Alamogordo Bombing and Gunnery Range, known today as Holloman Air Force Base, and White Sands Proving Grounds, now White Sands Missile Range. This road in the park, built by the army during World War II, was used to service power lines for the bombing range.

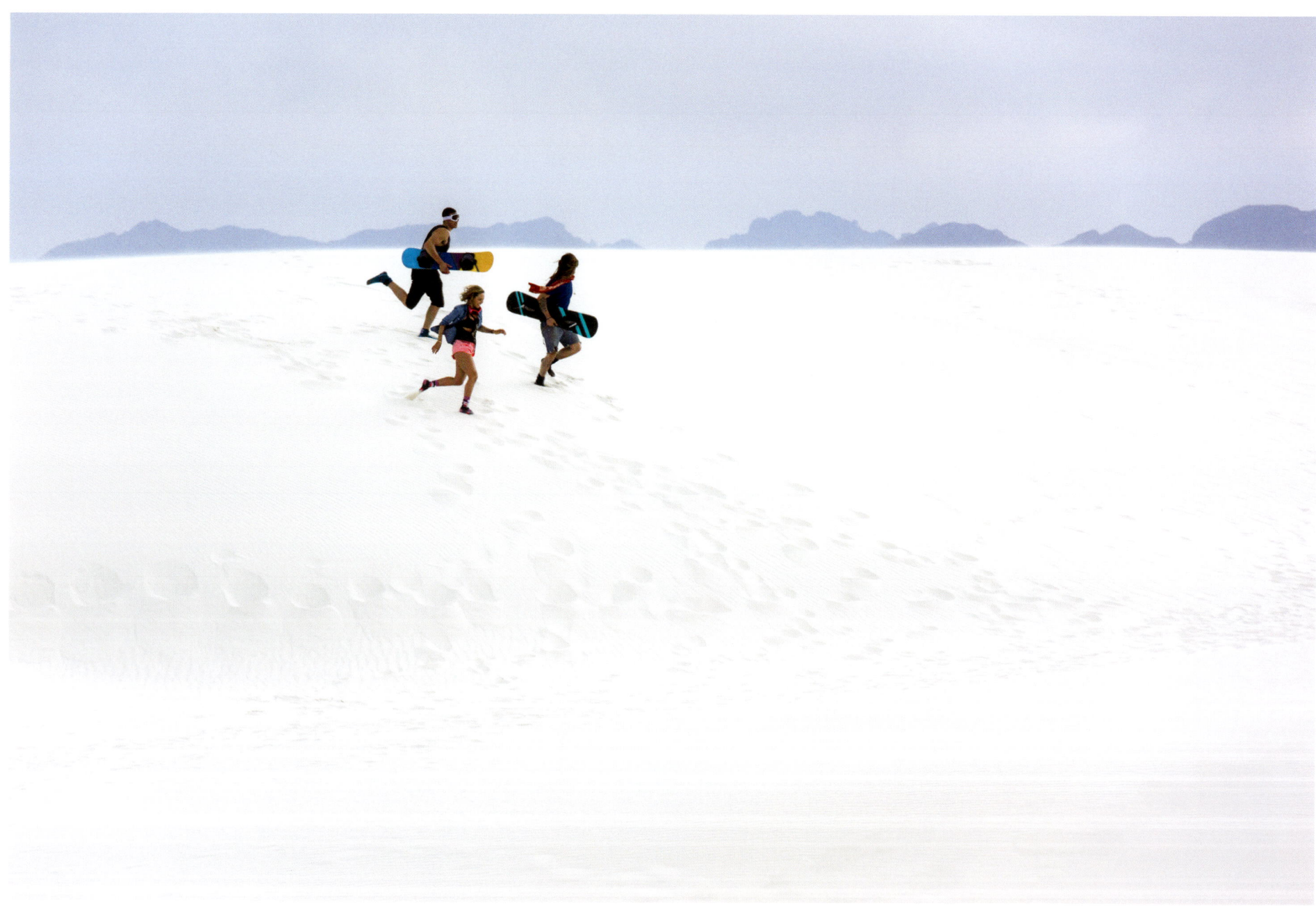

Snowboarders on Dunes, Spring.

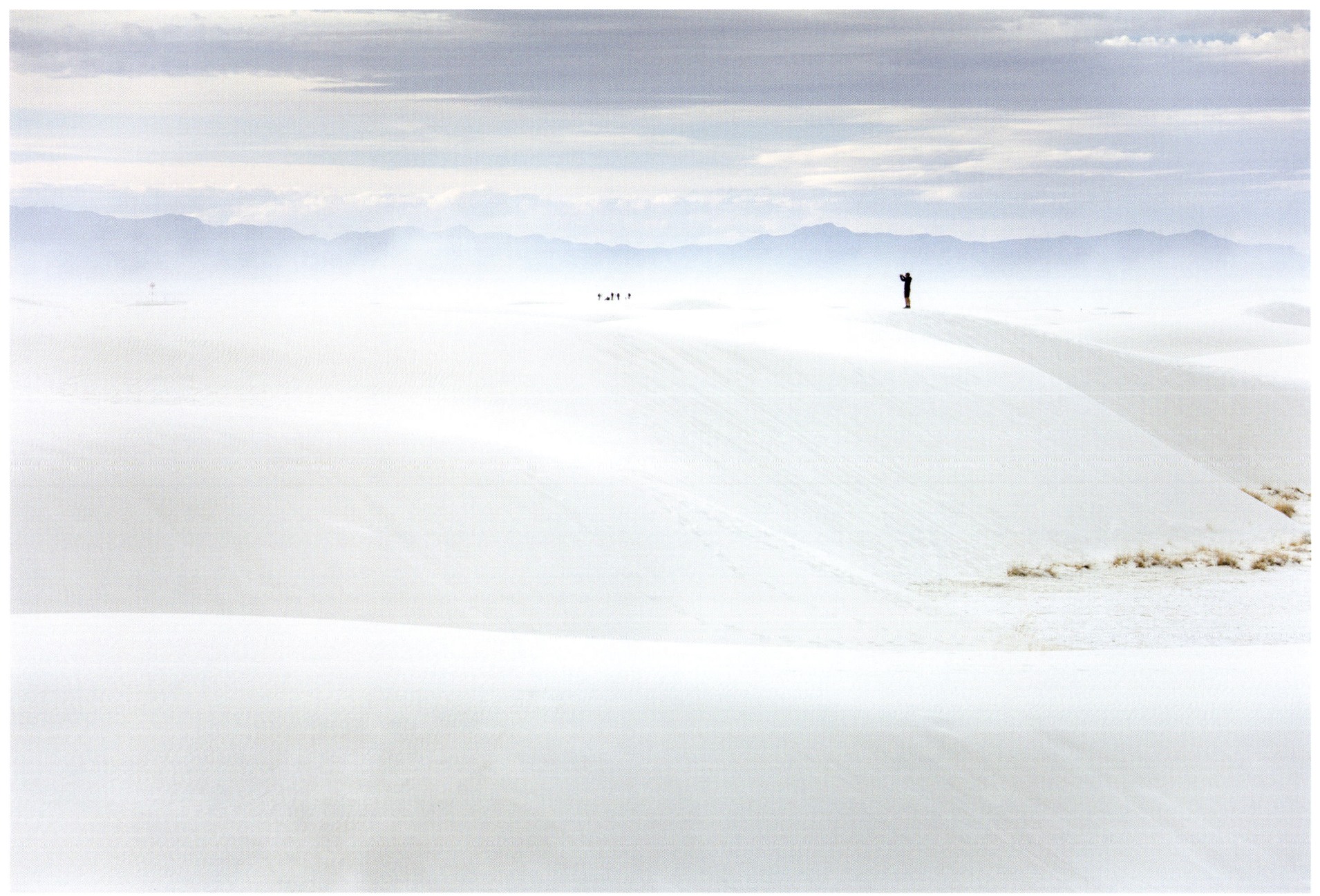

Taking Pictures with Cell Phone of Winds, Spring.

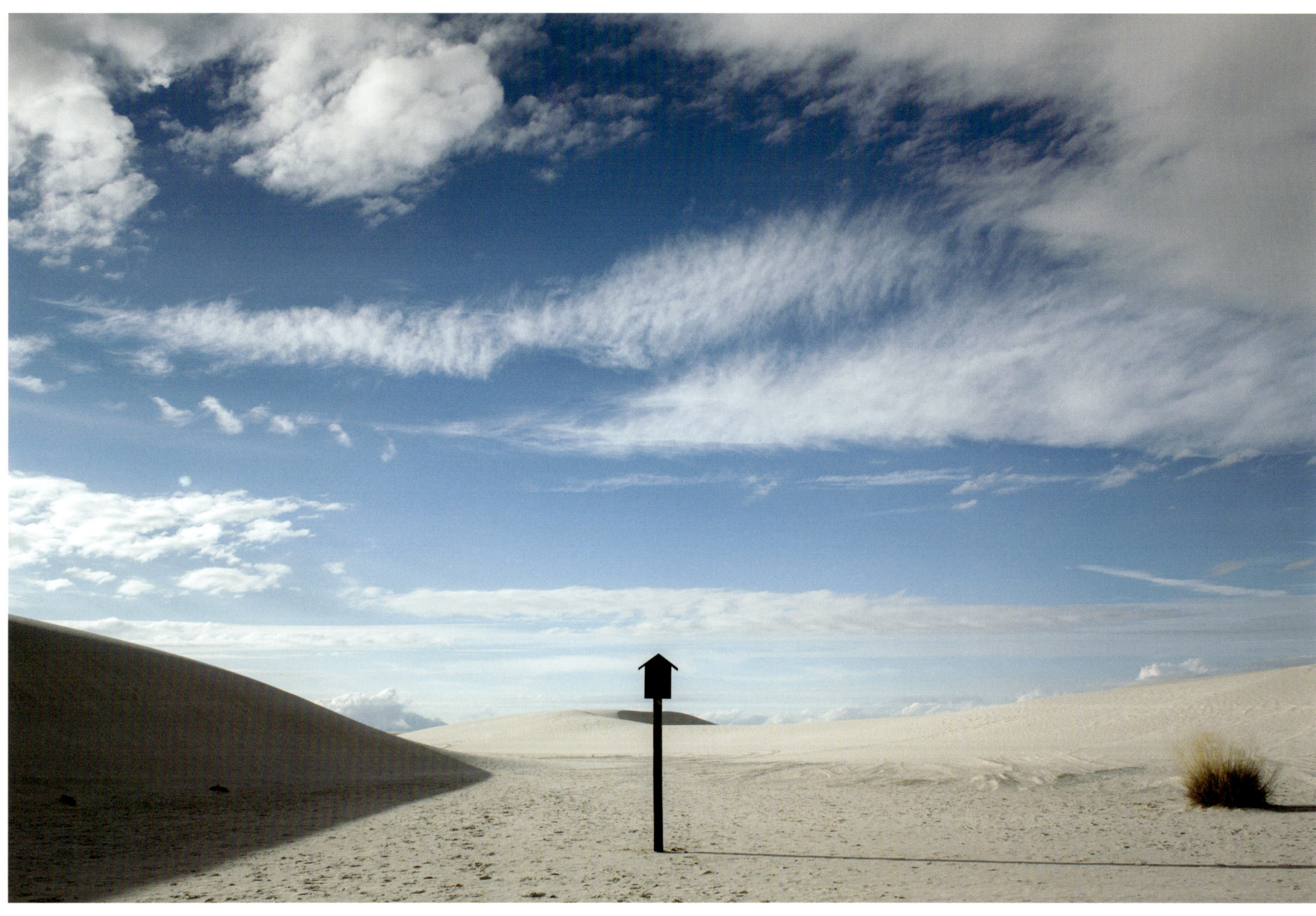

Trail Head Marker to Alkali Flats, Spring.

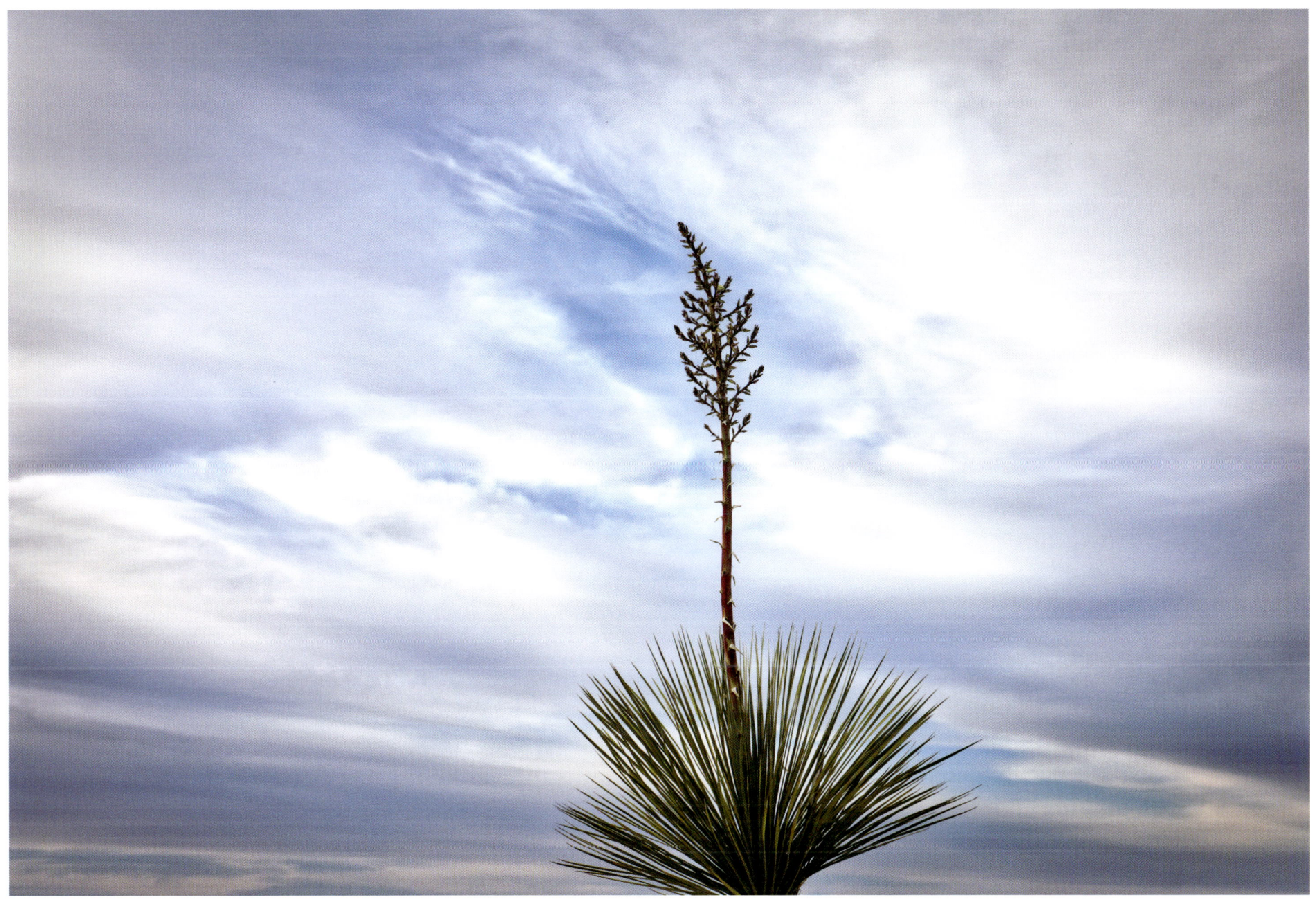

Yucca with New Growth, Spring.

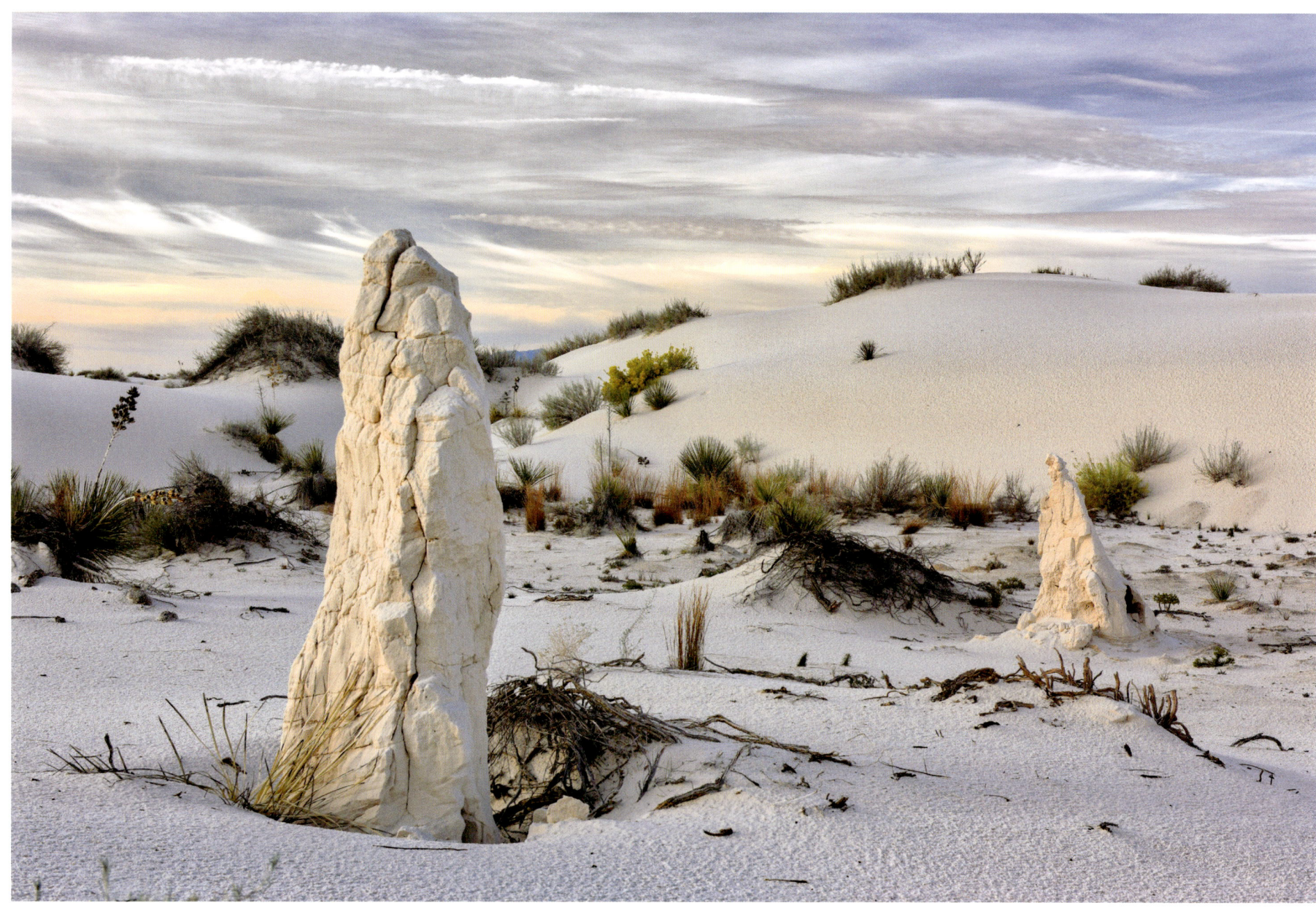

Pedestal Remains, Dawn, Autumn.

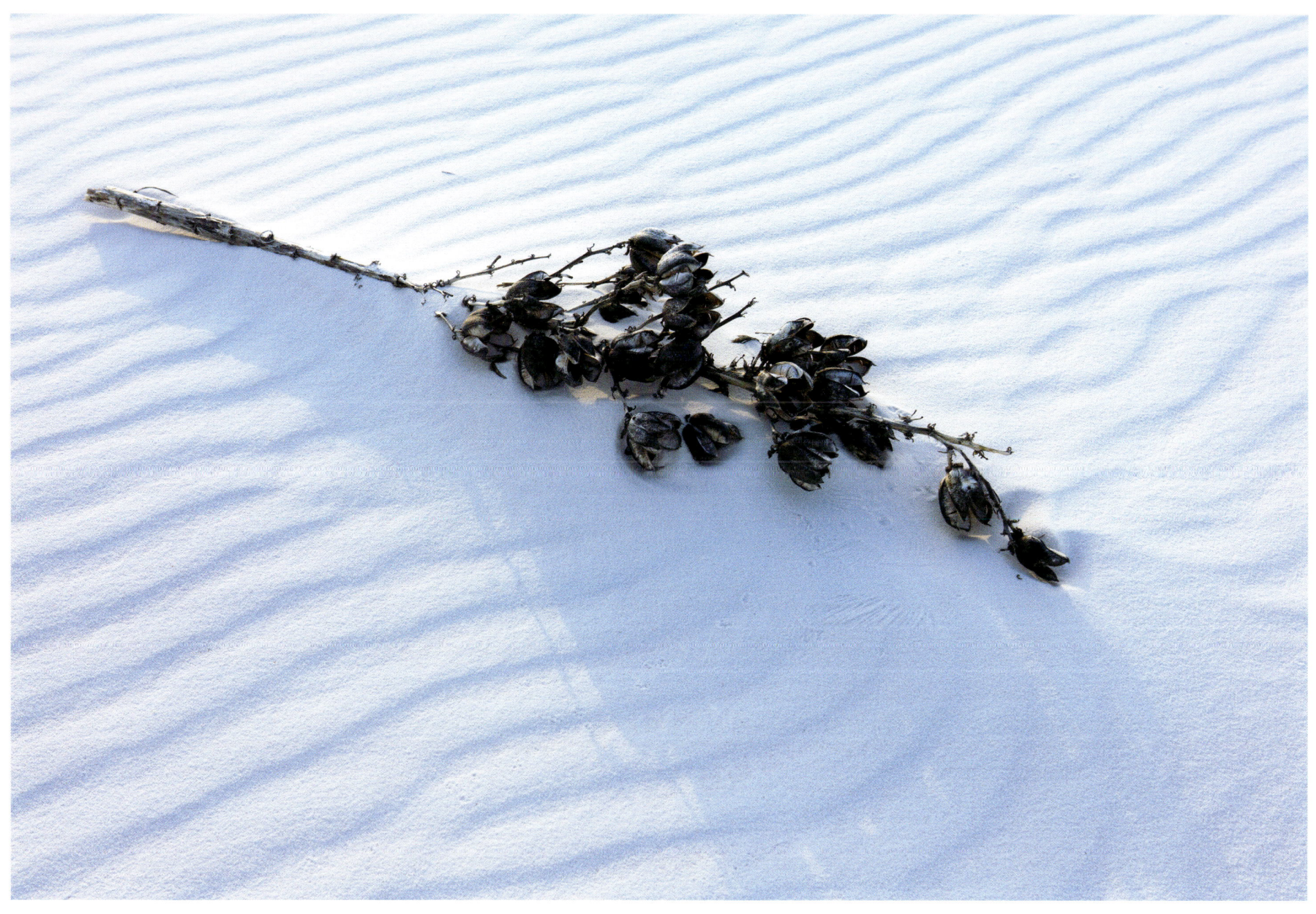

Fallen Yucca with Sand Ripples, Late Winter.

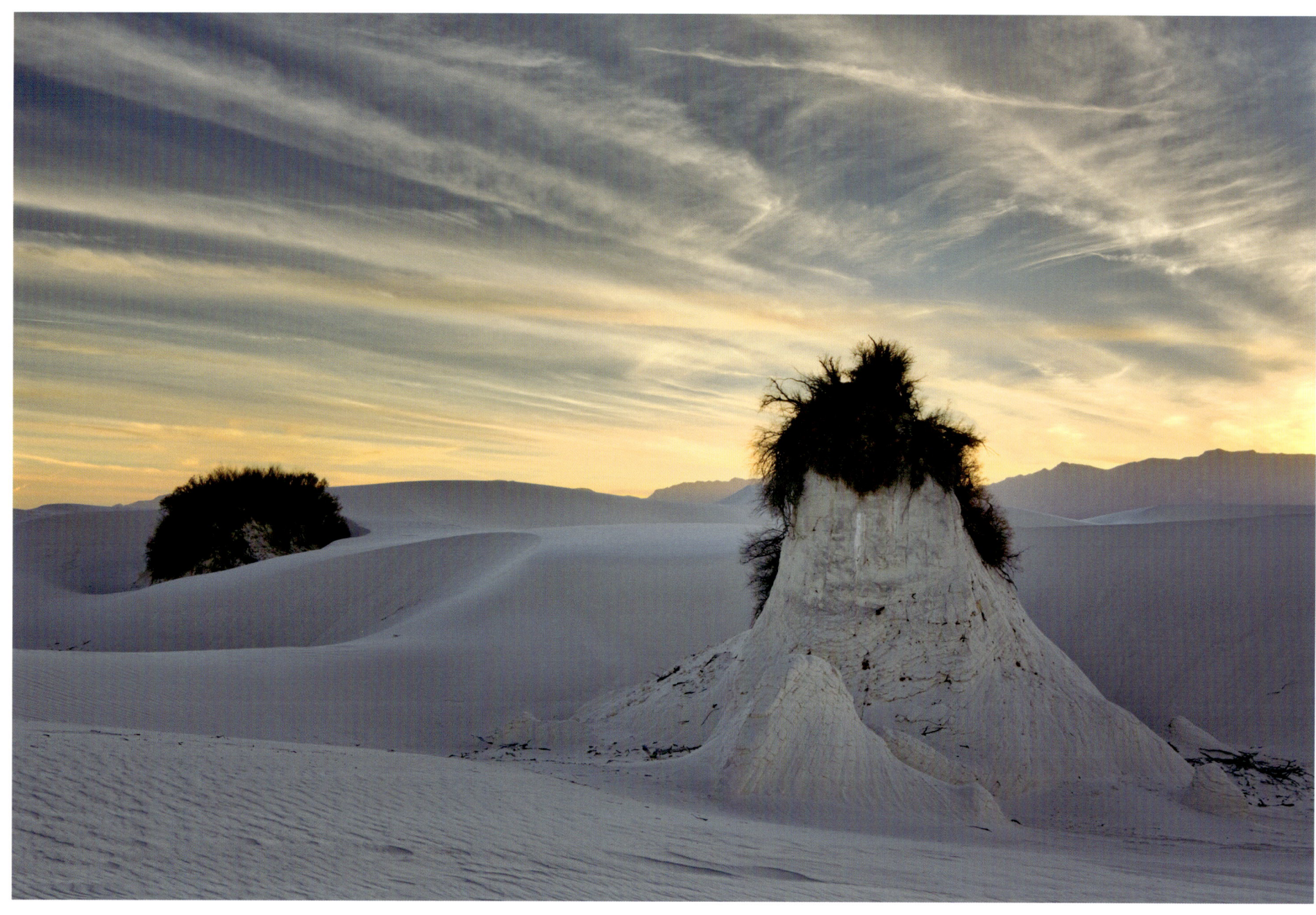

Salt Cedar Pedestals and Dunes, Sunset, Summer.

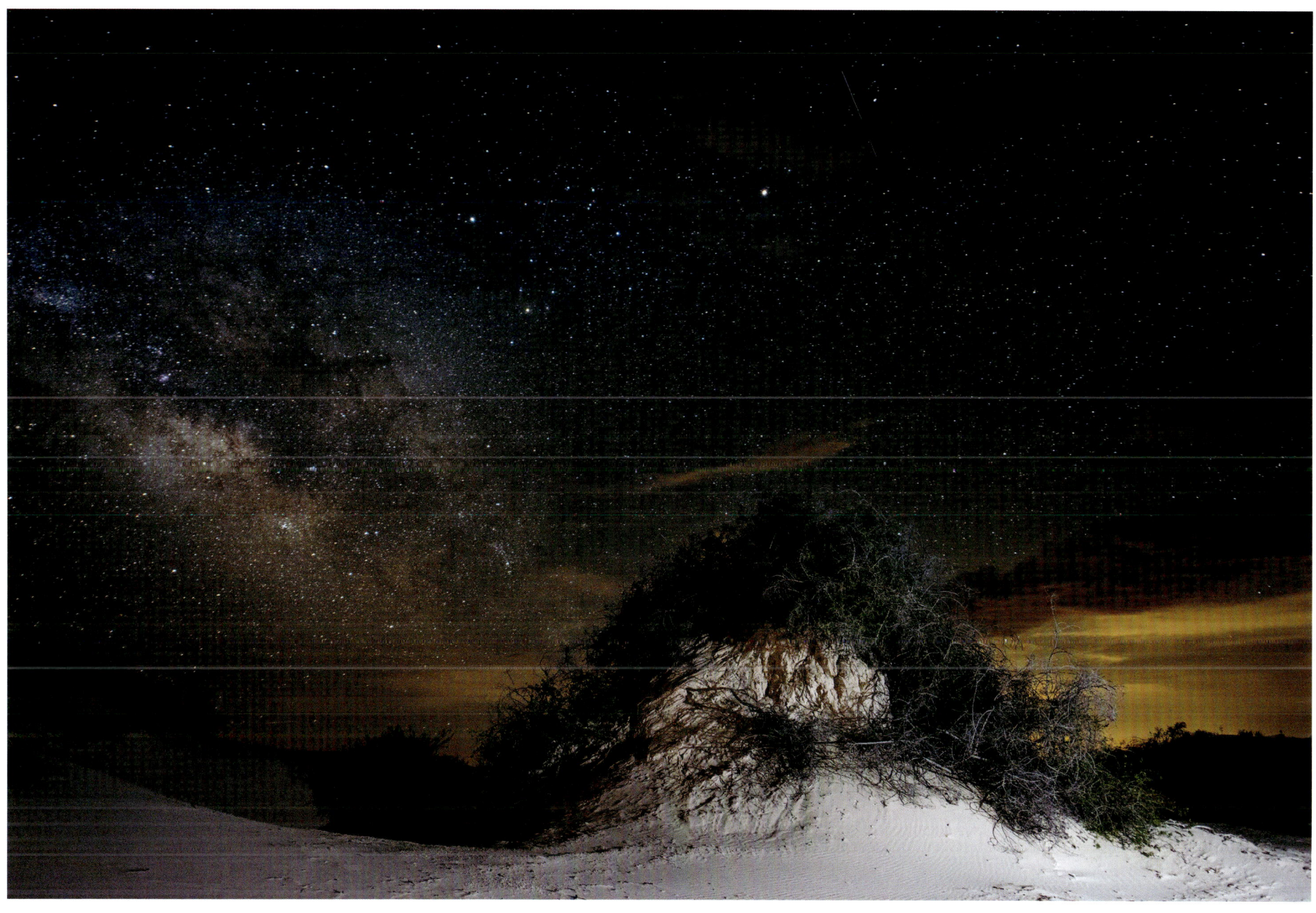

Sumac Pedestal and Milky Way, Autumn.

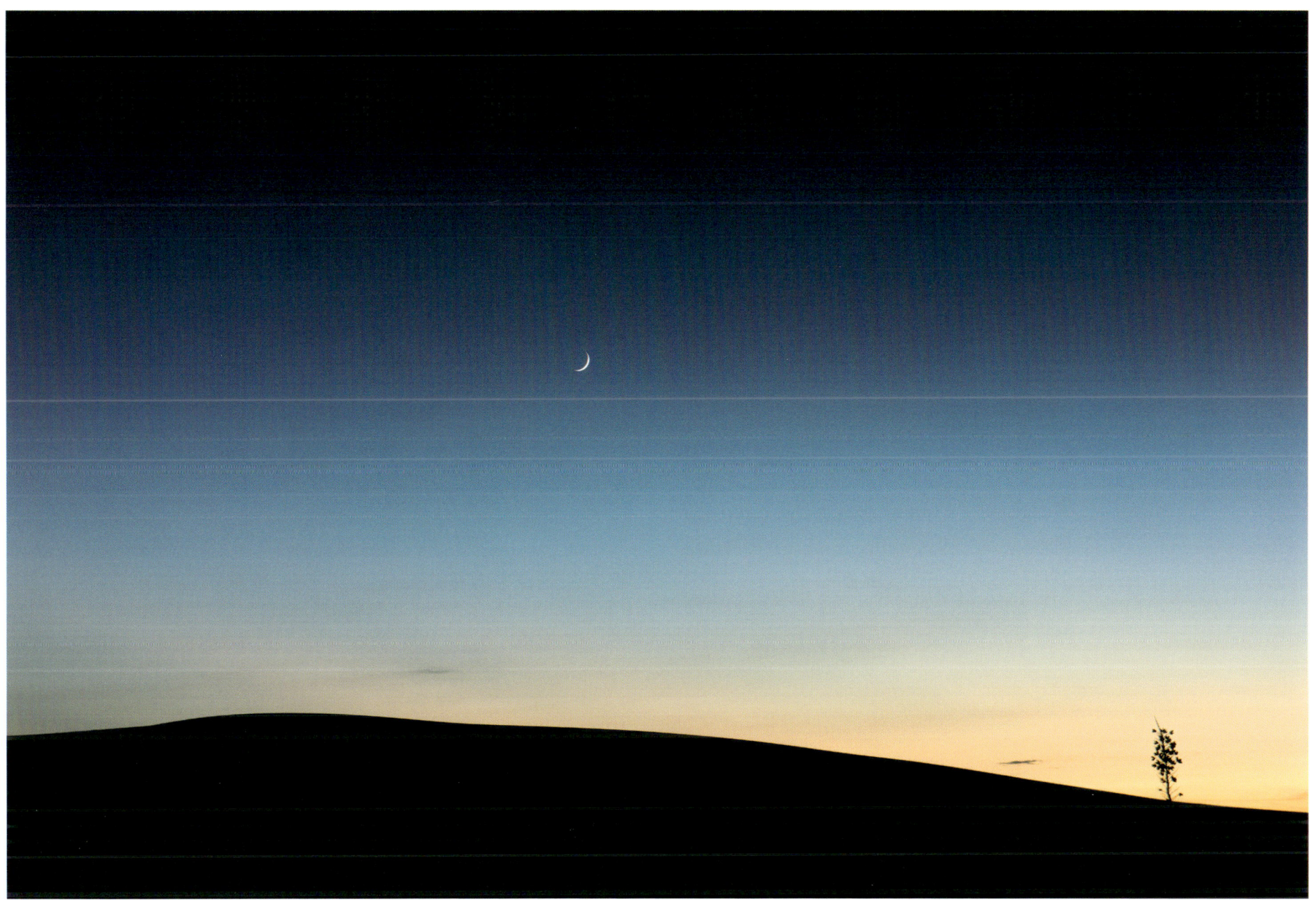

Under a Crescent Moon, Twilight, September 26, 2014.

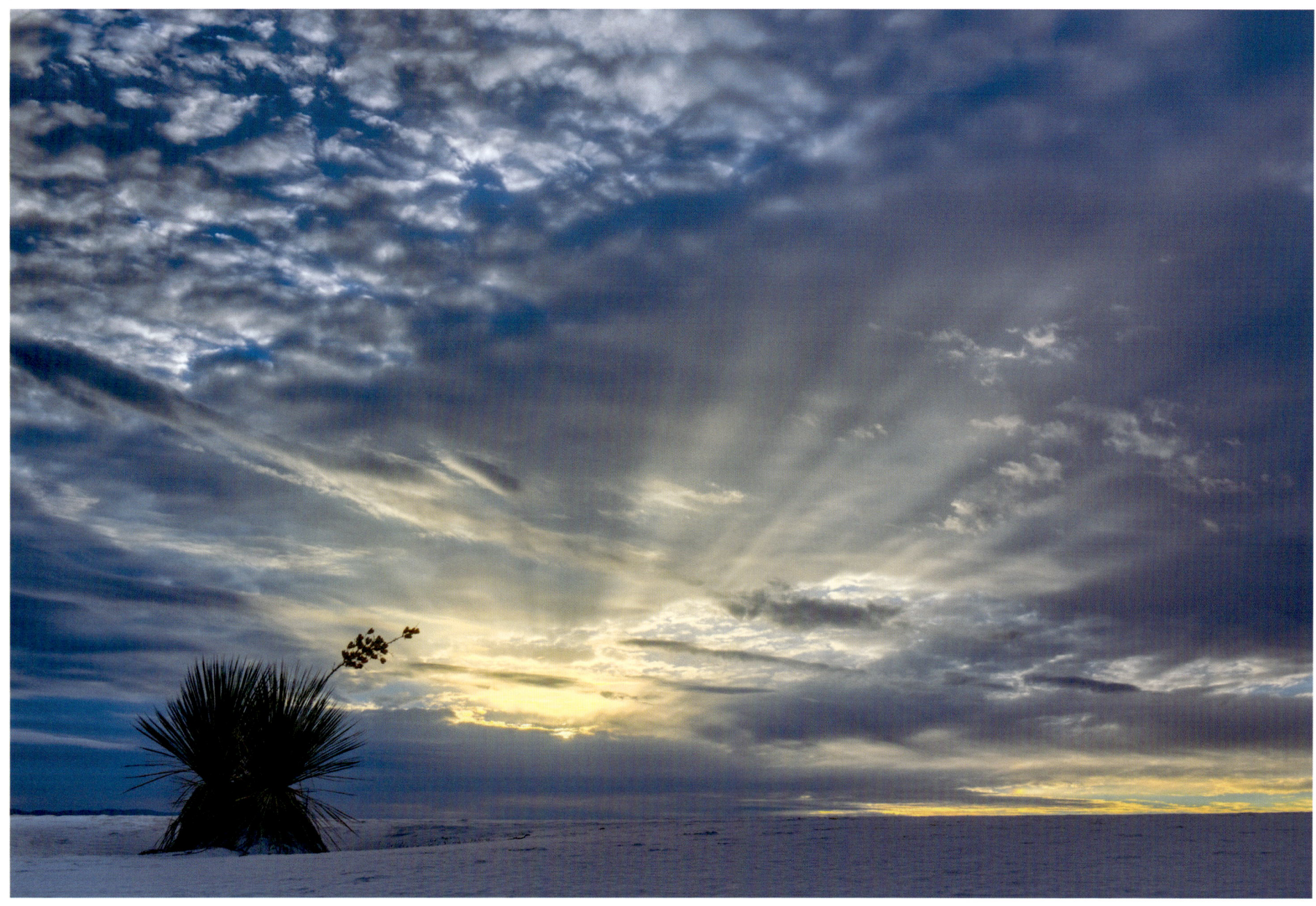

Yucca with Sun Rays, Autumn.

White Sands Meditations

Jeanetta Calhoun Mish

A TIMELESS PLACE

It's a windy June day, and as we drive south on New Mexico Highway 54, we can see white whirlwinds from fifty miles away. It's an easier trip for us than it was for travelers in the past—we're protected from the heat and wind, we carry water in the car, and, instead of the two miles an hour we might manage if walking alongside a carreta or carrying a pack, we approach the sands at sixty-five miles an hour. I wonder what it was like for the ancients, the Spanish, the Apache, and the early settlers—day-hiking doesn't accurately approximate the difficulty of living on this land where water is scarce. I know I can always go home. This was—and is—their home. Yet, austere as it is, there is a grandeur to the Tularosa Basin, in the way it's embraced by mountains and crowned with a lava flow. It is a monument to resilience.

Named for the red reeds—tules—found along the banks of the Rio Tularosa, the Tularosa Basin of south-central New Mexico is shaped like a philtrum—the groove above our upper lip that some traditions say is the print of an angel's finger, put there to hush the child's ability to speak of the soul's prebirth experience. The Basin and its geological first cousin on the west side of the San Andres, the Jornada del Muerto, feel like old souls, perhaps even more so than the rest of New Mexico—partly because of their mythic status among human beings.

A HAUNTED PLACE

In her small book entitled *Tales of the Tularosa*, Mrs. Tom Charles describes the spirit of the dunes as she saw it for the first time, in 1910:

The eddy took shape as it neared the summit of the dune; it filled out—it was a woman. Right at the crest she stood erect and bent forward, as if peering into the shadows beyond the hill upon which she stood. Pavlo Blanco, the White Wraith, dressed in her flowing wedding gown. She poised for an instant, still looking, then ran along the rippled edge of the dune. She disappeared with a sound that was halfway between a sigh and a sob.

There is much to ponder in the knowledge that more than one culture has seen—and continues to see—the figure of a woman in the swirling eddies that rise up from the dunes, dancing, sometimes curtseying or bowing to get a closer look at interlopers. From at least the time of the Apache, women and women's spirits have been associated with White Sands. The Mescaleros' White Face Woman is linked with the dunes, and her name, evocative of the way the sands leave a sheen of white gypsum covering everything, seems to tie her even more closely to the area. Perhaps White Face Woman is the protostory for the Legend of Pavla Blanca. The many pale vortices that form and just as quickly disappear over the sands have been envisioned by later inhabitants of the area, Spanish and Anglo alike, to be the spirit of a woman. The term "Pavla Blanca" seems to be a phonetic spelling of a misheard Spanish word, "pavura" meaning "dread" or "terror," a term that referred to the entire White Sands area. According to Ray John de Aragón's *Enchanted Legends and Lore of New Mexico: Witches, Ghosts, and Spirits*, the story behind the ghost of White Sands is that of a young Spanish woman who searched the white sands for her sweetheart, who had gone missing

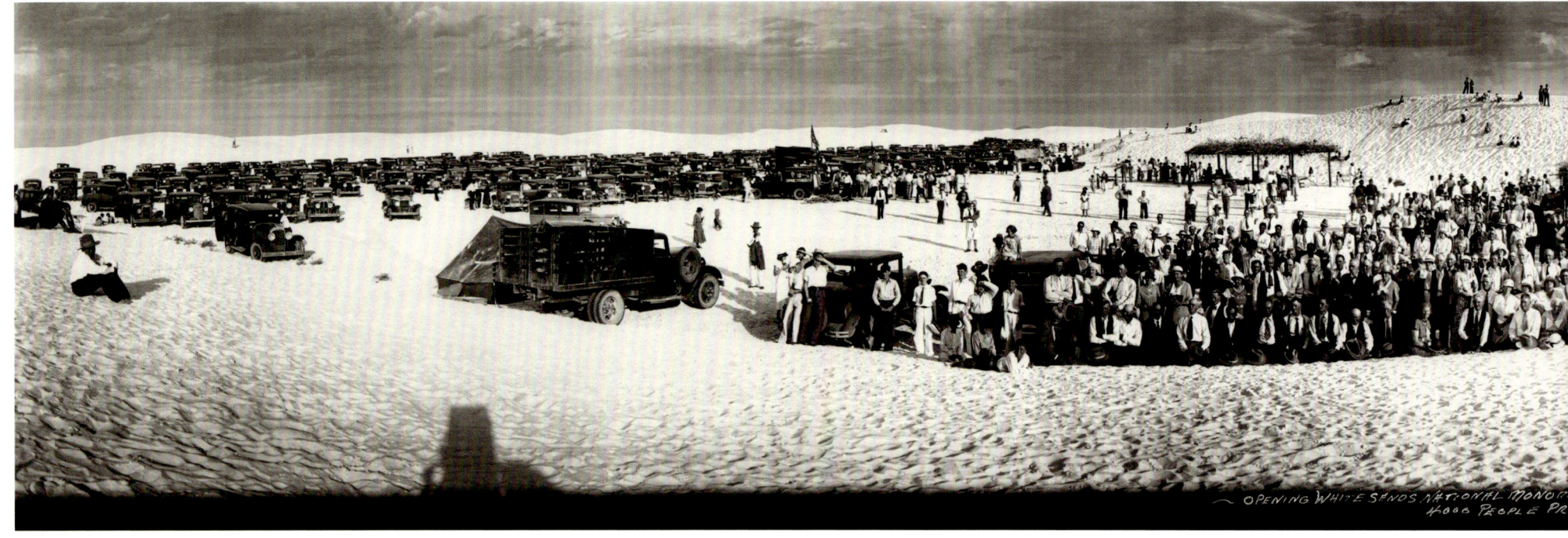

OPENING WHITE SANDS NATIONAL MONUMENT
4000 PEOPLE PR

from the Coronado Expedition. She died in the sands and, so the legend goes, her spirit is still looking for him. The name "White Dread," originally descriptive of the sands, became attached to the swirling white sandstorms that take the shape of a woman—a white wraith that can be seen from space.

A PLACE OF THE DISTANT PAST

In geographic terms the Tularosa Basin and its white sands are relatively young, having come into being as a result of the Rio Grande Rift—a pulling apart of the earth's crust. The geologic changes that brought about the Rift began in the early Miocene Epoch, between 35 and 29 million years before the present time, when the earth's hard shell began to spread apart.[1] While the Rift and the Basin are geological adolescents, the deposition of hydrous calcium sulfate—gypsum—that forms the dunes is the result of processes which are much older. The story of geography is one of cycles, and that of the Tularosa Basin is no exception. During the middle Permian period (275 million years before present) the southern third of New Mexico was covered in a shallow sea known today as the Hueco Seaway. In the late Permian (260 million years before present) those seas began to dry up, and just like mineral deposits appear on your water glasses or on your sink fixtures if you have "hard" (high mineral content) water, as the sea water evaporated, it left behind extensive salt and gypsum (*yeso* in Spanish) deposits.

However, it's not obvious to the casual observer where those deposits lie. The first thought would be that Lake Otero, an ancient lake bed in the White Sands National Park area, was once a part of the inland sea. However, Lake Otero is not the remains of the Hueco Seaway. In one of the magical moments of geology, we have learned that the bottom of the old seabed is now the uplifted Permian period rocks exposed in the San Andres mountains on the west side of the Tularosa valley (Chronic). The old seabed is also below your feet—the Basin floor drops several kilometers as the walls rise. The Yeso Formation is sandstone, red beds of ancient soils—all that remains of the former sea.

Who could have witnessed the tearing of the earth, felt the shuddering, heard the deep underground rumble and the sudden crack of repeated earthquakes? Not humans. And—although there was extensive volcanic activity in

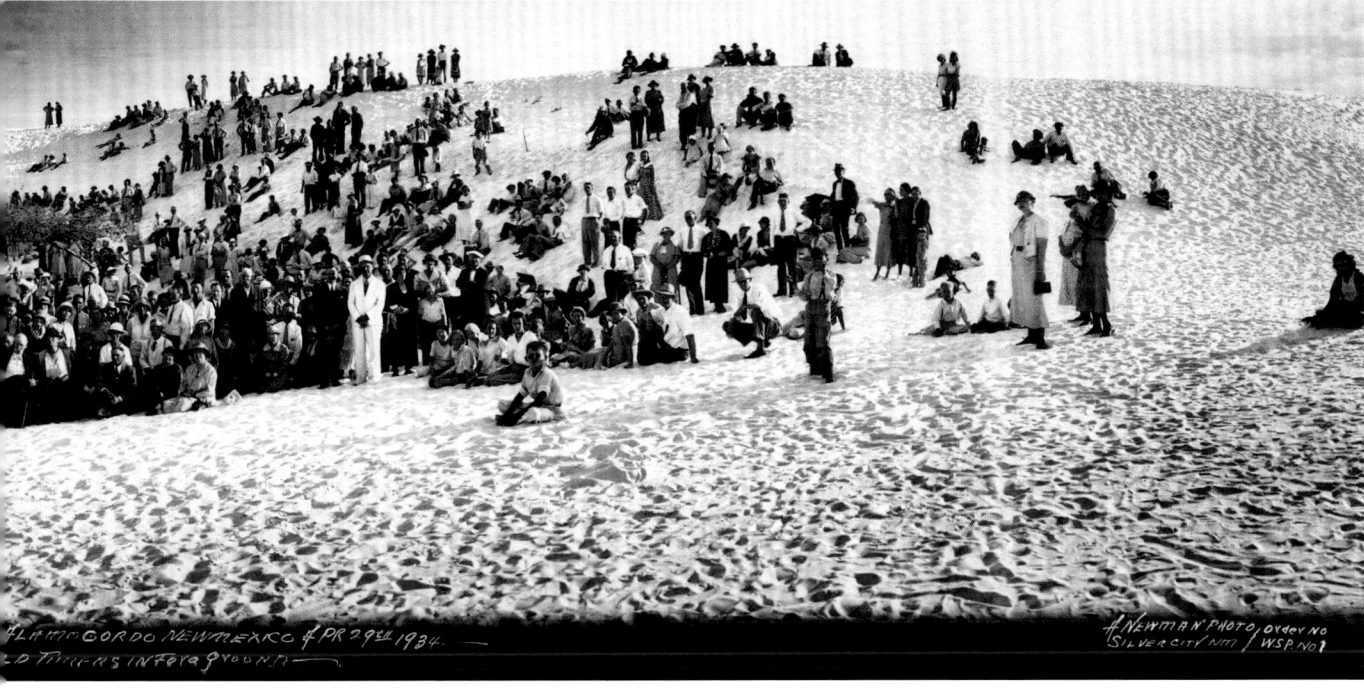

Opening White Sands National Monument, near Alamogordo, NM,
April 29, 1934. Photograph by Almeron Newman, Silver City, NM.
Courtesy of the National Park Service.

the area before, during, and after the Rift began to sink
between two faults—the voles, the saber-tooth cats, and
the three-toed horses must have been startled by the
shivering of their grasslands, and the vibrations in what is
now the Gulf of Mexico surely disturbed the early whales.

Another wet and cool period during the late
Pleistocene epoch (one million years before present)
was essential to the creation of White Sands. In the
Pleistocene epoch, the land now known as the western
United States could lay claim to some of the largest
lakes in the world: the Great Salt Lake in Utah is a lake
from the Pleistocene as is the Lake Otero playa (a dry
lake bed that temporarily fills with water) and Lake
Lucero, a ten-square-mile remnant of Lake Otero and
its drainage basin, both found in "Alkali Flats,"

situated between the dunes and the San Andres
Mountains. Lake Otero was formed at least forty
thousand years ago, during the last ice age when there
was more water in the Basin. During this period, a
glacier formed on Sierra Blanca and rain and snow fell
on the mountains in the area.

Rain, groundwater, and snowmelt from the mountains dissolved gypsum (calcium sulfate), salt (sodium
chloride), and other soluble minerals embedded in the
rocks and carried them into the Basin. With more water
came more gypsum. However, during the late Pleistocene and early Holocene epochs, the water in Lake
Otero evaporated. For thousands of years afterward,
wetter and dryer periods alternated, and when the most
recent dry period occurred—the one we're living in
now, which began about seven thousand years ago

during the middle Holocene—Lake Otero dried up
entirely, leaving behind gypsum crystals, many of them
small enough to be easily broken down and carried
away by the wind.[2] That process of dissolved gypsum
precipitating—that is, being left behind after evapora-
tion—continues today at Lake Lucero each time it rains
then settles in for a dry spell.

Humans followed bison or mammoths or the
now-extinct indigenous horses and camels to the
Tularosa Basin twelve thousand years or so before
the present time. They camped, among other places,
near Lake Otero, which was then surrounded by a
grassland much like the great prairies of the Midwest
Packrat middens from the last ice age (late Wisconsin)
preserve plant remains for study by archeologists, so
we have some idea what the Basin was like in the

distant past.[3] Today, evidence of human settlements and hunting sites are found throughout the Tularosa Basin, and fossil footprints of Pleistocene mammals are still visible along what was the Lake Otero shore, due west of the Space Harbor.[4]

A PLACE OF DUNES

The earliest known published account of what is now the White Sands National Park appeared in the *American Naturalist* in 1870:

> Salt Plains of New Mexico.—Brevet Major General August V. Kautz, U. S. Army, writing from Fort Stanton, New Mexico, informs me that there is a valley of some two hundred miles long and twenty wide, lying between the Sierra Blanca and the San Andreas and Occura [sic] mountains, in that Territory, in which there is no stream, and only a few alkaline springs and salt lakes, or ponds. Where the road from Ft. Stanton to El Paso crosses it, about sixty miles south of that post, is a plain of white sand, apparently granulated gypsum, which has drifted into mounds, forty and fifty feet in height. Water of a strongly alkaline character is obtained by digging a few feet, and around the edges of this district, salt marshes exist, where in the dry seasons, great quantities of almost pure salt may be collected. The sand is so white and the plain so extensive as to give the effect of snow scenery. As I do not remember to have seen a description of the place in print, I send you this note with a specimen of the sand forwarded by General Kautz.[5]

Strictly speaking, the White Sands are an *erg* (sand sea), a term defined as an area that contains more than 48 square miles of aeolian (wind-blown) sand. The white sands dune sea is 275 square miles—27 miles long and, on the average, 10 miles wide. Unlike other natural formations like mountains, dunes move at a human-recognizable rate: the most active ones are moving toward the northeast at a rate of up to thirty feet per year, pushed along by prevailing winds that blow from the southwest.[6]

Dunes are categorized by their shapes, and of the six primary types of dunes, four are present at White Sands: dome, barchan (crescentic), transverse, and parabolic. Dome dunes are just what they sound like: low mounds of sand. They are found immediately downwind of Lake Lucero, as they were the first dunes to form from the gypsum sands. It is the dome dunes that are moving at thirty feet per year. Barchan dunes are crescent shaped, transverse dunes are made up of several barchan dunes joined together, and parabolic dunes are the mirror image of barchan dunes. Parabolic dunes are created when plants grow into the dune and hold the arms of barchan dunes in place, causing their shape to invert. Barchan dunes offer an insight into how all dunes are formed: dunes form wherever the wind slows down—when the wind slows down, it drops its load of sand particles. Anything from a depression in the landscape to a plant to a rock can slow the wind down enough that sand drops out.

In another mechanism of dune building that is more difficult to explain, the sand itself can cause its own accumulation. It does this by slowing down the wind that carries it and when sand grains collide with other sand grains. Once a sand dune has reached a certain thickness and angle (known as the *angle of repose*), avalanches begin to occur, and sand tumbles down the dune on the "slipface" or leeward (downwind) side, a process that, through repeated avalanches, moves the dune forward, and the process of dune building begins again.

The language of dunes is poetic: parabolic (the mathematical representation of a gravitational effect) and barchan (from the Kazakh language), both crescent shaped like a waxing or waning moon. Domed like a cathedral's cupola vault, designed to mimic the eternal heavens. Aeolian, a word come down to us from the Greek god Aeolus, the god of wind—dunes are aeolian structures, meaning they are created by the wind. Ah, but "angle of repose" is the most magical phrase of all. The angle of repose in this case is not the position I take when reading poetry on my couch; instead, it is the steepest angle to which a dune (or loose rock, snow, or other granular material) can be piled without slumping, without grains beginning to tumble down the slope. Think of this when you walk the dunes— look for the tiny avalanches that presage larger avalanches. Contemplate that, as you think of the angle and the impending avalanches, you, yourself, are in repose—in a state of tranquility. You have become one with the dune.

Dune fields are living, breathing, moving macroorganisms. They are ecosystems; that is, they serve as habitat to animals and insects and plants; the dunes at White Sands, no matter how desolate they may look, are no exception. The interdune area—the mostly level sand sheets between the dunes—are essential to the flora and fauna of White Sands. The water table in some interdune areas is so close to the surface that a freshly dug shallow hole will fill with water, albeit water not drinkable by humans. Here, in these areas that are sheltered from the wind by the dunes and where groundwater is close to the surface, is where most of the plant life of White Sands puts down its roots.

The NPS White Sands website informs me that there are six distinct ecological units in the White Sands, each of which has its own array of plant life. Among the wildflowers you might see at White Sands are centaury (not the century plant, but a pink gentian), wooly paperflower, sand verbena (which smells like lilac), stick-leaf, and yellow evening primrose. Soaptree yucca is also a common plant in the dunes. It has evolved to stay ahead of the encroaching sand by elongating its stem whenever a dune threatens to overtake it, growing toward the sky as much as a foot per year. Skunkbush sumac and hoary rosemint can do the same, just not as quickly as soaptree yucca. Dunes that are more stable are hosts to, among other plants, the lovely light-pink blossoms of ephedra, the happy yellow-blossomed greenthread, the scarlet "claret cup" hedgehog cactus, and the purplish, feathery seedheads of alkali sacaton bunchgrass.

The most unusual plant in the dunes is the night-blooming cereus (*Cereus greggii*), a member of the cactus family. When it is not blooming, the plant's gray stems can appear to be dead. But, once a year, the cereus—*la Reina de la noche*—pushes out elongated buds and—on one night, for only one night—the cereus blooms. When this occurs, all the cereus plants in an area bloom at the same time. The white, double-petaled flowers fill the air with a scent sometimes described as an intense vanilla.

Let us consider now the Queen of the Night. How does she intuit the perfect evening to unfold her expansive, waxy blossom? And how does she tell her sisters it is time to unwrap their corsages? She waits four years or more to send out her first bud and then waits again for the perfect summer night when the stars sing una canción ranchera *to the sky. All the sisters hear the song and open their white flowers at once, like a hundred embroidered silk handkerchiefs dropped for a gentleman's attention. La Pavura Blanca, attracted by the flowers' rich perfume, whirls by and picks a single white blossom to pin in her hair before continuing the search for her beloved.*

It's not only plants that make their home in White Sands National Park: there are approximately 144 species of birds, 23 small mammals, 371 species of insects, and several types of reptiles in the dunes.[7] Badgers, kit foxes and grey foxes, porcupines, and cottontails and jackrabbits are common in the dunes, as are pallid bats and four species of pocket mice. Several species of lizards and snakes live in the dunes, including the nonpoisonous western coachwhip and Sonoran gopher snakes and the poisonous western diamondback and prairie rattlesnakes. There are even toads and one species of fish, the endangered White Sands pupfish, which lives in Lost River, a stream that enters the park dunes from the east and then, after about two miles, disappears into the sands.[8]

Among the small mammals of White Sands is the Apache pocket mouse, which has evolved to be lighter in color than its counterparts in other places. Similarly, the pocket mouse in the Malpais is a darker color than it is in other habitats. Camouflage is an important adaptation for survival of the little mouse, whose buff white fur matches the sand and makes it more difficult for predators to see him. The Apache pocket mouse isn't the only dunes animal to make use of camouflage coloration: the bleached earless lizard, the little-striped whiptail lizard, the Cowles prairie lizard, the spotted ground squirrel, and two species of camel crickets have all evolved to a permanently lighter color after generations of living in White Sands.[9]

Bird life in the White Sands and surrounding areas is much more diverse than one might imagine. Birds commonly seen at the Sands include the wise and talkative Chihuahuan Ravens, which surely carry on important conversations with Northern Mockingbirds and Western Meadowlarks. Of the raptors who hunt in White Sands, the Northern Harrier and the American Kestrel are most often in the skies. White Sands birds range in size from the Great Horned Owl, whose adult wingspans can reach 5 ½ feet, to the tiny Say's Phoebe, whose entire body is only six inches long. The fancy-flying Common Nighthawk likely inspired more than one airplane, like those that rule the airspace in the Basin. Then, there is the beautiful desert cardinal, which looks like a cardinal with reversible feathers: they are mostly gray, with cardinal-red accents. There are other birds that are not as common at White Sands, but visitors should stay alert—they might be lucky enough to see one of the rare species, like the West's fanciest dresser, the Violet-Green Swallow, or perhaps even the majestic Golden Eagle.

There are flora and fauna in the White Sands area that are not native but have been introduced, and, strangely enough, two species were introduced by agencies charged with protecting New Mexico's plant and animal life. In 1966 the New Mexico Department of Game and Fish introduced the oryx, a large African antelope, to White Sands Missile Range in order to provide hunters with big game.[10] Free of their natural predator, the African lion, oryx flourished in the Tularosa Basin then expanded into the National Park area, and they are now a nuisance animal that over-grazes and damages the native plants in the area. Yearly oryx hunts on the Missile Range have been unable to fully control the population, and the park has had to resort to large fences to keep the oryx out—but tracks seen on a trip to Lake Lucero in 2013 suggest that the fences can't entirely control the oryx, despite the best efforts of park employees. Similarly, between 1899 and 1915, the US Department of Agriculture introduced the tamarisk, commonly called exotic saltcedar, to the Southwest. It has run amok wherever water and saline soils are found. Although it is a lovely tree covered with clouds of pink blossoms in the spring, it grows and spreads quickly, choking out native plants and monopolizing available water. However, the agencies involved are now trying to control or eradicate both the saltcedar and the oryx. Also, many of the agencies concerned with wildlife, including the military and tribal groups, are participating in the reintroduction of the desert bighorn sheep to northern New Mexico and the Mexican gray wolf to New Mexico, although the White Sands Missile Range is a "backup" area for future releases. The program has brought the wolf's numbers in New Mexico up from zero identified individuals and breeding pairs in 1998 to eighty-three individuals and five breeding pairs in 2013.[11] Beginning in 1999 the New Mexico Department of Game and Fish captured and relocated desert bighorn sheep to the San Andres

mountains, just west of White Sands. In 2015 there were an estimated 115–135 bighorn in the San Andres.

We humans are so anxious to meddle. We often mean well: the saltcedar was meant to hold back the banks of rivers, the oryx—well, the oryx was meant for sport, for human recreation. The Mexican gray wolf was near extinction because we brought our cattle to the Basin, and to a wolf a cow looks like dinner, so the wolf was exterminated for being hungry. Not so different, then, from those who brought the oryx to the Basin for the hunt. White Sands should give us pause: the earth has been maintaining itself and revitalizing itself and remaking itself for millennia without our intercession; perhaps we need to think in centuries instead of years.

A PLACE AND ITS PEOPLE

The most well-known and earliest group of Paleoindians of the early Holocene period are the Clovis people, named for the New Mexico town because the first extensive Paleoindian archeological site was found near there.[12] Several Paleoindian sites, dating from the early to mid-Holocene epoch (our current geological moment) up to about 5500 BC, have been identified in the Tularosa Basin. The people who followed the bison were primarily hunters who lived on meat and wild plant foods such as nuts, berries, greens, and tubers— wild potato or turniplike plants. While it was originally thought that Paleoindians did not build shelters but instead took shelter only in caves and overhangs, the 2005 discovery in western Colorado of the remains of a Paleoindian Folsom-period pole-and-brush shelter with associated mud daubs suggests that at

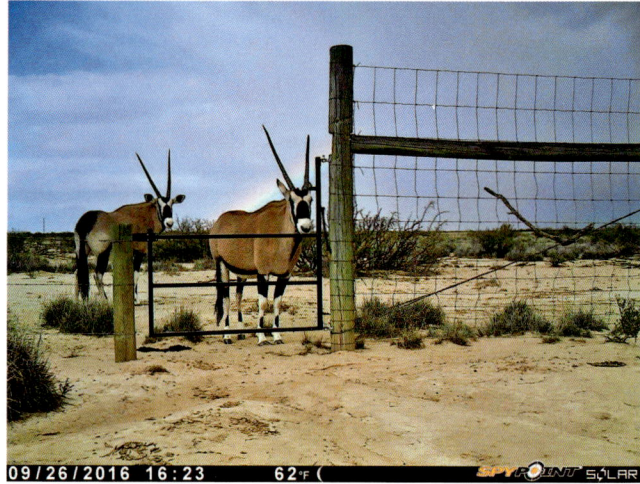

09/26/2016 16:23   62°F (

Oryx and rainbow. Photograph made with trail camera. Courtesy of the National Park Service.

least mid- to late Paleoindian cultures sometimes built semipermanent shelters, probably for use in the winter.[13] The Folsom Period was also named for a town in New Mexico, where the first identified site of post-Clovis occupation was found.

In the White Sands, time slows until its passage is uncountable by the human mind. Space converges—it would be so easy to lose your way, one dune merging into another into another. Nothing but cerulean sky above, no sound other than the whisper of blowing grains of gypsum. This is the center of the Mescalero homelands, cradled by the four sacred mountains—all about a twenty-four-hour walk away. To the east is one of the four, Sierra Blanca, where the People came into this world. Even before the Apache, surely this mysterious place was sacred to the ones who lived in the caves of the San Andres and Sacramentos, who hunted in the Basin, who gathered wild plants on the riverbanks, and who built fire pits in the sands. Be still as you stand in the dunes—perhaps this place will become sacred to you as well.

The Paleoindian cultures evolved into the Archaic cultures, and their occupation of the Tularosa Basin was widespread, both on the Basin floor and in the foothills.[14] The Archaic cultures' eating habits began to vary from their forebears': they ate more plant foods than their predecessors—plants like agave and yucca and goosefoot (a close relative of quinoa)—and, using ground stones, they prepared flour from ricegrass and mesquite bean pods. They gradually gave up big game hunting for easier-to-manage game like deer and rabbits. Most importantly, around 2500 BC the Archaic cultures began to cultivate beans (perhaps

the native tepary beans), amaranth, and *maíz* (corn), the product that is now ubiquitous in our lives. Along with the cultivation of corn came the use of trough metates and heavy manos for grinding.

Think oceans of grasses and wildflowers. Of packrats scurrying to collect their winter stores. Of camels where dunes had not yet formed and of small indigenous horses grazing where mustangs do today. One set of footprints overlays many others: my footprints in the Basin's alluvial fill echoing the footprints of a Clovis woman who was searching for tubers and nuts to feed her children. Recognize that someone else's footsteps will overlay mine.

Native cultures of the Tularosa Basin that followed the Archaic groups are familiar to us today because of their pottery. Late in the Formative period, as it's called, the people also started building in the pueblo style using adobe. Two of the many Formative villages of the Basin—known today as the Lake Lucero and Huntington sites—were located along the banks of Lake Lucero. It seems that by 1200 BC the people of this period may also have made use of "summer houses" and "winter houses," and, archeologists say, permanent group settlements were on or near the foothills both east and west of the Basin, in areas with year-round, reliable water sources. Ruins on the Basin floor appear to be smaller, seasonal habitations, perhaps used when gathering seasonal wild foods or hunting small game. The white sands supplied early Basin residents with gypsum, used as a pigment for decorating pottery, teepees, shields, and bodies and, later, applied as stucco. White Sands was also a source of salt—such an important mineral that it had been

used in various times throughout history as currency. Religious practices flourished and solar calendars were in use, perhaps borrowed from the Casas Grandes people to the south. Most foods eaten during this period came from agriculture rather than from gathering. Irrigation systems were built. But it's the pottery that defines this culture for us today: the black on white Chupadero, the Three Rivers red on terra-cotta, Jornada Polychrome on red, and the stunning, seemingly modern designs on pots made by the Basin peoples' western cousins, the Mimbres.

A simple pot. A useful thing: to carry water in, to prepare food in, to cook in. Who was the first person to put paint to clay? A woman, I think   she would be intimate with her pots, she would know them by heft and shape, by purpose and strength. The act of bringing art into the world is driven by the desire for beauty. Or, perhaps, was the first red line in the center of a pot a reminder that this or that particular one was especially well-suited for a hot fire? For whatever reason, aesthetic or functional, that first black circle or red line made it impossible to ever again forget that the pot was a blank slate, a clean canvas, a space that desired decoration.

As had occurred many times before in the long life of the earth, a major drought occurred in New Mexico from AD 1276–1299, and by 1350 the Tularosa Basin was empty of permanent settlements. Perhaps the people went elsewhere, looking for a place to live that had more reliable water sources. Perhaps they went south to central Mexico or east to the Sacramentos. No one knows for sure. But when the Spaniards arrived in the 1540s, it was the Apaches who ruled the

Tularosa Basin. Dietmar Schneider-Hector, author of *White Sands: The History of a National Monument*, has succinctly and accurately described the Apache presence at White Sands: "From 1610 to 1821, in spite of the Spanish presence, the white sands country remained an Apache domain."[15]

We learned that these natives lived on rabbits, hares, and deer (which they hunted and found in abundance), and on the corn, calabashes, Castile melons and watermelons (resembling winter melons) which they sowed and cultivated. They also ate fish and mescal, the pulpy part of the agave (lechuguilla), a plant half a yard tall with fleshy green leaves on the stumps. By boiling these plants they made a very sweet preserve, similar to quince preserve, which they called mescal.[16]

Espejo traveled El Camino Real de Tierra Adentro, "the royal road" of the Spaniards that followed pre-existing Native trails; evidence of the royal road—wagon ruts, earthen swales, and gravestones—can still be seen today. El Camino Real swerved to the west of the San Andres and the Tularosa Basin, avoiding the Apache in its march through the life-threatening Jornada del Muerto. However, some few travelers, like La Pavura Blanca's beloved, must have explored the Basin, since broken carretas have been found half-buried in the swirling sands. Perhaps the carts belonged to someone camped at paraje Robledo, a resting place for weary travelers twenty-five miles from the Sands, named for Pedro Robledo, a member of Oñate's expedition who died and was buried there. What stories were told about the White

Sands by Camino Real travelers gathered around the fire? Surely there were days in March when the white sand lifted into the air like a community of souls reaching high enough to be witnessed from Robledo.

For the Mescalero Apache, the White Sands are more than just a salt lick or an interesting feature: they are also a spiritual place. The sands are within the boundaries of the Apache world, a physical and spiritual space delineated by the four sacred mountains: Sierra Blanca, Guadalupe Mountains, Three Sisters Mountain, and Oscura Peak. Moreover, according to some sources, a version of the story of White Face Woman (alternately White Shell Woman), first woman to the world and mother to the hero twins, pinpoints White Sands as the place where she came to rest in her abalone shell once the great flood waters receded. There is evidence that the Apache used gypsum from the sands to whitewash their homes, a practice that was taken up by later settlers and continued well into the early twentieth century. The Apache still consider the Basin a part of their homeland today.

To see the earth from space is to gain a different perspective on our planet and our place in the greater scheme of things. The white sands are easily visible from the International Space Station (245 miles above the earth) and, appearing as a snowflake against a darker background, the area was seen by astronauts looking back at earth on their way to the moon. This is truly a monumental place, a place that demands meditation and respect. Geological eons marked by gypsum sands. Inhabited by a locus genii, a "guardian spirit," who watches over it and reminds us that places have their own meaning and vocabulary beyond that which humans bring.

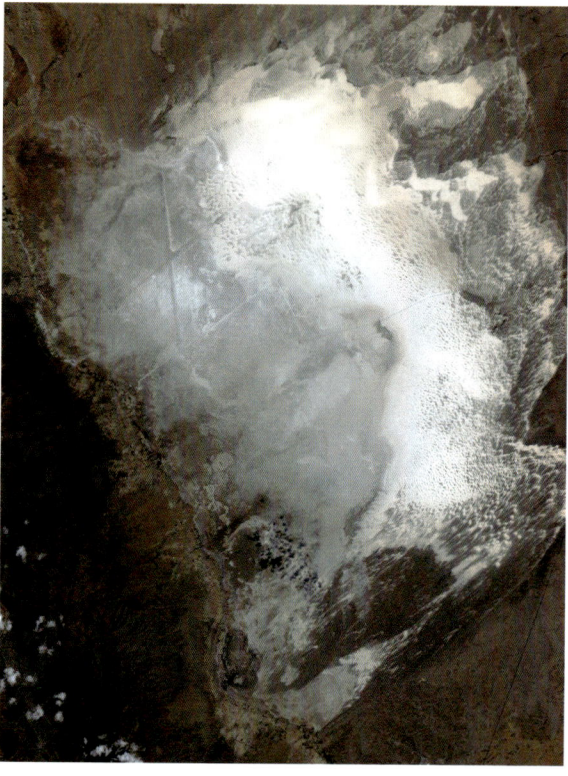

White Sands National Park as Seen from Space. NASA image created by Jesse Allen using the Advanced Land Imager onboard NASA's Earth Observing satellite.

Despite occasional forays into the area for salt, the Spanish conquistadores and colonialists didn't linger long in White Sands. There was no gold, and no permanent settlements were established in the Sands during this period. On *entrada* period maps, the area to the east of the San Andres and north of El Paso is an empty space labeled, if noted at all, as *Las Salinas*. In 1821, after the Mexican Revolution, Nuevo México's Spanish governor Facundo Melgares swore allegiance to the Mexican government. Nuevo México and White Sands were then governed by Mexico until 1848, when the Treaty of Guadalupe-Hidalgo, signed at the end of the Mexican-American War, ceded the territory north of the Rio Grande and Gila rivers. Soon after, in 1855, Ft. Stanton was built, followed by Ft. Selden in 1865. The Americans had come to stay.[17]

After the establishment of Ft. Stanton (near Ruidoso), more settlers arrived in the Basin because the fort promised protection against Apaches resisting incursions into their homelands. Kit Carson and Black Jack Pershing were stationed at Ft. Stanton, although at different times. Buffalo Soldiers from Ft. Selden helped Ft. Stanton soldiers pursue Victorio and Geronimo. Billy the Kid was held at Ft. Stanton, under protection as a witness to a murder. The Army also improved a trail which began south of White Sands and wound through San Augustin Pass and onto the plain of the Camino Real. In 1861 a group of Hispanic farmers, tired of losing their crops and homes to floods on the Rio Grande, moved their settlement to the Basin and established the town of Tularosa; another group established La Luz. Texas cattle barons arrived, too: in 1875 my distant cousin John Chisum drove ten

thousand cattle past the White Sands on his way to the railhead in Engle.

THE TWENTIETH AND TWENTY-FIRST CENTURIES

In 1897 Jose and Filipe Lucero built ranches on the west side of Lake Lucero, which was named for these brothers who also served as sheriffs and deputies of Doña Ana county. The Luceros and other ranchers settled the Basin at a time when the native grasses grew "high as a horse's shoulder," before overgrazing led to its demise.[18] Ruins of a Lucero ranch corral, on the north side of the park accessible through the missile range, can still be seen near the western edge of Lake Lucero: a windmill, recently toppled; a water tank; weathered fence posts; and barbed wire.

The Luceros weren't the only ranchers in the Basin: among them were Thomas J. Bull and W. W. Cox, whose land was taken under eminent domain for the White Sands Missile Range, and Oliver Lee, owner of the largest ranch in New Mexico, whose name is remembered today because he was accused but acquitted of murdering Las Cruces judge Albert Jennings Fountain and his nine-year-old son. The remains of Fountain and his son were never found—most believe they still lie beneath the white sands. After his acquittal in 1907, Oliver Lee sold his Alamo Ranch. Part of it became the townsite of Alamogordo, and another section eventually became Oliver Lee Memorial State Park.[19]

And there was Eugene Manlove Rhodes, cowboy, sharpshooter, novelist, and poet, who established his ranch in what is now Rhodes Canyon (within the White Sands Missile Range). In the following passage

from his novel, *Pasó Por Aquí*, Rhodes's love for the landscape of the Tularosa Basin is evident:

The Plain was dark and cold below him; the mountains took shape and grew, the front range of the Rockies—Capitan, Carrizo, Sierra Blanca, Sacramento, with Guadalupe low and dim in the south: the White Sands were dull and lifeless in the midway plain. Bird twitter was in the air. Rabbits scurried through the brush, a quail whirred by and sent back a startled call; crimson streaks shot up at the sky, and day grew broad across the silent levels. The cut banks of Salt Creek appeared, wandering away southeast toward the marshes. Low and far against the black base of the Sacramento, white feathers lifted and fluffed, the smoke of the first fires at Tularosa, fifty miles away. Flame tipped the far-off crests, the sun leaped up from behind the mountain wall, the level light struck on the White Sands, glanced from those burnished bevels and splashed on the western cliffs; the desert day blazed over this new half world.[20]

From 1880 to the turn of the century, the Tularosa Basin was the wild, wild west. Along with the cattle ranchers came the cattle rustlers, like John Kinney and his gang, who were so successful that they ruined several ranches by stealing their herds. Judge Fountain and his son were killed in the midst of a crackdown on cattle rustlers—or, depending on who you ask, in the middle of a land-and-water grab and consolidation of power by cattle barons to the detriment of individual ranchers. After the rustlers were rustled up and the gunslingers dead or in jail, the influx of settler families helped calm the communities of the Tularosa Basin.

Settlement of the Basin increased, and towns like Alamogordo were established once the El Paso and Northeastern Railroad arrived in 1898. At the same time, a movement—or, rather, a series of movements—arose that many historians call "boosterism." The Tularosa Basin had become "the place to be"—cultured society was evolving, business was booming, and the healthy air called to those with tuberculosis and other respiratory problems. The Sands themselves became a place for recreation rather than a site of range wars and impromptu burials.

Visitors had been exploring the White Sands for as long as humans lived in the Basin, but tourism in America—tourism available to middle- and working-class people—was a new phenomenon made possible at first by the railroads then by Henry Ford. Alamogordo, especially, was eager to celebrate its arrival into the twentieth century, and leading city citizens seized upon tourism and the White Sands as a way to do so. As early as 1889 people were advocating for a national park in the area, but shortly after statehood in 1912, US Senator Albert B. Fall (New Mexico) introduced one of "at least four national park bills" that he would pursue over the next ten years.[21] With the creation of the National Park Service (NPS) in 1916, the possibility of creating a national park in south-central New Mexico—in the Tularosa Basin and, perhaps, in the surrounding mountains—became more viable.

What did we bring, we humans, to this place? Did we bring gifts or burdens or some of both? What do the Sands say about our violence against one another? I listen closely from the top of Three Rivers's petroglyphed hills but cannot comprehend the wind's answer. I listen again from the top of a dune, but the raven refuses to translate his call.

After Albert Fall was appointed secretary of the interior in 1921, he continued advocating for a national park in New Mexico. In fact, one of the proposals overseen by Secretary Fall was the "Southwestern All-Year National Park," which included portions of the Malpais, the White Sands, the Sacramentos, and the Mescalero Apache Reservation. It was during the organization and promotion of the "All-Year Park" that Tom Charles became a leader in the southern New Mexico national park movement. However, because of the difficulties involved in parceling out a section of the Mescalero Reservation, the inclusion of Elephant Butte and its dam (which was completed in 1916 and controlled by the US Bureau of Reclamation), and suspicion of its oddly shaped boundaries (which appeared to add value to Fall's sixty-thousand-acre ranch) the "All-Year Park" was not approved.

Yet Tom Charles continued his quest to have White Sands recognized by the NPS. In a pamphlet entitled *Story of the Great White Sands*, Charles noted that the value of commercial gypsum was, at the time, five cents a ton and that the "New Mexico Tourist Bureau finds that every automobile leaves an average of $21.50 in the state before occupants see the attractions which interest them." Pointing out that, at those values, "it takes 430 tons of white sand to equal one tourist," he continues,

So far as "making anything out of them," there is

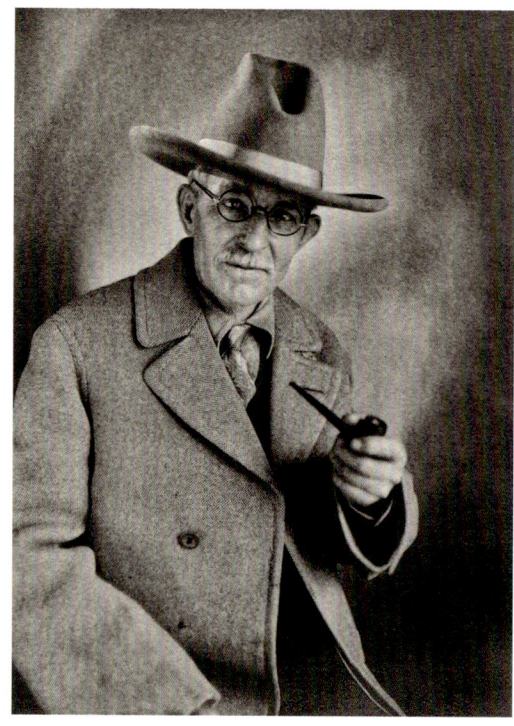

Portrait of author Eugene Manlove Rhodes. Photographer unknown. Courtesy of the New Mexico State University Library, Archives and Special Collections.

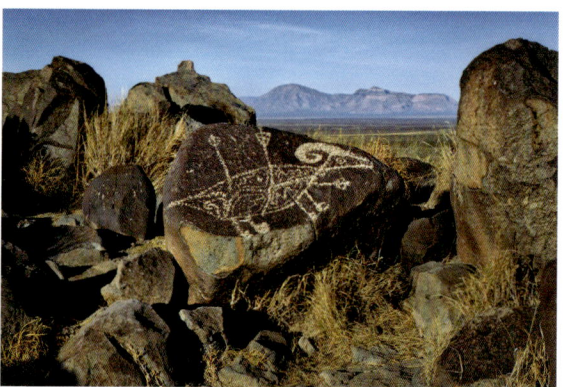

Petroglyph of Bighorn Sheep with Arrows, Three Rivers Petroglyph Site, Bureau of Land Management, Tularosa, New Mexico, 2016. Photograph by Craig Varjabedian. Three Rivers Petroglyph Site is located fifty-six miles north of White Sands National Park.

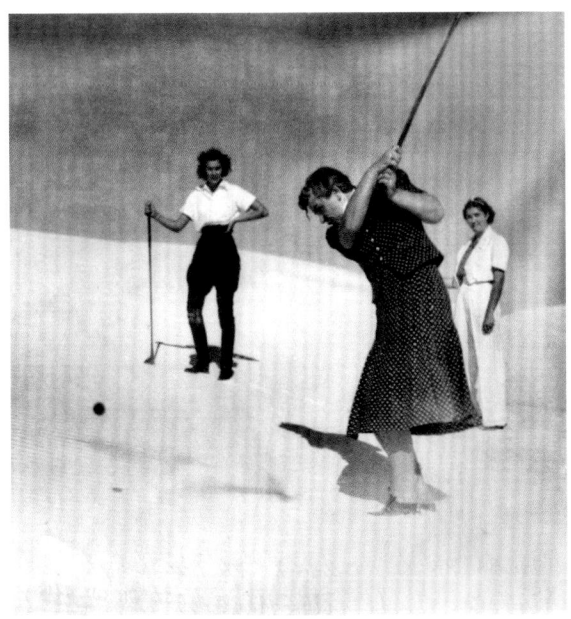

Golfing with black golf ball, Dorothy Birdwell of Alamogordo in jodhpurs, ca. 1940s. Courtesy of the National Park Service.

only one question to answer; do we want to sell the Great White Sands at five cents per ton [the price of gypsum] or at $21.50 per inspiration? Do we want to sell them in inspiration to be spread over the pages of National Geographic and similar publications or do we want to sell them at five cents per ton to be made into plaster and buried in the walls of city skyscrapers?[22]

Tom Charles's decade of championing the White Sands as a "pleasuring area" was finally rewarded with congressional approval of the White Sands National Monument on January 18, 1933.[23] The monument encompasses 225 square miles—143,733 acres.

Roosevelt's New Deal also benefitted the monument: the visitors' center was built by the WPA, and both WPA and CCC workers helped improve old roads and build new ones. The CCC helped improve water supplies by building catchment basins. Although the dunes had been used for recreation before 1933, recreational use increased dramatically after it achieved monument status. During its first year, the newly christened monument tallied twelve thousand visitors—a thousand a month, in a period when Americans were just starting to "take to the road." In 1935 National Geographic published a photo essay on White Sands by George A. Grant, chief photographer for the NPS, thereby introducing it to the world.

Monument. For centuries the word carried the meaning "man made" and also the idea of memorializing human presence and ingenuity. The pyramids. The Parthenon. The Eiffel Tower, the Lincoln Memorial, the Vietnam Veterans' Wall. What then, does it mean, that in the early twentieth century in America, our perspectives shifted and allowed us to think of natural spaces as monuments—as monumental? As worthy of respect and awe and preservation? What do we memorialize in these sands, what lessons have we learned that allow us to see a dune field as nature's equivalent to human structures? And what do we lose when we think of only the monumental structures of nature and not of her less picturesque areas as worthy of respect?

Early White Sands visitors were creative in their use of the dunes: some people skied the white sands, either downhill or behind an automobile; some played softball; some picnicked as they do today. There are photos of women playing golf in the sands during the 1950s—perhaps they were perfecting their sand-trap shots. A photo from the 1970s captured a wedding at White Sands—it appears the entire wedding party wore white. Today, hiking and sledding the White Sands are favorite activities.

From the beginning, White Sands attracted visitors from all over the world as it does today. By 1948 there were more than 100,000 visitors and more than half a million by 1965. In recent years the number of visitors has averaged around 500,000. And, just as the New Deal contributed to White Sands, White Sands in turn contributes to the local economy: according to a 2016 NPS report, the park's 555,794 visitors spent about $29.3 million in communities surrounding the park, supporting 437 jobs in the local area.

However, unlike most national parks and monuments, White Sands is nearly surrounded by military installations: only 40 percent of the 275 square miles of dunes are within the park's boundary; the other 60 percent lies within White Sands Missile Range.[24] In order to tell the story of White Sands, it is also necessary to discover how White Sands Missile Range and Holloman Air Force Base came into being. The Tularosa Basin, particularly the White Sands, is—or was, at least in 1937—one of the most desolate areas of the United States, and while desolation is usually considered a negative attribute, for the military it's a feature. While desolate, the area was not uninhabited: huge ranches claimed both private and leased public lands in the Tularosa Basin. The ranchers had the area to themselves until January 20, 1942, when Roosevelt, by executive order, established the Alamogordo Bombing Range in the Tularosa Basin. Ranchers were told to take their livestock and leave the area, and they were given lease agreements that were supposed to last only until the end of the war.

According to Jim Eckles's *Pocketful of Rockets*, the Germans' use of the V2 rocket changed the military's outlook on the Tularosa Basin—it was suddenly needed to test rockets. So, after a short experiment in "joint use" of the land between the military and ranchers, an experiment that led to ranchers finding live rockets near their homes, ranch families were moved permanently out of the missile range area. Many of the ranchers felt they were unfairly compensated, and the court battles went on for years. Today, few people can remember when there wasn't a missile range in the middle of the Basin. "Joint use" is now an agreement between the military and the NPS: Lake Lucero is within the boundaries of the national park—access is through the White Sands Missile Range. Visitors to White Sands National Park who wish to visit Lake Lucero must sign up for a ranger-escorted trip that takes them through the missile range, a trip the military helps facilitate.

We drive through the missile range in a convoy, warned at the gate that we need to stay close to our fellow adventurers, to keep the line of cars grouped together. We are not to stop until we reach our destination, Lake Lucero. Until now, we have only seen this part of the Basin from a distance—the alluvial fans of the San Andres, the western edge of the dune field, the evidence of perched aquifers in canyons and of seasonal streams. We arrive at a parking area at the edge of the road, and, once parked, all of us—maybe thirty people—exit our vehicles and listen to the park ranger's short talk about safety and a reminder to take nothing and leave nothing behind. We linger at the ruins of a corral and tank, built and used by the Jose Lucero family. We peer at animal tracks in the sand, identifying a kit fox, a coyote, and an oryx. And hundreds of rabbits. We hike up over a little rise, and there is the lake, dry today, no water above ground. The lake fools the eye—from here, it shimmers like a mirage. From there, it looks like a snow-covered field. As our compatriots walk out on the lake, they look like amateur ice skaters in a Christmas movie, moving carefully on the spongy ground. We forget for a while that weapons are tested not far from here, on the missile range.

Despite the presence of the missile range, the phrase "White Sands" may be best known for another military usage: in 1945 the white sands and their residents, animal and human alike, witnessed, from a mere forty-five miles away as the crow flies, the detonation of the world's first atomic bomb. So much has been written and said by so many passionate and artistic people that, instead of giving such an existentially important event a short gloss here, let us share a moment of silence.

Silence.

Today, some of the grasslands that were overgrazed in the ranching years have regrown on the mostly uninhabited missile range, and cattle have been removed from the park area. Moreover, with the military's cooperation and in partnership with the San Andres National Wildlife Refuge and the White Sands National Park, many animals, especially large mammals, are returning to the Tularosa Basin: bighorn sheep, mountain lions, mule deer, pronghorns, golden eagles, and hawks. The land is healing itself, much like radioactive areas of northern Russia, where flora and fauna have reclaimed a land uninhabitable by humans. The White Sands, the mountains, the *animals* predated human incursion—and, it appears, they will survive us.

THE DUNES AND THE ARTS

There is no doubt that, like the rest of New Mexico, the Tularosa Basin and the White Sands have drawn artists of all kinds, since at least the Mogollon period. The artists of the petroglyphs at Three Rivers surely had spent some time in the Sands—the dune's white blossom on the landscape is clearly visible from the top of the petroglyphed hills.

Among the many artists attracted to White Sands was painter, landscape artist, and muralist Ray Strong,

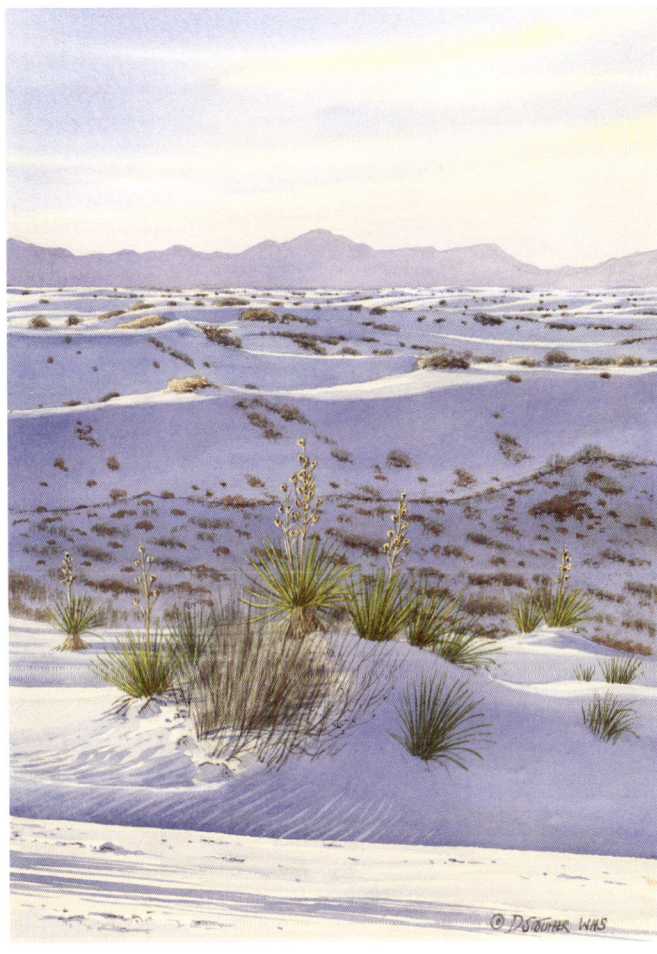

White Sands Reverie. Watercolor painting by Dan Stouffer. Courtesy of the artist.

who painted the dioramas at the park headquarters as well as murals at Mt. Lassen and Mt. Rainier.[25] A 1934 photograph of Strong working on the dioramas is on display at the Tularosa Basin Historical Society along with the dioramas themselves. Artists such as Peter de La Fuente, Michael Hurd, Eanger Irvine Couse, Cyrus LeRoy Baldridge, Dan Stouffer, and John Z. Thomas found and continue to find the Sands an inspiration. A quick internet search reveals that artists are still drawn to the Sands: one artists' sale site (among thousands) features fourteen paintings of White Sands.

The film industry has likewise found White Sands a unique setting for feature films, television shows, music videos, and documentaries. According to an NPS information sheet available at the White Sands National Park website, roughly two dozen feature motion pictures have been filmed at White Sands; the films have been directed by such luminaries as Stephen Spielberg, Harold Ramis, Michael Bay, and Sam Peckinpah and have included actors such as Clint Eastwood, Willem Defoe, George Clooney, and Ewan McGregor. Eugene Manlove Rhodes's novel *Pasó Por Aquí* was made into a film entitled *Four Faces West* with Joel McCrae in the leading role and a young John Astin ("Gomez Addams") in a small part. More recently, the first two *Transformer* movies, *The Men Who Stare at Goats*, and *The Astronaut Farmer* were filmed at White Sands. The White Sands International Film Festival is held every year in September; it attracts film stars such as Lou Diamond Phillips and Jeffrey Tambor.

While the NPS information sheet lists several additional television shows and films, it does not include films or television shows that feature White Sands as a setting or that use archival materials from White Sands. A favorite White Sands reference is an episode of *The Twilight Zone* entitled "A Hundred Yards Over the Rim" (1961), a Western starring Cliff Robertson. While the episode was not filmed at White Sands, it features White Sands as a setting—almost a character. One of the classics of early science fiction, *Destination Moon*, a 1950 film based on a Robert Heinlein story, used archival material from the missile range. According to Michael Shinabery of the New Mexico Museum of Space History, the opening sequence of the film is a "rocket [launch that] appears to be actual footage from White Sands Proving Ground's Launch Complex 33."[26] For the opening scene of his 1956 movie, *Around the World in 80 Days*, Michael Todd filmed the launch of a Corporal missile at the missile range.[27] Music videos filmed at White Sands include Pink Floyd's "The End," Boyz II Men's "Water Runs Dry," and Martina McBride's "How Far."

Not only have music videos been filmed at White Sands, but songs and a ballet have also been inspired by the park. The ballet, which premiered at Flickinger Center for the Performing Arts in Alamogordo, is named for and based on the "Legend of Pavla Blanca." The ballet is an entirely New Mexican production: "The score and libretto were written by Alamogordo resident JD Droddy and choreography is by Ann Gavit, Anne Bishop and Sara Jackiewicz of the New Mexico State dance program."[28] Music inspired by White Sands includes the mystic-pop group Maquiladora's album *White Sands*, the band Oppenheimer Analysis's song "New Mexico," Planet P Project's song "White Sands," and several original tunes available on

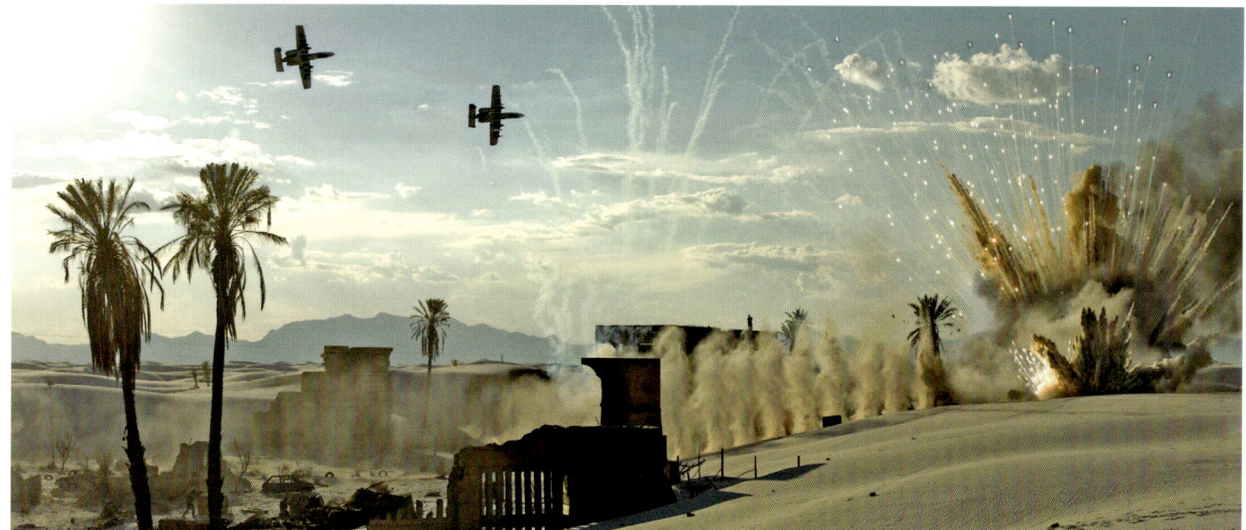

A scene from *Transformers: Revenge of the Fallen*, is filmed at the White Sands Missile Range. Courtesy of the United States Air Force.

YouTube. During "Full Moon Nights," held monthly between May and October, White Sands National Park invites musicians to play for the public out on the dunes.

Photography has been a part of the White Sands story for more than a century. Photos of the area by visitors, scientists, and others from as early as the late 1800s have been documented, and many are available in the photography collections curated by the University of New Mexico and archived in New Mexico Digital Collections. It was George A. Grant's photo essay that introduced White Sands to the national imaginary. Laura Gilpin, one of America's premier large-format photographers and platinum printers, visited White Sands in 1947, and she selected at least one of the images, *White Sands #3*, for her last touring exhibition. Master photographers Brett Weston, Ansel Adams, and Jack Welpott also photographed at White Sands. Like photographers before him, Craig

Varjabedian has found the Sands irresistible in their unique response to light and shadow.

A PLACE, TIMELESS: A FINAL MEDITATION

As I was writing this essay, I was also in the process of organizing family photos that came into my possession after the deaths of my mother and grandmother. Halfway through one large box of photographs, a snapshot marked "1989" on the back fell out of the box. When I turned it over, there was my mother, standing in White Sands. I don't remember her telling me she visited White Sands, but there she was, barefoot and smiling.

I was not sure when I started this essay that I was the right person for the job, being a fairly recent transplant to New Mexico, but finding the photograph of Momma in the Sands made me realize something that should have been obvious: the park is a national

park—it belongs to all of us. And, like other compelling, spiritual places on this planet, it belongs to none of us. I thought of Georgia O'Keeffe, who said of Pedernal Mountain, "God told me if I painted it enough, I could have it." What she meant, I believe, when she said "have it," was that if she dedicated her art to revealing the many faces and moods of the mountain to the rest of us, then she had earned a claim to kinship with it.

I claim a kinship with the White Sands, with its sere basin, its startling cerulean sky, its strange sublimity. I think often of its history, both human and geological. I wish I could have seen the Basin covered in grasses as high as a horse's shoulder, and I hope that, one day, I can experience a magical summer evening when la Reina de la Noche unfurls her blossoms.

I recollect the moment I spied the first petroglyph at Three Rivers and the gasp of recognition that escaped

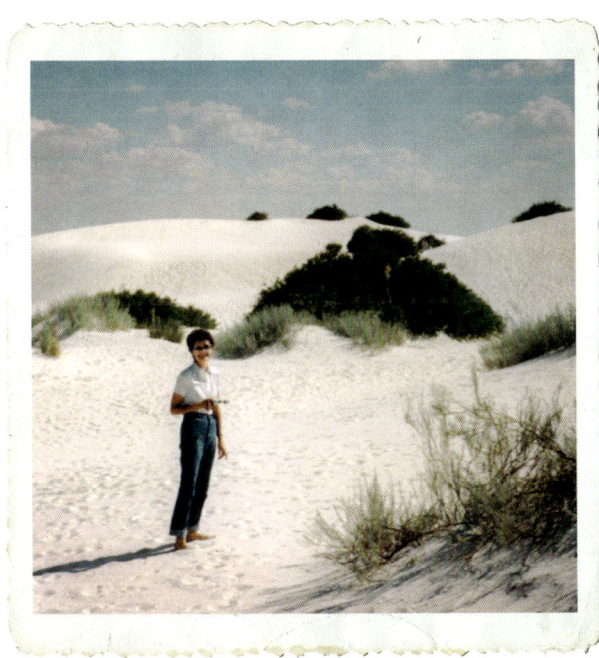

Calhoun Mish's mother, Myrna Teague, at White Sands National Monument, 1989. From the Mish family collection.

unbidden from my heart. I hold in the center of my chest the horizontal timelessness that abides among the dunes, and I feel the vertical spike of sacredness that anchors me in the center of the world. I think of the other artists who came before me, the pot makers, the santeros, the church builders, the moccasin makers, the writers, the poets, the songmakers. The photographers and painters and sculptors.

I worry that some day we will forget our cultural awakening to the monumental in nature. I mourn for those whose lives were inexorably changed or taken by technologies developed there—and I pray for peace in their names. I celebrate the return of the wolf and the bighorn sheep while hoping that other nonhuman inhabitants of the basin never need to be reintroduced.

The dune winds still whistle in my ear; the visual memory of stark white sands settles me for meditation. These days, La Pavura Blanca calls to me across the dunes in my mother's voice; she holds a bouquet of cereus and is accompanied by a guardian coyote. I listen closely, as I did to the wind and the raven, and I think I hear her say, "Tell everyone. Tell everyone this place is sacred. Tell everyone they can find their solace here."

NOTES

1. "Rio Grande Rift FAQ," http://aconcagua.geol.usu.edu/~arlowry/RGR/faq.html.
2. Fryberger, "Geological Overview of White Sands National Monument."
3. Walker, Church, and Seymour, *Basin and Fan*.
4. Eidenbach, ed., *Prehistory of Rhodes Canyon*.
5. George Gibbs, "Salt Plains of New Mexico."
6. National Park Service, "White Sands National Monument."
7. Dodge, *Natural History Story*, 5–6.
8. New Mexico Department of Game and Fish, "White Sands Pupfish."
9. Kain, "White Animals at White Sands."
10. Welsh, *Dunes and Dreams*.
11. US Fish and Wildlife Service, "Mexican Wolves in the Wild."
12. Eidenbach, ed., *Prehistory of Rhodes Canyon*.
13. Dold, "Stiger's Very Old House."
14. Eidenbach, ed., *Prehistory of Rhodes Canyon*.
15. Schneider-Hector, *White Sands*, 32.
16. de Espejo, "Journey to the Provinces and Settlements of New Mexico."
17. Schneider-Hector, *White Sands*.
18. Sonnichsen, *Tularosa*.
19. Welsh, *Dunes and Dreams*.
20. Rhodes, *Pasó Por Aquí*.
21. Schneider-Hector, *White Sands*.
22. Charles, *Story of the Great White Sands*.
23. Qtd. in Schneider-Hector, *White Sands*.
24. Welsh, *Dunes and Dreams*.
25. Strong and Karlstrom, "Oral History Interview with Ray Strong."
26. Shinabery, "Destination Moon."
27. "TV-Movies Eye Range for Public," *Wind & Sand*.
28. Moore, "Ghostly Dance."

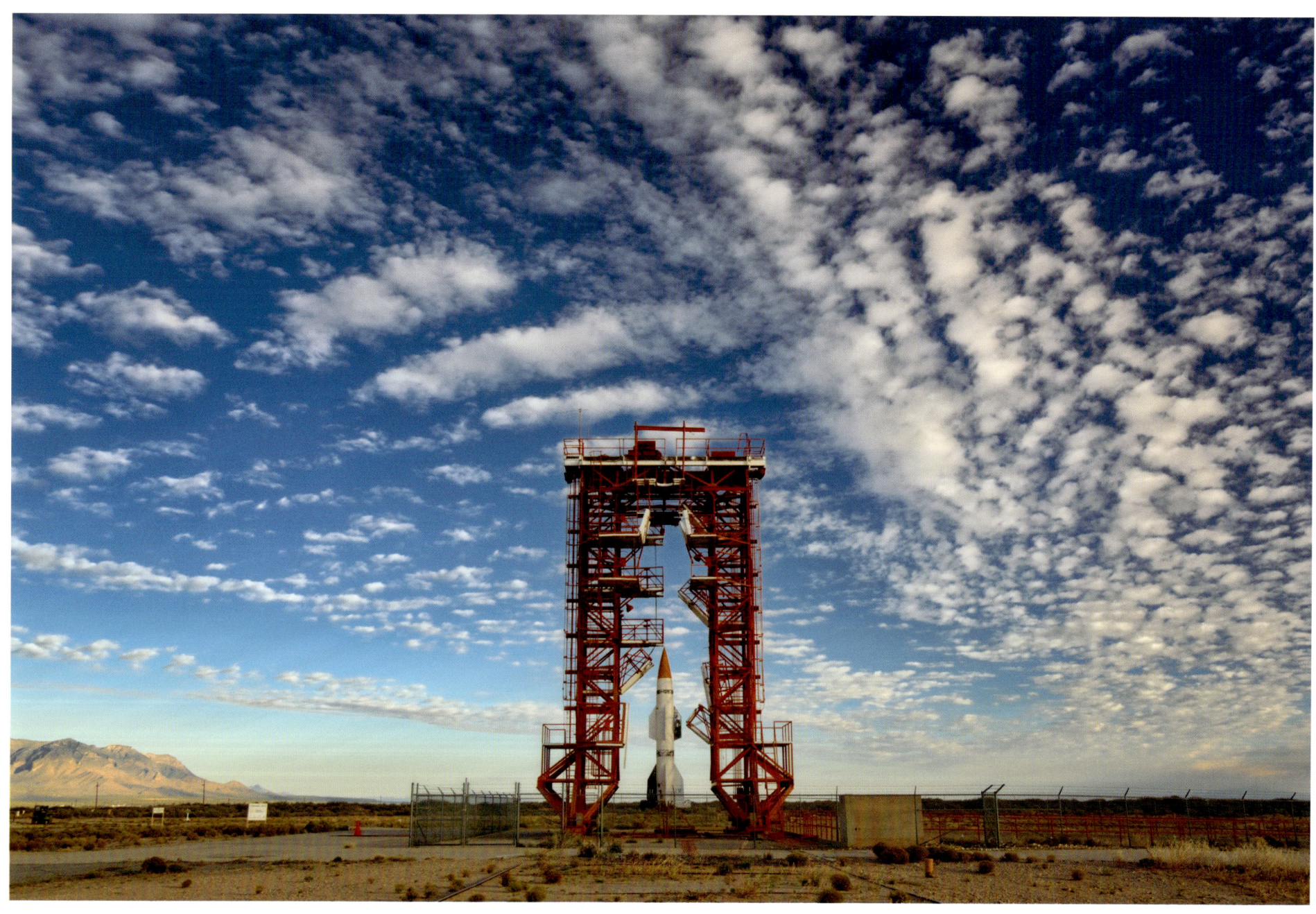

Von Braun V-2 Gantry Crane with Hermes A-1 Missile, Launch Complex 33, White Sands Missile Range. The German V-2 Rocket Gantry Crane stands over a Hermes A-1 missile at Launch Complex 33. The gantry, erected in 1946, gave technicians easy access to various levels of a rocket or missile during preparation for launch. Before firing, the gantry, which is sitting on rails, was rolled out of the way. A plaque located near the gantry reads, "This unique structure was used in the development of America's first modern rockets and is where man took the first step to the moon."

The Other Side of the Boundary

WHITE SANDS MISSILE RANGE

Jim Eckles

THE ARMY'S DUNES

White Sands Missile Range occupies a very large space in southern New Mexico, hefty enough to easily squeeze in Delaware and Rhode Island. It extends north and south about one hundred miles and is forty miles wide in most places. Within its boundaries are two mountain ranges, most of the Tularosa Basin, some of the Jornada del Muerto, and an assortment of playas, lava flows and Mogollon pueblos.

Also within its boundaries are the remaining gypsum sand dunes, those not protected in White Sands National Park. It turns out more than half of the gypsum dunes are on the missile range. They extend north from the park boundary, along the eastern edge of old Lake Otero and the missile range, to a few miles southwest of the village of Tularosa.

Because of the shifting nature of the dunes and their caustic environment, the missile range has almost no development in its dune field. With so much other land, the military has found it easier to place facilities and sites on friendlier ground.

This means the missile range's dunes, without any visitors, are just as pristine as most areas found within the park. The range has restrictions on using the dune field, but they are not as stringent as those of the National Park Service (NPS). Just a few years ago, scenes from the first two *Transformers* science-fiction movies were filmed in the missile range's dune field—look for very white dunes. It was a large project that could not have been accomplished inside the park.

Looking at its basic dimensions, one would assume the missile range is 4,000 square miles, but that is not the case. It is only 3,200 square miles, or 2,000,000 acres. One reason is the very jagged boundary with its many severed corners and cutouts. However, the main reason is the presence of the San Andres National Wildlife Refuge and the White Sands National Park within the missile range's borders. These entities are islands of Department of Interior land floating in a sea of Department of Army property and have to be subtracted from the total.

The wildlife refuge is isolated up in the San Andres Mountains and has little impact on the missile range. The national park, however, sits on the eastern border and extends right into the heart of the range's daily business.

SHARING THE NEIGHBORHOOD

One obvious question is why a military test facility, where dangerous stuff happens, has a 225-square-mile public park smack-dab in the middle of it. The main reason is timing. White Sands was originally established as a national monument in 1933 by presidential proclamation. This was years before any military needs arose in the Tularosa Basin and, as the old adage goes, "possession is nine-tenths of the law." Being a long-established NPS holding helped when World War II started.

On July 9, 1945, the missile range was created by appropriating the real estate used for the Alamogordo Bombing Range during World War II. It would have been logical at that time to include the monument's property in the new testing facility, to make one continuous expanse of military property with no large inholdings. However, the war's conclusion ended the incredible urgency that drove extensive American sacrifices during the war years. Citizens were tired, heartbroken, and just wanted to return to normal life.

The park already existed, and trying to abolish it to create more military facilities wasn't going to happen. It was realistically and politically impossible. From two thousand miles away in Washington, DC, leadership simply decreed that the two organizations would have to learn to live with each other.

Having a civilian entity, normally open to the public all the time, completely surrounded by the missile range, with its secretive and dangerous testing, created an unusual and interesting relationship for both sides. During those first few years, we'll say there was friction between the two organizations as they tried to work out the details glossed over by Washington officials.

For the national monument, it meant safety restrictions for visitors and issues such as noise, military encroachment, and access difficulties for staff. For the missile range, it meant keeping those visitors safe, arranging mission schedules to minimize impact on the monument's operations, tailoring flights to avoid public land, and continuously educating the range's workforce about the agreed upon restrictions concerning monument property.

TESTING TO SEE IF AN ITEM BEHAVES AS ADVERTISED

White Sands Missile Range needs such a large footprint because it is charged with safely conducting weapons testing for the Army, Navy, Air Force, and foreign military services. Also, the missile range provides testing support for other government agencies like NASA, the Department of Transportation, and the Federal Aviation Administration. Finally, some private companies avail themselves of the range's state-of-the-art facilities.

Basically, the test range's most valuable asset is its vast empty space. This allows heavy objects to be sent careening through the air at supersonic speeds, sometimes colliding with each other and falling harmlessly to the ground. In fact, since 1945, more than forty-two thousand rockets and missiles have been safely fired at the missile range. Any youngster who loved playing with firecrackers and bottle rockets would find working at the missile range a dream come true.

Like other places in the country during 1942, landowners (ranchers in this case) were originally forced to leave their property for the creation of the Alamogordo Bombing Range and to accept lease payments for the duration of World War II. Plans to return the property after the war hit a major glitch when military officials realized they needed to learn more about the newfangled rocket technology emerging from Germany and at home. The old bombing range met most of the military's criteria for their vision of what a missile testing range should look like.

The White Sands Proving Ground was established as the place in America to test and investigate rockets, especially the V-2 "Vengeance" weapon from Germany. The proving ground, later changed to "missile range" in 1958, took up the same property as the bombing range, and leases with ranchers were simply extended.

The private property inside the new missile range accounted for less than 4 percent of the total. The rest was state and federal land originally leased by ranchers for grazing purposes. The privately held acres were finally purchased in the 1970s and 1980s.

In addition to its characteristics as a weapon, the V-2 rocket turned out to be a fabulous scientific research tool. The V-2s were used by military and civilian researchers to test and measure our atmosphere, study the effects of weightlessness, photograph the earth from space, and measure what happens to plants and animals when exposed to high levels of cosmic radiation. These early flights strongly suggested that a large mammal like a man would one day be able to survive a rocket flight.

Because of that work, the original launch complex is now a national historic landmark and is credited as the place where the space age began for the United States. The other national historic landmark on the missile range is Trinity Site, where the first atomic bomb was tested on July 16, 1945—the place where the nuclear age began.

This use of a rocket to "sound" or explore the upper atmosphere and carry experiments to the edge of space is the longest-running program at the missile range. Even today, rockets sponsored by NASA, with payloads built by university students, are still fired by the Navy at White Sands, which is run by the Army. It is truly a cooperative effort.

All of these rockets and missiles and the hundreds

of remotely controlled aircraft used as targets have come crashing down on the missile range—well, most of them have. Early on, when the technology was still young, there were occasional incidents where vehicles crashed outside the "sandbox." The most famous was a V-2 that flew south instead of north and hit the ground with a resounding *kaboom* just outside Juarez in July 1947. To say the least, it was front-page news in the *El Paso Times* the next day.

KEEPING A CLEAN HOUSE

With all of that action, most people assume the missile range is a bombed-out, crater-pocked moonscape. It is not. When I used to fly VIP tours over the missile range, I'd often ask visitors how much debris they saw on the ground during the helicopter ride. Most of the time they would think about it a moment and realize they hadn't seen any.

For decades the missile range has actively hunted down the debris from tests and removed it from the landscape. One reason for this is to analyze the remains of the missile, to perform a kind of autopsy on a machine. Another reason is to keep the place neat and tidy so when there is a need to search for a particular test vehicle, personnel aren't confused by a lot of other junk strewn across the desert. Finally, removing the debris lowers the safety risk on the range for humans and wildlife.

Speaking of wildlife, a common question for missile range personnel concerns the safety of animals like the African oryx that frequent the flats of the Tularosa Basin. They wrongly assume that a few oryx

randomly wandering hither and yon across hundreds of square miles of the Basin are somehow in grave danger from occasional falling debris. The chances of an animal being struck are astronomically small. This lack of understanding probabilities must surely contribute to the popularity of American lotteries and casinos.

The reality is that the missile range, with its very restricted access, has huge swaths of land that are now de facto wildlife refuges. There are very few roads into the mountains, and many of them are questionable four-wheel-drive-only routes. As a rule there are no planned missile impacts in the mountains—they act as a buffer zone—so the only people who go up the roads are a few hunters and the infrequent wildlife biologist or botanist. Get off the roads and into the backcountry and there are places that haven't seen a human being in a decade or more.

In fact, many scientists say much of the land on the missile range that was heavily grazed by cattle and goats until 1942 is returning to its natural state, maybe how it was before 1850.

Of course, officials at the missile range did not set out seventy years ago to develop a nature laboratory. Much of the unused land is a result of the testing business and the need to keep people and valuable facilities out of the line of fire. Whole areas were simply not used.

Early attitudes about the landscape and the neighbors at the monument were very self-centered. The Cold War boomed from the 1950s through the 1980s, and personnel at the missile range felt they had a mission to defend the very future of the nation.

Weapons of all kinds were tested to make sure they could stop the Soviets in Europe or anywhere else.

Niceties about sand dunes, boundaries, noise, and impacts on visitors were not driving considerations. In fact, when reading the history of White Sands during those years, one gets the impression the military simply bullied the monument into submission. Changing those military attitudes was a slow process.

ATTITUDES HAVE EVOLVED AND IMPROVED

Sure, there were and still are a few missile range personnel who would love to simply asphalt the whole Tularosa Basin. But, in general, missile range attitudes about the park are now the polar opposite from what they were in 1950.

Most of the missile range's workforce appreciates the landscape, the flora and fauna populations, the diverse human history in the area, and what the park represents. It has been a decades-long educational process that has been helped by a more stable workforce. The lack of constant turnover has created a group of people who are at home in southern New Mexico. They and their families use the national park and have come to appreciate its wonder.

These are the people who have shown the way for continuing improvements in the relationship between the two entities. They have opened the lines of communication, listened, and are willing to try different approaches.

Now, when a missile test's safety footprint overlays the park's picnic loop, the range doesn't simply call and expect the area to be evacuated. The evacuation is discussed by the two sides, dates are adjusted, and times are set that are convenient for each party. Usually the test time will be set early in the morning so the park doesn't actually have to evacuate the dunes drive; they simply delay opening it until the firing is complete.

The park and its visitors are encouraged to report noise from aircraft flying too close or too low if it bothers them. There are flight rules around the park for both the missile range and Holloman Air Force Base next door. Violators can often be identified and re-educated.

In the end, each organization would probably be very happy if the other simply didn't exist. Life would be much easier. However, the missile range's workforce has grown to appreciate the value of having White Sands National Park nearby. They understand that the park does nothing for the nation's defense, but they have come to appreciate that White Sands National Park certainly makes the country worth defending.

PHOTOGRAPHS OF WHITE SANDS MISSILE RANGE

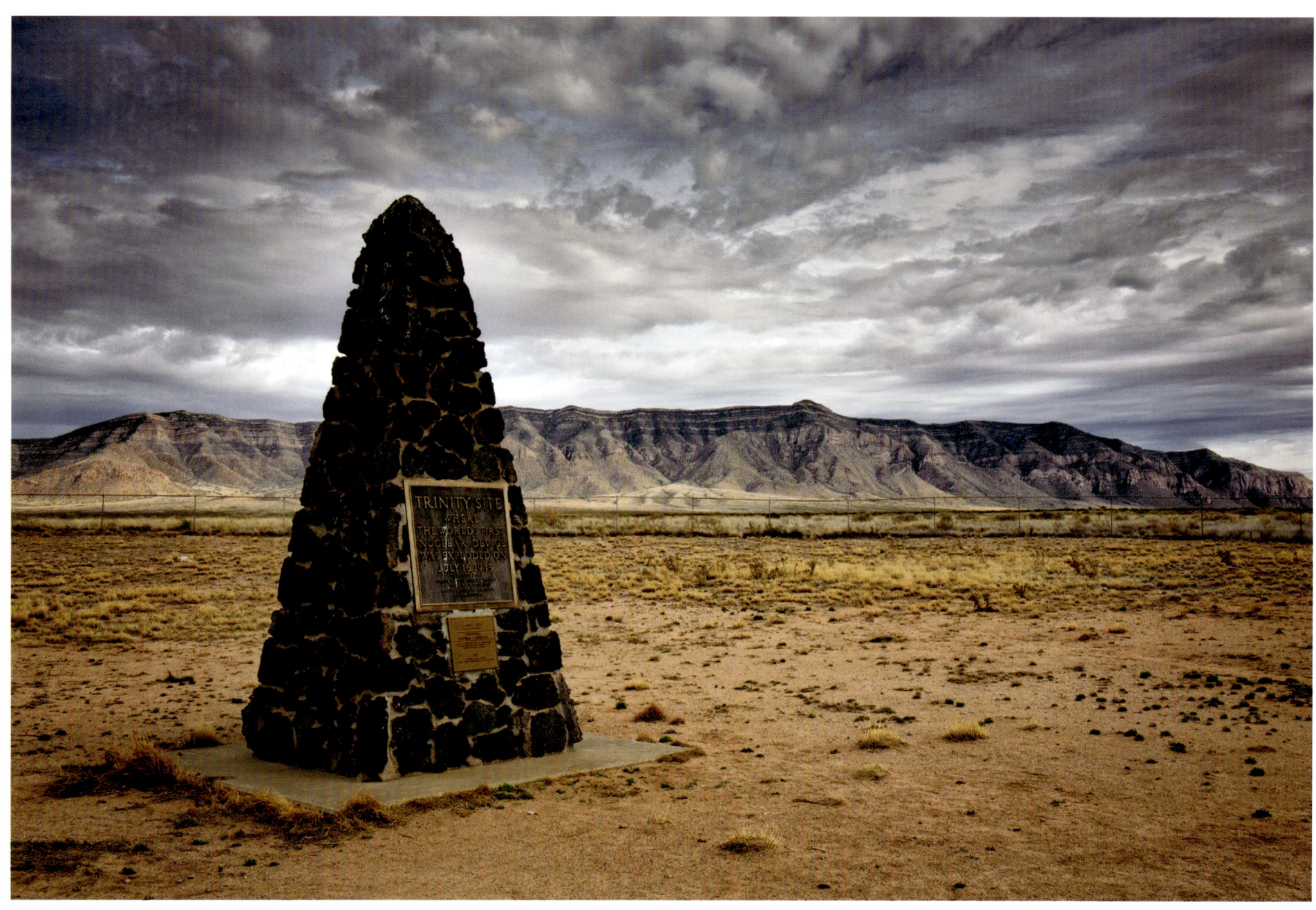

Obelisk, Trinity Site, White Sands Missile Range. This lava-rock obelisk marks exact ground zero at the Trinity Site. It sits between what would have been the four legs of the one-hundred-foot steel tower on which the first atomic bomb was exploded. The tower was vaporized in the explosion. The lava comes from the Valley of Fires flow on the east boundary of White Sands Missile Range. Erected in 1965, the plaque reads in part, "Trinity Site where the world's first Nuclear Device was exploded on July 16, 1945."

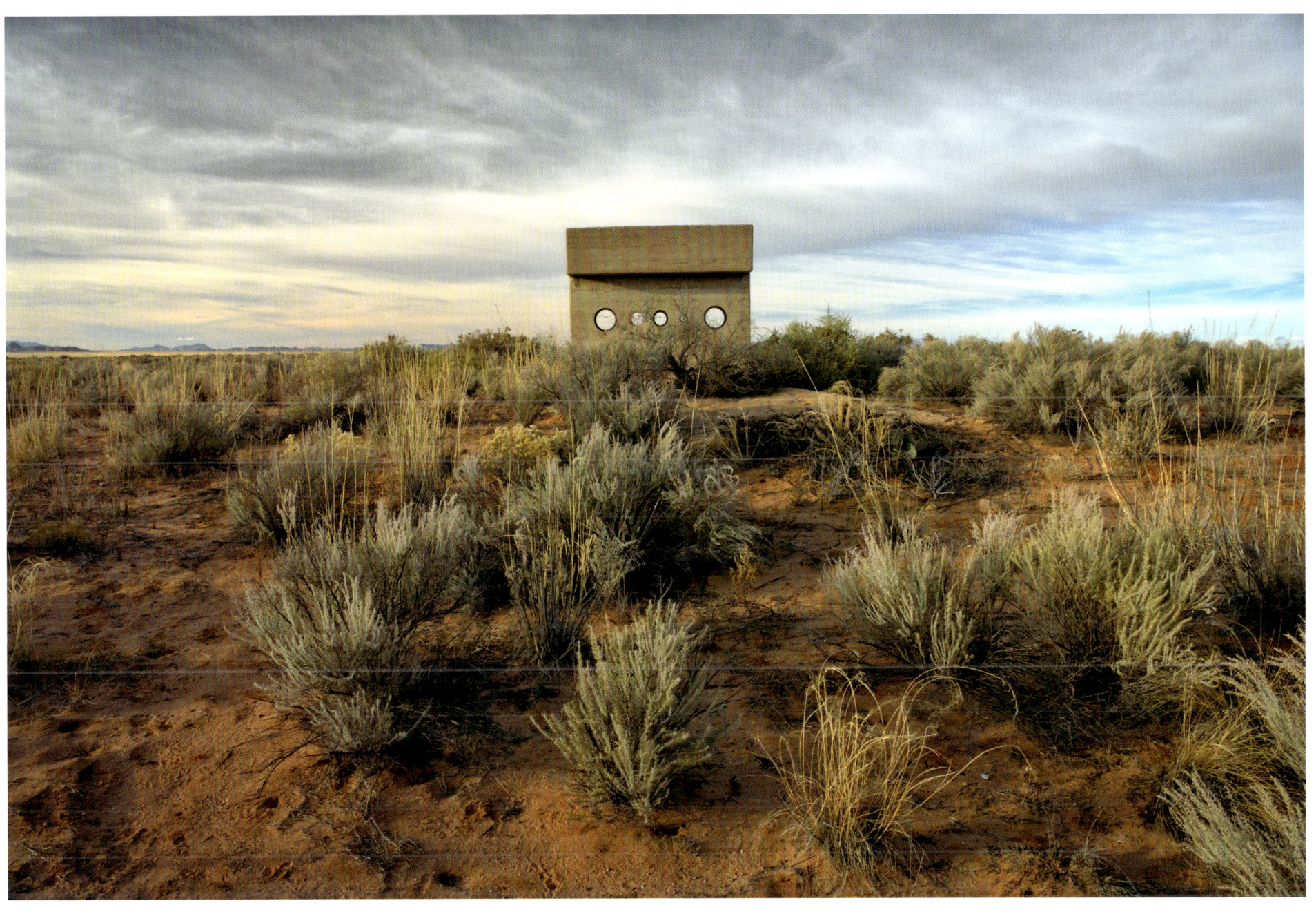

North 10,000 Camera bunker, Trinity Site, White Sands Missile Range. The camera bunker is located ten thousand yards north of ground zero at the Trinity Site. Berlyn Brixner took most of the iconic photos of the first atomic bomb's explosion from this location. This is one of the few artifacts left from the test that ushered mankind into the atomic age.

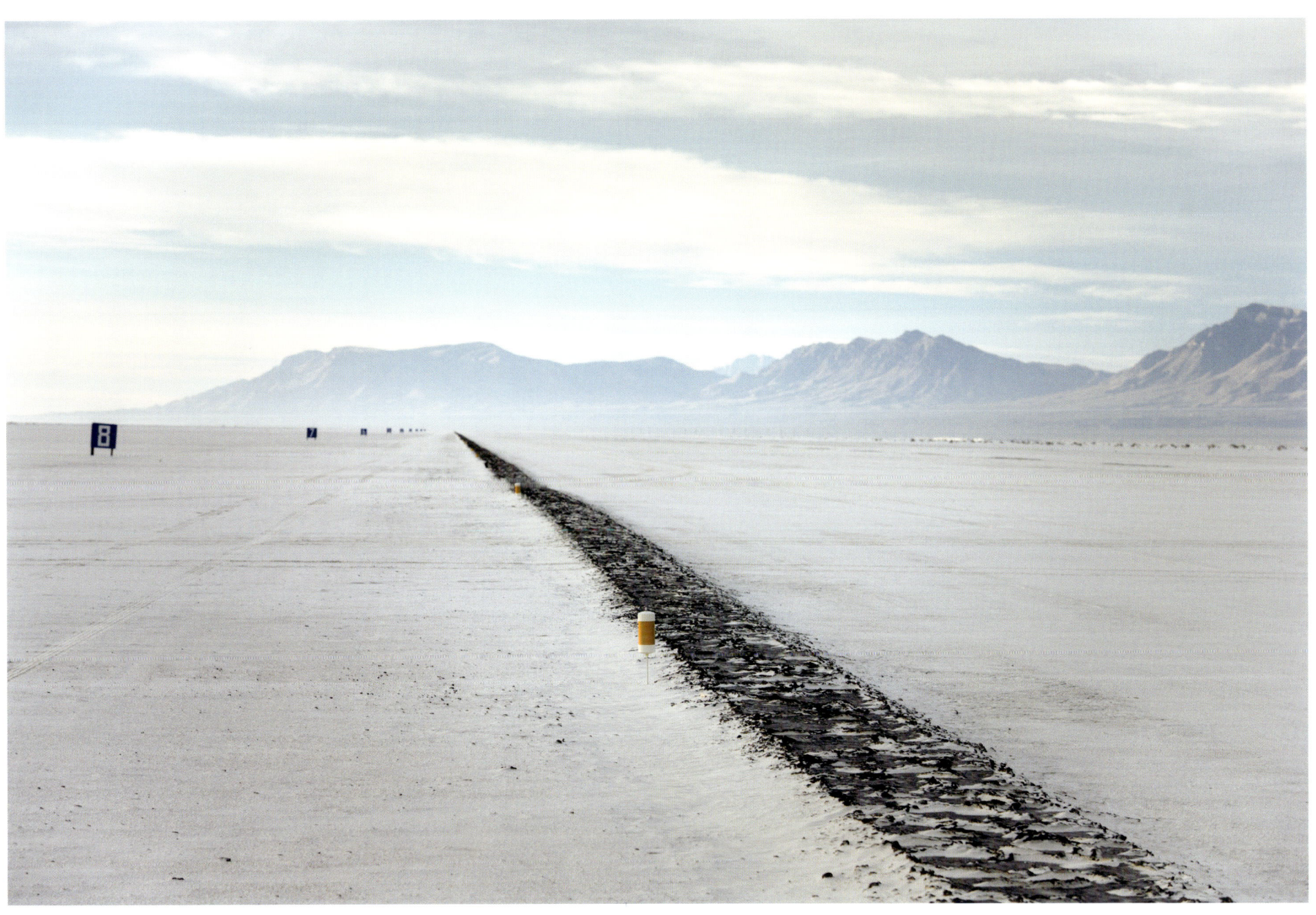

Space Shuttle Runways, Space Harbor, White Sands Missile Range. Asphalt still marks the edge of one of the Space Shuttle runways at the missile range's Space Harbor. Space Shuttle Columbia landed here on March 30, 1982. Since the abandonment of the Space Shuttle Program, the two runways are slowly returning to being part of the huge gypsum-based lake bed that makes up the missile range.

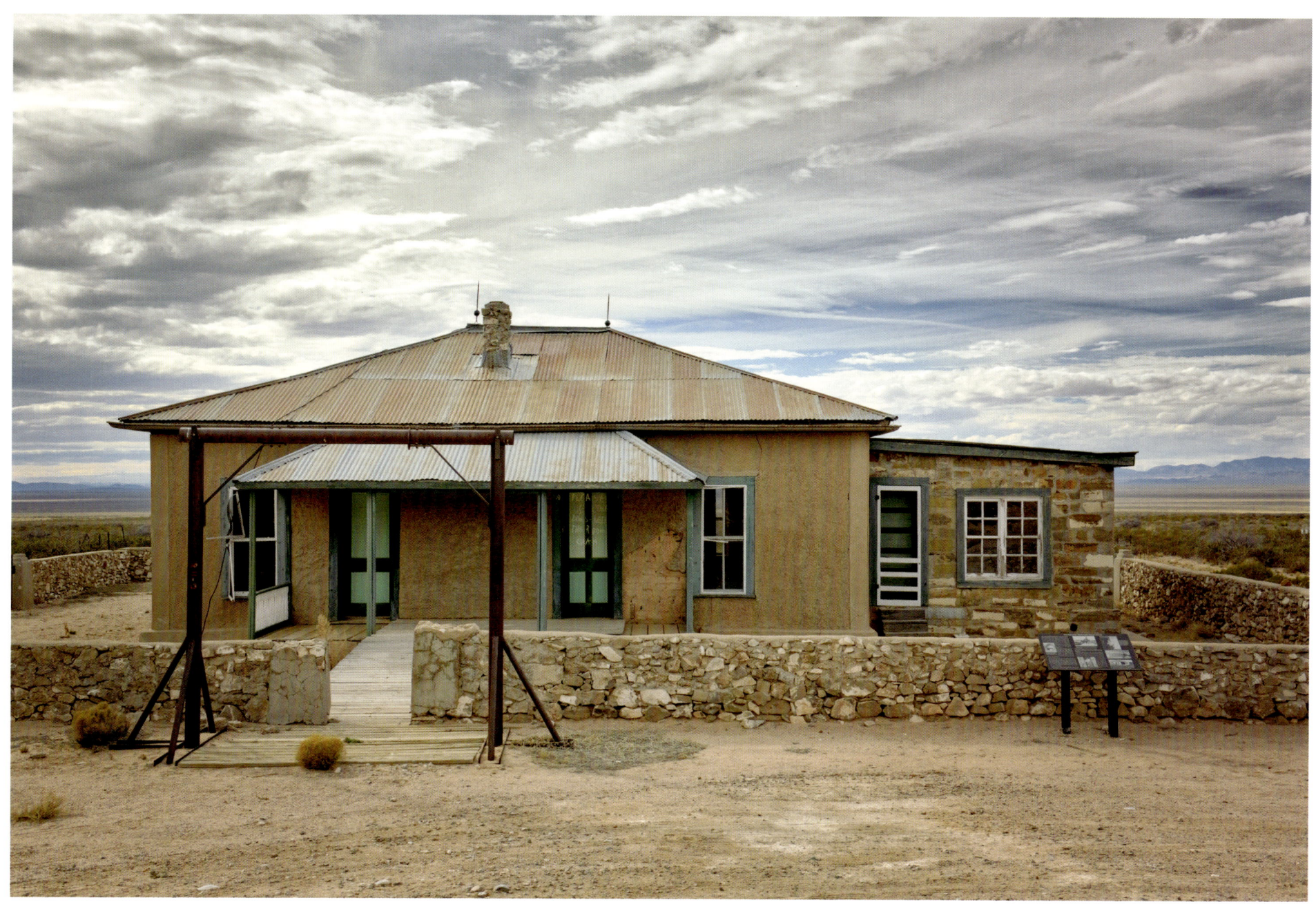

Schmidt/McDonald Ranch House, Trinity Site, White Sands Missile Range. The Schmidt/McDonald ranch house sits just two miles from Ground Zero at Trinity Site, where the first atomic bomb was exploded on July 16, 1945. The house was constructed by rancher Franz Schmidt in 1913 to accommodate his growing family. The last owner before World War II was George McDonald. The right-hand door leads into the house's master bedroom, which was used by Los Alamos scientists as a clean room for their assembly of the first atomic bomb's plutonium core. The house is part of the Trinity Site National Historic Landmark.

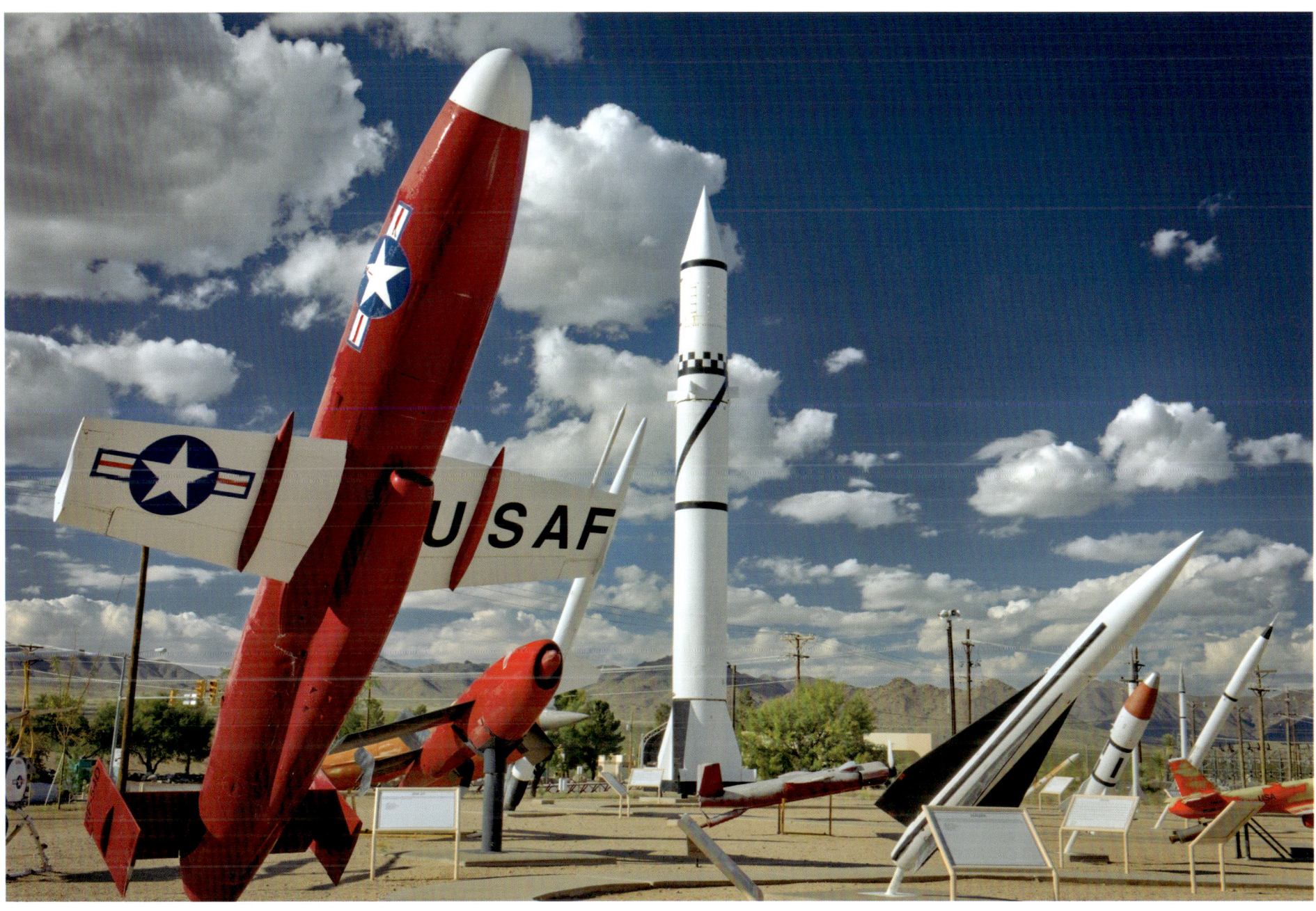

Missile Park, Museum, White Sands Missile Range. The Missile Park at the White Sands Missile Range Museum has dozens of rockets, missiles, and other vehicles on display. The red US Air Force vehicle is a Crossbow, an air-launched missile designed to home in on ground targets emitting radar signals. The tall missile in the background is a Redstone, designed by Wernher von Braun's team. Redstone components were used to put America's first satellite into orbit and send Alan Shepard into space.

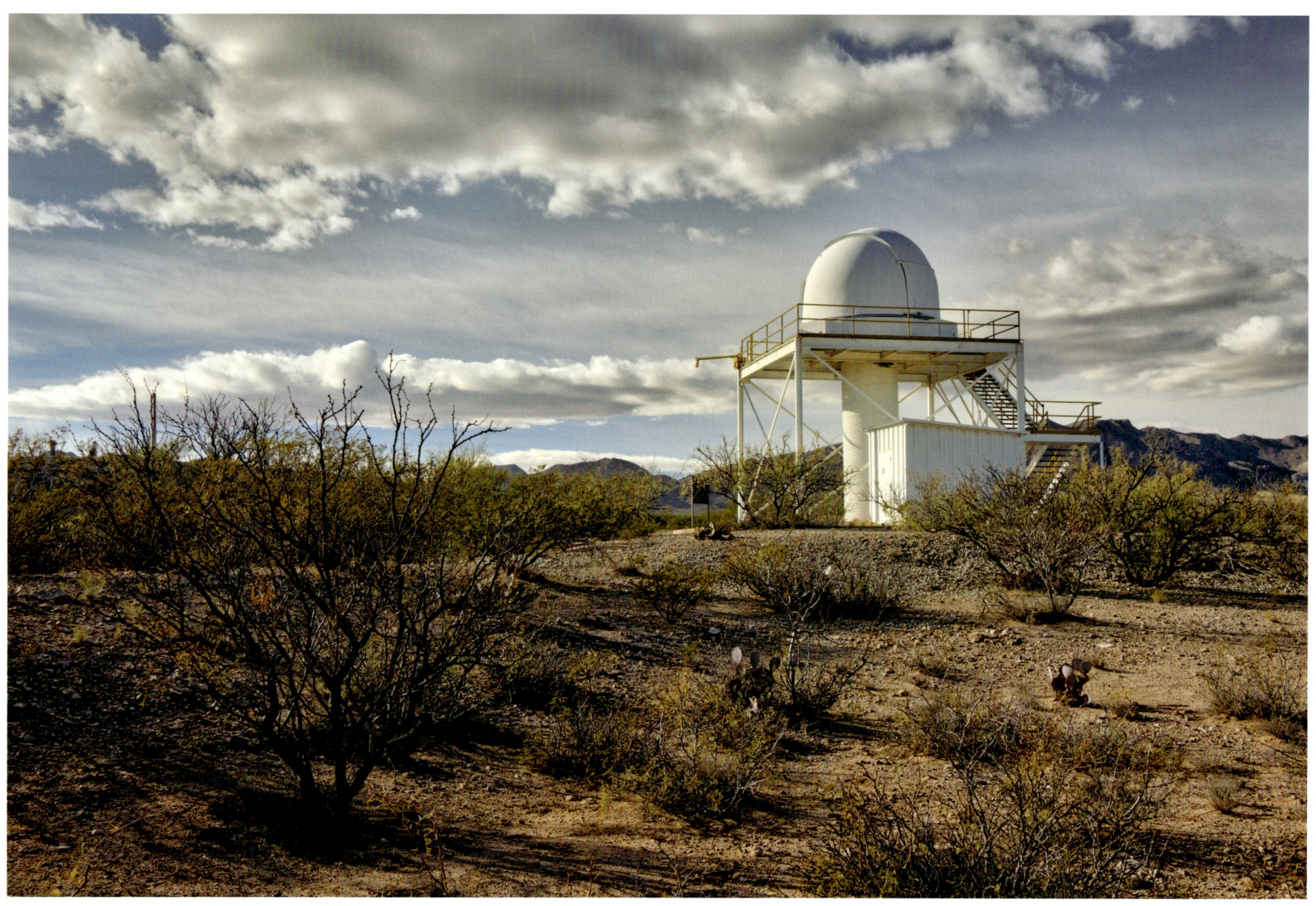

Astrodome, White Sands Missile Range. A typical astrodome found on White Sands Missile Range. Like many astronomy domes, this one was installed to house a large telescope with a camera attached. There is a removable cover over a vertical slot or opening in the dome so the camera can see out and track a missile or its target. As the operator rotates the telescope to record the mission, the dome rotates in unison with the instrument.

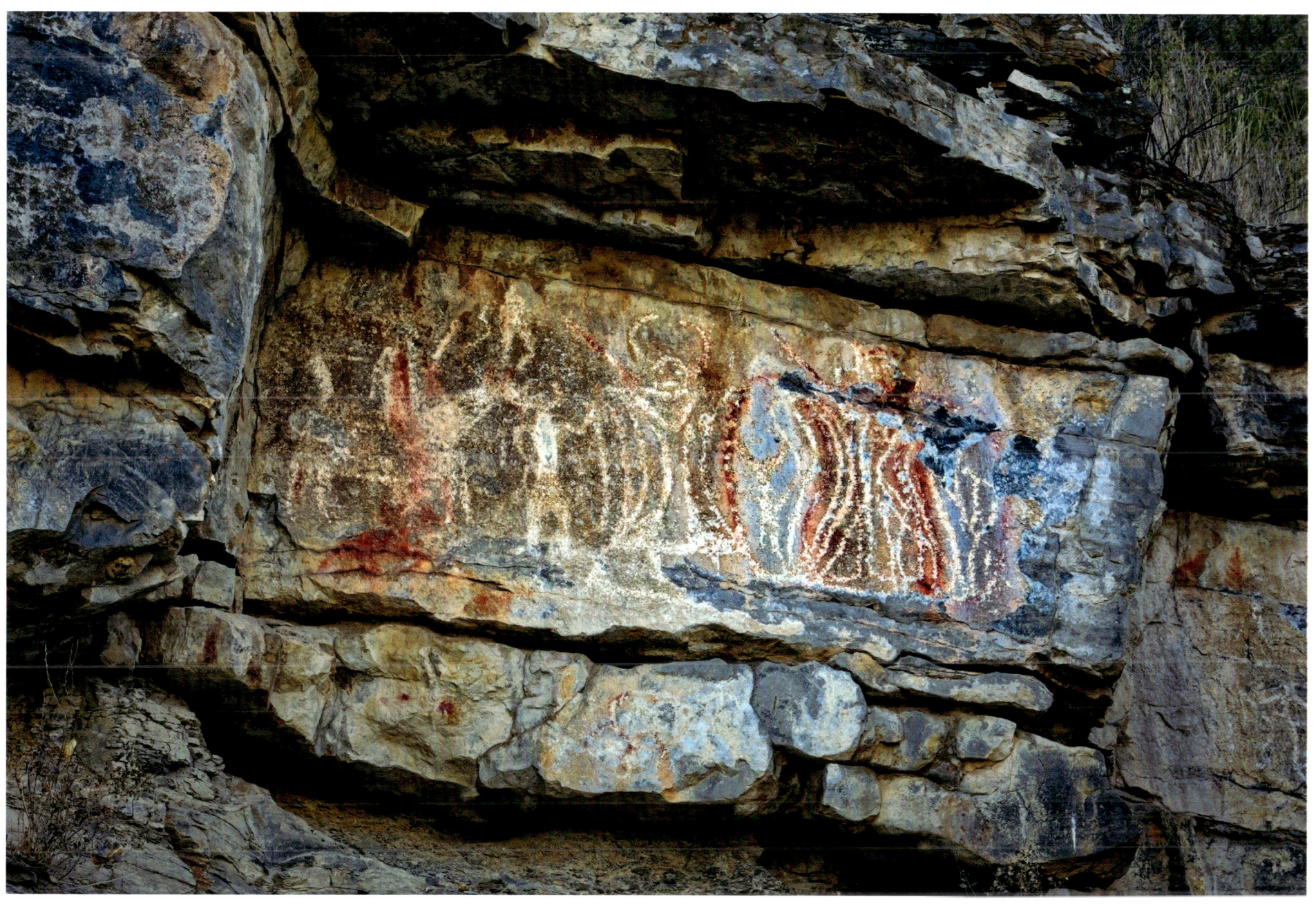

Petroglyphs, Hembrillo Canyon, White Sands Missile Range. Apache petroglyphs in Hembrillo Canyon. The reason experts say they are Apache and not earlier is because of the figure on horseback, which would indicate post-European contact. Just west of this "rock art" site is the Hembrillo Battlefield, where Buffalo Soldiers from the US Cavalry fought Warm Springs Apache warriors led by Chief Victorio in April 1880.

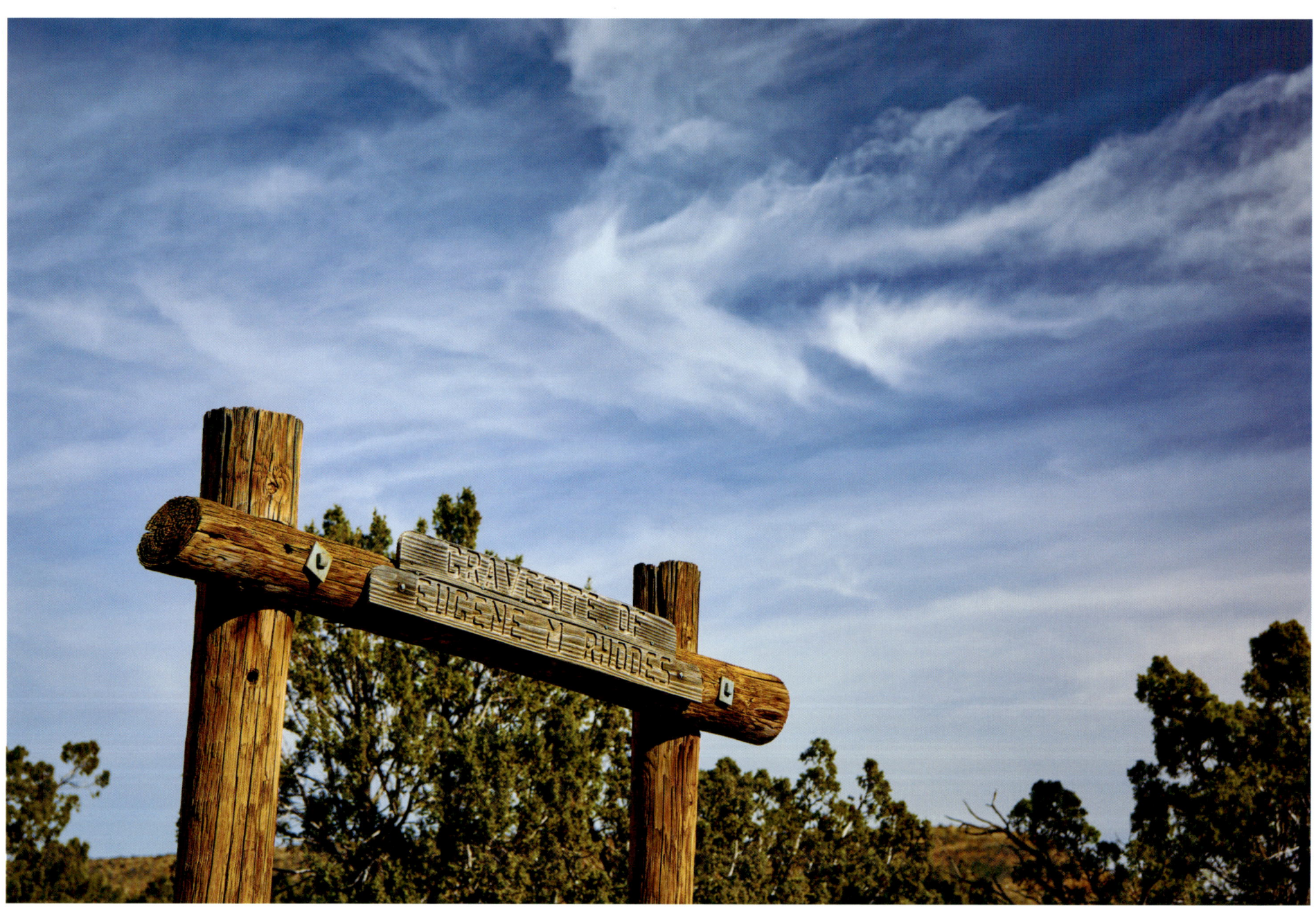

Grave of Eugene Manlove Rhodes, San Andres Mountains, White Sands Missile Range. The grave of author Eugene Manlove Rhodes is nestled in the juniper and piñon trees at Rhodes Pass in the San Andres Mountains on White Sands Missile Range. Rhodes once had a ranch just downhill to the east in Rhodes Canyon. The missile range has allowed an annual tour to the gravesite for decades.

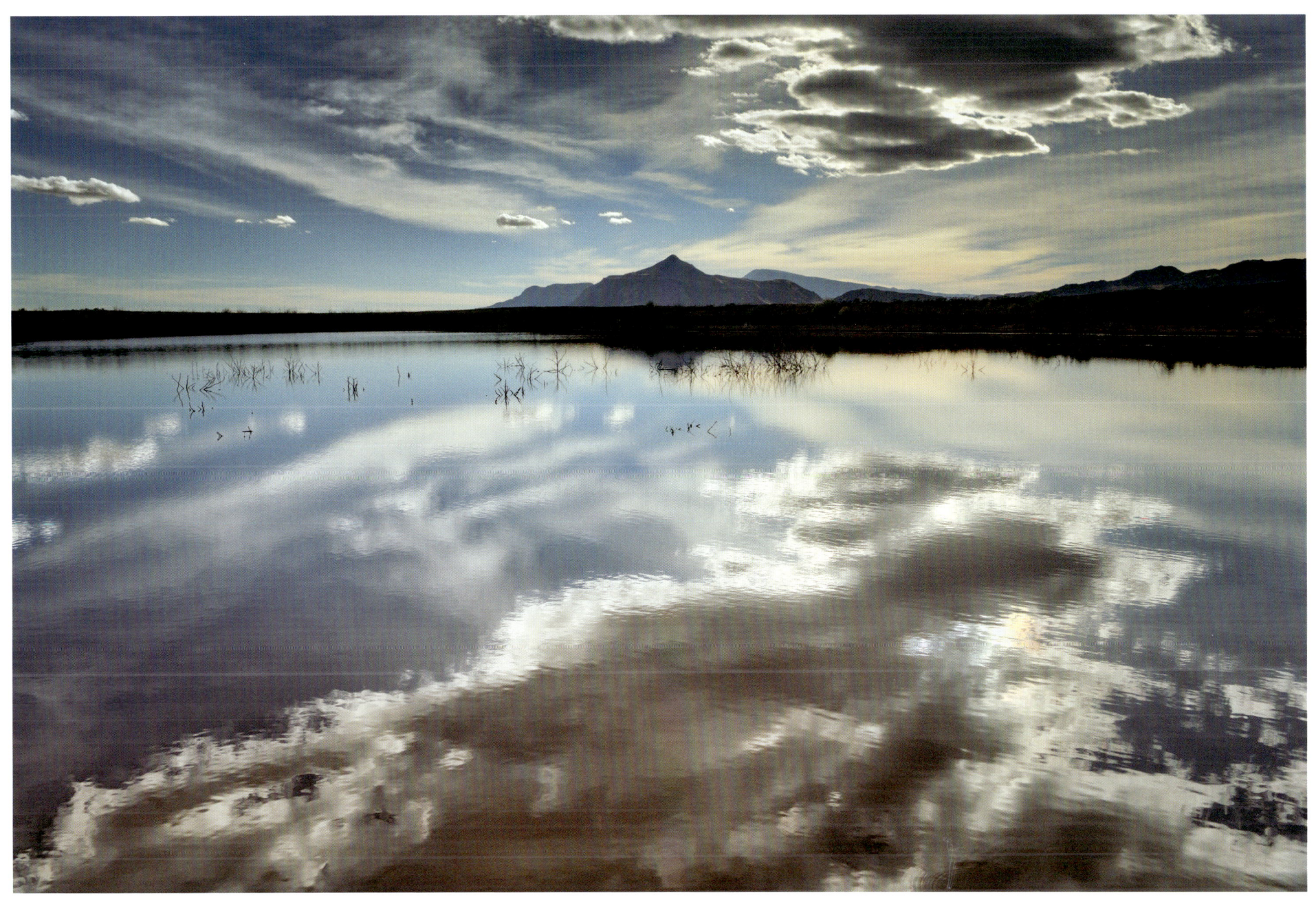

Red Tank and Capital Peak, White Sands Missile Range. Red Tank was constructed by the Civilian Conservation Corps (CCC) in the 1930s and usually has water in it year round. Capitol Peak stands out in the background.

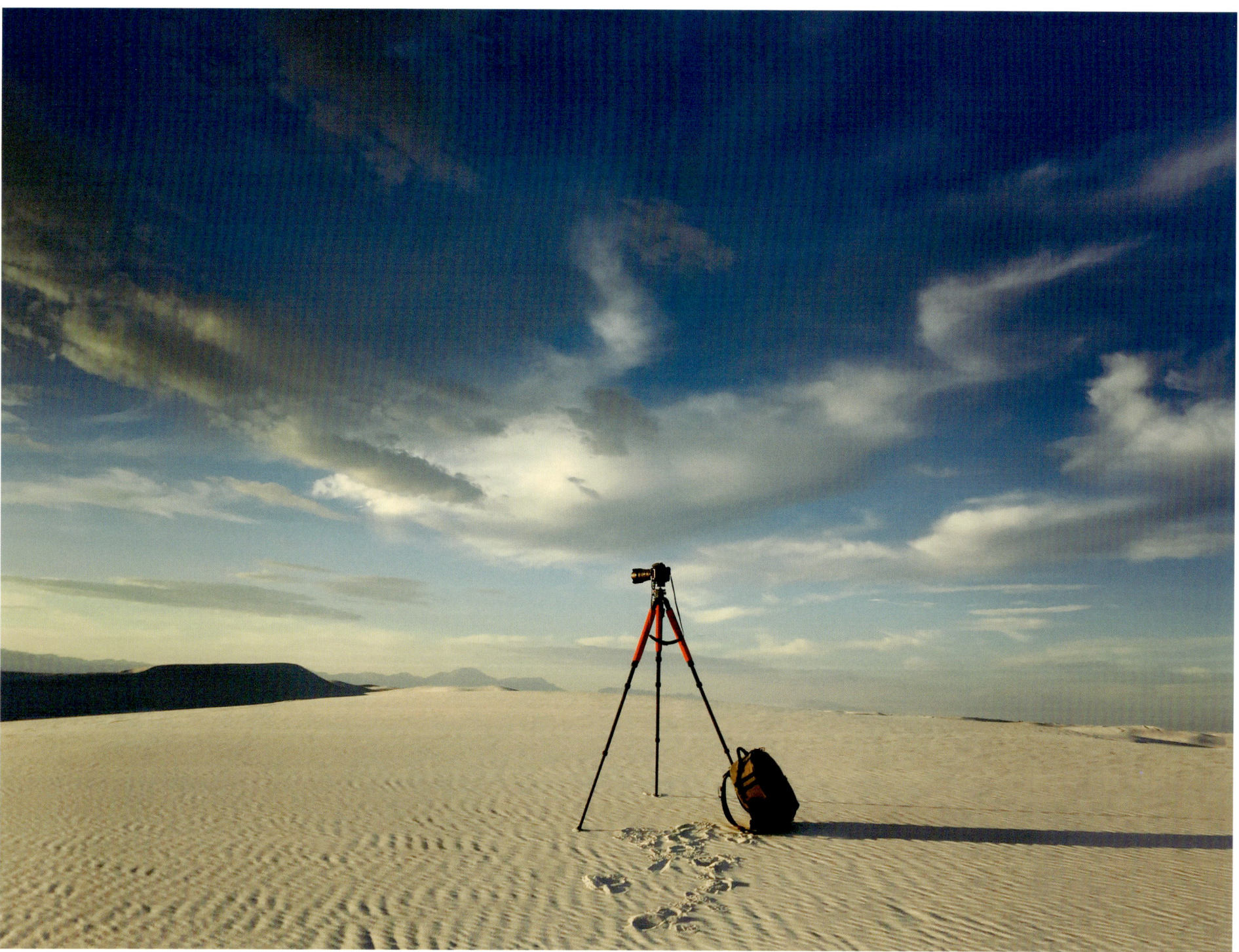

Into the Great Light

Craig Varjabedian

The Photographer's Nikon Camera, Tripod, and Backpack on the Dunes, Sunset. Photograph made with Apple iPhone.

So Boss, with enthusiasm radiating so constantly around us, is it any wonder we get so excited over our area?

—Johnwill Faris, "Southwestern National Monuments Monthly Report," October 1939

It's spring break at White Sands National Park, probably the busiest time of year at this national park. When I drove through the gate this morning, Terry Wilder, the park ranger at the entrance, told me that he expected more than ten thousand visitors in the park today. It looks like he's right. As I drive the loop road through the park, there probably isn't a dune that's not occupied by some group of people—families, perhaps, and others who have set up a base camp at the top of a dune to spend the day together having fun sliding down these gypsum sand dunes in brightly colored snow (sand) saucers. As I have wandered among these sledders over the years many of them have told me that waxing the bottom of the saucer is the secret to improving the speed of these sand chariots.

I came to White Sands for a different experience. While I delight in watching my fellow visitors enjoy the park, I am looking for something else—something contemplative, restorative, deeper. I am a photographer—an artist who creates with light. Back about thirty years ago I came to this place for the first time in search of beautiful moments—confluences of light, shadow, atmosphere, and feeling that I might capture with my camera. What I discovered was something miraculous. Over the years, between other photo projects, I would make my way back to White Sands so I could walk among the gleaming dunes and reset myself—to visually and emotionally prepare for the next body of work I would make. My friends say that I keep returning to White Sands to find my smile. I think they're right.

LIGHT AND MAKING PICTURES

I swear to you, there are divine things more beautiful than words can tell.

—Walt Whitman, "Song of the Open Road"

Like many artists, I came to New Mexico because I had heard about its extraordinary light. On the first morning after my arrival in Santa Fe, I remember watching the sun come up over the mountains and wishing that I could collect that magical light in a mason jar. White Sands puts on just as great a light show. From the beautiful color of the predawn light to the almost psychedelic sunsets—in fact throughout the day—the light at White Sands seldom disappoints. And of course, no two days are ever the same. Just as a day could begin with a beautiful sunrise, it might end with a hellacious storm—both beautiful in their own ways. I think Forrest Gump's remark about life being like a box of chocolates is an apt way to describe the light and the weather at White Sands. You never quite know what you're going to get until you are there, experiencing it from the top of a gleaming-white sand dune.

Photography is a curious art, combining emotions, visual stimuli, and aesthetics with the science of optics, and in the case of digital photography, the capture and manipulation of pixels. At times, though, the technology can get in the way of making a deeper connection with what is being photographed. F/stops, shutter speeds, ISO, lenses, tripods, computer software, and so much more have to be considered to record an image well. But making a great photograph requires more than technology. When I worked for photographer Paul Caponigro years ago, he would talk about working to attain "a state of heart," a gentle space offering inspirational substance that could purify one's vision. Paul would often speak about a spirit he called "otherness" that a photograph must have in order to fully engage the viewer. For me, a good photograph must be an open-ended conversation; it must contain an invitation to the viewer to wander and to linger and to stay awhile. If it's merely a record of having been somewhere, no matter how well composed or beautiful the image, I am left empty. A good photographer must follow the trail of their feelings to their source but not necessarily reveal them entirely. And so as I hike among the dunes, I work hard to quiet my mind and seek that state of heart, to tune out the distractions of the world in order to connect with a deeper presence that I sense within this landscape of great light. From the first time I encountered it, this kind of raw essence has been my teacher, often whispering guidance on when and where I should train my camera. In the end, I want to create photographs of those magical, evanescent moments that are consonant with what it was like to stand there and witness them.

At White Sands, the pictures do not always come quickly or easily. You have to know the technical side of photography as well as you know how to brush your teeth and then somehow be able to push that all aside and become a child again, filled with wonder and amazement. You have to get in sync with the subject somehow, to fall in love with it. You have to get away from preconceived ideas about how the subject is "supposed" to look and just allow the subject to be what it is so that the spirit that called you in the first place can live in the photograph. Making good photographs, in short, is a joyful experience, but it is hard work.

One of the things I continue to be struck by is the vastness of White Sands, and I sometimes have to struggle to decide how to frame what I see. If I shoot with a wide-angle lens, for example, the picture sometimes captures too much information, obscuring the thing that called me to make the photograph in the first place. In her 1976 autobiography, Georgia O'Keeffe spoke about painting the "fragments of things because it seemed to make my [her] statement as well as or better than the whole could." And so I started photographing the fragments of White Sands: a yucca plant, the shadow of a dune created by another, windswept patterns in the sand, and so many other things. As the seasons passed and the sun made its slow journey across the horizon, I began to see how every feature of the desert was bound to the rest—the curve of a dune to the wind's patient shaping, the sweep of a hawk's shadow to the restless patterns in the sand. Gradually, these connections emerged with such quiet certainty that I could no longer see them as separate. When I raised my camera, it was not always to capture an instant but sometimes to honor a living whole. The images carried the language of the place— its heat and hush, its drift and sudden movement— and they spoke to me in a way that engaged both the reasoning mind and the more ancient, wordless chambers of the heart.

> It is the photographer, not the camera,
> that is the instrument.
>
> —Eve Arnold, American photojournalist

The pictures in this book were made with a full-frame Nikon digital camera. A D810 DSLR with an arsenal of Nikon zoom and prime lenses in focal lengths from 14 to 200 mm along with a Sigma 150–600 mm lens was more than adequate to produce the varied images I made for this body of work. The Nikon 24–70 mm f/2.8E ED VR lens, however, deserves special mention. My go-to optic for most of the photographs I make, it was used to create many of the pictures in this book. You may be asking why I made these pictures with a Nikon camera. My high school teacher Norm Stewart had a Nikon FTN SLR film camera with a couple of lenses—good technology for the time. He got excellent results and spoke glowingly about the camera and why he acquired it. Stewart allowed me to use his camera a few times, which is how I too fell under the spell of Nikon. As time went on, I noticed over and over that photographers whose work I admired also made pictures with Nikon cameras. So the choice of my first 35 mm camera and the camera I work with today was probably inevitable.

Over the years I have had the opportunity to work with just about every brand and type of camera out there. I have made noteworthy pictures with many different kinds of cameras and lenses and have learned that each of them has a distinct personality uniquely its own. Pictures made with a Canon camera with Canon lenses, for example, look different to me from those made with a Sony camera and Sony lenses. I'm not talking just about image sharpness nor am I trying to wade into the perennial argument about which camera is best. I am speaking about something much more subtle that can be seen and perhaps even felt if you look with care at enough pictures made with different cameras and lenses. I like what I see in photographs made with a Nikon camera and lenses. It's in the color and the sharpness and the way a Nikon lens will describe and render space in a photograph. It works well for me. And creating art is, in part, about the choices of tools and materials that help the artist achieve the intended expression.

They say that the best camera is the one you have with you. They are right. Photographer Ernst Haas was often quoted as saying, "There is only you and your camera. The limitations in your photography are in yourself, for what we see is what we are." Today a lot of the pictures I see being made at White Sands (and many other places too) are taken with cell phones. For quick images, or when my Nikon camera isn't handy, I use my trusty Apple iPhone. The quality of the images the phone is capable of making often surprises me. But I sometimes find the camera app included with the phone limiting. There are scores of additional camera apps for smart phones. For the iPhone I have been using ProCamera by Cocologics with excellent results. And for an Android phone, I've heard good things about the ProCam X—Lite :HD Camera Pro app available at Google Play. Additionally, a fully charged cell phone offers a bonus. If you get lost out on the dunes, you can call 911.

Thus shadow owes its birth to light.

—John Gay, "The Persian, Sun, and Cloud"

One of the biggest challenges of making photographs at White Sands is the extreme contrast on a bright day, which often exceeds the capabilities of digital cameras. With a normal exposure you may be unable to record all the highlight or shadow information of a scene in a single capture. Because I am looking to make photographs and eventually finished prints that are rich, smooth, and brilliant and that have depth and substance, I need my image file to contain information in all areas of the scene. In my resulting photographs I want to feel the heat of the sun and the texture of the sand and, as much as possible, the quality of light that I see as I look through the camera. Yet I am not trying for a literal transcription of the scene. Rather, I want to share through my photograph a particular moment when light, shadow, atmosphere, and feeling came together and called me to a specific place to make a photograph. This is when the technique called HDR (High Dynamic Range) photography comes to the rescue. Making a series of camera captures from underexposed to overexposed and then processing them either in the camera, if the camera is able, or combining them utilizing a computer and software, can make an image file with detail in both the highlights and the shadows. Many of the pictures in this book were made this way and were processed on a computer utilizing Luminar Neo software from Skylum, which is available for the both the Mac and PC. Photomatix from HDRsoft is another piece of highly recommended HDR software.

Safety doesn't happen by accident.

—Standard Oil Company of California, 1941

Safety is important at White Sands. While it is not a common occurrence, there are stories about people who have hiked out into the dunes, have gotten lost, and sadly have even perished. When I first began photographing at White Sands I was told by a National Park Service (NPS) law-enforcement officer that of all the people who get lost out on the dunes, it is frequently photographers they have to search for and rescue. I can see how this happens. You hike out into the dunes and you notice a shadow, say, developing on the slip face of a dune, or a beautiful sunset, and you begin looking for a subject that you might want to include in the frame with it. You wander and you explore and then, all of a sudden, you can't find your way back to the place where you parked your car. You can't always rely on finding and tracing your footsteps in the sand to find your way back, because they may have been erased by the wind. While the Alkali Flats trail out into the dunes is marked with bright-red posts, most hiking locations at White Sands are unmarked. Carrying with you several bottles of water, a fully charged cell phone, and even a GPS device will go a long way to ensure that you return home safely. The Park Service also suggests bringing along a lightweight space blanket to either keep you warm or protect you from the sun if necessary and a whistle to make noise in the event you get lost.

As I write this, a flock of kids has descended on a nearby table, having just returned from playing out on the dunes. Their chaperone, possibly someone's mother, is preparing picnic food for the hungry horde. One of the kids walks over to a car parked nearby, rolls down the windows, and turns up the radio, at which point I am shaken out of my contemplative state by the strains of a song popular in dance clubs years ago, Haddaway's "What is Love?" It was used in an old *Saturday Night Live* skit, and the kids start bobbing their heads in unison to the beat like the characters in the sketch. As I sit laughing, watching the performance, my mind flashes back to a conversation I had with park ranger Becky Burghart a few years ago. She said that one of the most remarkable things she had discovered at White Sands was that the place could become whatever the visitor wanted it to be. "You can craft your own experience here," Becky told me. So if you come to White Sands to go sledding down a dune, attend a full-moon concert, enjoy a picnic with your family, savor a contemplative moment, go on a ranger-led walk across the dunes, or even photograph exquisite confluences of light, shadow, atmosphere, and feeling, as I set out to do, there is something here for you. And perhaps, in the end, this is the true and amazing gift of White Sands National Park.

ACKNOWLEDGMENTS

The gift of a book is the result of many helping hands. And while any list of appreciations such as this is bound to be incomplete, I want to express my deepest gratitude.

To the National Park Service, the US Department of the Interior, and the good people at White Sands National Park, particularly Marie Frias Sauter, superintendent; David Bustos, resource program manager; Rebecca Burghart, former chief of interpretation; Eugenio Ibarra, park ranger; Jonathan Knapp, physical scientist-geologist; Patrick Martinez, biological technician; Terry Wilder, visitor use assistant; Jackson Jakeway, intern for the NPS Geoscientists-In-the-Parks Program, and Molly Murphy, former archaeologist intern.

To the command at White Sands Missile Range, especially Camilla Montoya, public affairs specialist, and Erin Dorrance, former chief of public affairs.

To the writers of the essays in this book: Jeanetta Calhoun Mish, poet, writer, and literary scholar; Dennis Ditmanson, former superintendent at White Sands National Park; and Jim Eckles, former chief of public affairs at White Sands Missile Range.

To clients and friends who have supported my work over the years and who helped make this book possible: America Classics Car Club, Robert and Joan Behlman, John Berkenfield, Lawrence Blank, Cheryl Cathcart, John Cavallito, Robert W. Clevenger, Ron Cooper, Burton Kushner, Larry and Hannah Lattman, Howard and Ellen Lowery, Dale and Barbara Ouimette, Doug and Teresa Peterson, Tom and Lisa Redburn, James and Yolanda Scheihing, Bill Schultz, Russell Smith, and Kerry Stewart.

To the generous people who supported our Kickstarter crowd-funding effort: Stephen and Wayne Abby, Tomas Abreu, Tony and Gaynor Banham, Eric Banks and Lois Wilson, M. Robert Blum, Robert and Myra Bullington, Jeannie Camosy, Mike Castles, Randy Chance, Nat Coalson, Diana Cook, Carole Debeer, Katrina and Steve Dickerson, Jim Eckles, Andrew Epstein, James R. Fullerton, Donald and Barbara Gazibara, Deborah Glessner, Tye and Caroline Hardison, Gary Hein, Don and Kathy Holtzclaw, Craig Alan Huber, Scott A. Hutchinson, Kathy Imel, Michael R. Johnson, Mark D. Johnston, Kevin K. Jones, Robert and Sandra Kal, Clifford Land, Cindy Lantrip, J. David Levy, Paula Loftin, DiAnn L'Roy, Robyn and Walter Mehmke, Dolph and Jeanne Miller, Roland Miller, Kyran Mish and Jeanetta Calhoun Mish, Michael R. Mock, Sue Glover Mottinger, Debra Nunes and Janet LaPierre, Charles Ondrej, Leah Ostro, Clyde Parrott, Bill Polkinhorn Photography, Cathy Porter, Amy Reams, Lisa Richardson, Mike Rosebery, James Saxon, Stephen Schafer, Nicholas Schoeder, Robert W. Shea, John Ashley Simmons, Robert W. Stuhrman, Rhonda Troutman, Jim and Marjorie Van Hoy, Vicki Vaughan, Hank Voegtle, W. C. Waterbury Jr., and K. Wheeler.

To the following individuals who provided thoughtful feedback and comment on the essay "White Sands Meditations," Jeanetta Calhoun Mish joins me in thanking David Bustos, resource program manager at White Sands National Park; Dennis Ditmanson, former superintendent at White Sands National Park; Jim Eckles, former chief of public affairs at White Sands Missile Range; Jonathan Knapp, former physical scientist-geologist at White

Sands National Park; the late Larry Lattman, former president of New Mexico Institute of Mining and Technology; and Marie Frias Sauter, superintendent at White Sands National Park.

To the staff of the University of New Mexico Press, especially Stephen P. Hull, director; Felicia Cedillos, senior book designer; James Ayers, assistant director and editorial, design, and production manager; Elise McHugh, senior acquisitions editor; and Don Redpath, marketing and sales manager.

To the many other people I met along the way who have helped make this White Sands adventure a little easier: Tony Bonanno, photographer; Carol Ditmanson, Western National Parks Association; Jessi Fleming, Facebook; Beth Hadas, freelance editor; Roland Miller, photographer; Ernesto Ortega, former superintendent, NPS; and Margaret Stocker, former NPS volunteer at White Sands National Park.

To New Mexico State University Library, Archives and Special Collections, for permission to reprint Tom Charles's "Invitation" from his booklet *Story of the Great White Sands*.

To the corporate sponsors who have supported my work and that of the photography workshop program I teach for, Eloquent Light Photography Workshops in Santa Fe, New Mexico: Hahnemühle FineArt, HDRsoft Software, Skylum Software, NEC Display Solutions, Really Right Stuff, Sirui USA, Think Tank Photo, Topaz Labs, and Wine Country Camera.

To one and all who have purchased my books and/or acquired original photographic prints of my work over the years.

And finally to you, the audience for my work. Your kind words, your thoughtful comments on social media, your attendance at exhibitions, lectures, book launch events, and so much more—your contribution matters, and I thank you for it.

Craig Varjabedian

BIBLIOGRAPHY

WHITE SANDS

de Aragón, Ray John. *Enchanted Legends and Lore of New Mexico: Witches, Ghosts, and Spirits.* Charleston, SC: History Press, 2012.

Charles, Mrs. Tom (Bula). "The Great White Sands." In *Tales of the Tularosa.* Rev. ed. Tularosa, NM: Mrs. Tom Charles, 1953.

Charles, Tom. *Story of the Great White Sands.* Alamogordo, NM: n. p., 1938.

Chronic, Halka. *Roadside Geology of New Mexico.* Missoula, MT: Mountain Press Publishing Company, 1987.

Dodge, Natt N. *The Natural History Story of White Sands National Monument.* Globe, AZ: Southwest Parks and Monuments Association, 1971.

Dold, Catherine. "Stiger's Very Old House: Alumnus Rewrites Ancient North American History." *Coloradan* (March 2005): 16–17.

Eidenbach, Peter L. "Cultural History of the Tularosa Basin." National Park Service, 2014. http://www.nps.gov/whsa/historyculture/cultural-history-of-the-tularosa-basin.htm.

———, ed. *The Prehistory of Rhodes Canyon, NM.* Tularosa, NM: Human Systems Research, 1983.

Eidenbach, Peter L., Mark L. Wimberly, and Terry Knight. *Archaeological Reconnaissance in White Sands National Monument, New Mexico, 1978.* Tularosa, NM: Human Systems Research, 1980.

de Espejo, Antonio. "Account of the Journey to the Provinces and Settlements of New Mexico, 1583." In *Spanish Exploration in the Southwest, 1542–1706,* edited by Herbert Eugene Bolton, 163–95. New York: Charles Scribner's Sons, 1916. http://www.americanjourneys.org/aj-008/index.asp.

Felipe Lucero. n.d. Doña Ana Sheriff's Collection, C. L. Sonnichsen Special Collections. University of Texas-El Paso Libraries. http://cdm15823.contentdm.oclc.org/cdm/landingpage/collection/p15823coll3.

Fryberger, Steven G. "Geological Overview of White Sands National Monument." National Park Service, 2001. http://www.nature.nps.gov/geology/parks/whsa/geows/.

Gibbs, George. "Salt Plains of New Mexico." *The American Naturalist* 4, no. 11 (1871): 695–96. https://archive.org.

Kain, Susan M. "White Animals at White Sands." http://www.nps.gov/whsa/naturescience/white-animals-at-white-sands.htm.

Koontz, L., and Thomas C. Cullinane. *2016 National Park Visitor Spending Effects: Economic Contributions to Local Communities, States, and the Nation.* Natural Resource Report. NPS/NRSS/EQD/NRR—2017/1421. Fort Collins, CO: National Park Service, 2017.

Moore, S. Derrickson. "Ghostly Dance—New Ballet Based on Borderland Legend." *Las Cruces Sun-News,* June 29, 2012.

National Aeronautics and Space Administration, NASA Space Place. "White Sands, New Mexico, USA." 2000. Photograph taken May 9, 2000. http://spaceplace.nasa.gov/review/spuzzled/page16.html.

National Park Service. "Lake Lucero." https://www.nps.gov/whsa/learn/nature/lake-lucero.htm.

———. "White Sands National Monument." http://www.nps.gov/whsa/.

New Mexico Department of Game and Fish. "2015 Desert Bighorn Helicopter Surveys (Spring)." http://www.wildlife.state.nm.us/conservation/wildlife-species-information/mammals/bighorn-sheep.

———. "White Sands Pupfish." *Wildlife Notes*, 1996, rev. 2006. http://www.wildlife.state.nm.us/download/education/conservation/wildlife-notes/aquatic/White-Sands-pupfish.pdf.

Rhodes, Eugene Manlove. *Pasó Por Aquí*. In *The Best Novels and Stories of Eugene Manlove Rhodes*. Lincoln: University of Nebraska Press, 1987.

"Rio Grande Rift FAQ: Measuring Rio Grande Rift Crustal Deformation." A Joint Project of EarthScope, UNAVCO, University of New Mexico, University of Colorado at Boulder, Utah State University, Cooperative Institute for Research in Environmental Science, and National Science Foundation. http://aconcagua.geol.usu.edu/~arlowry/RGR/faq.html#what.

Schneider-Hector, Dietmar. *White Sands: The History of a National Monument*. Albuquerque: University of New Mexico Press, 1993.

Serling, Rod. "A Hundred Yards Over the Rim." *The Twilight Zone*. Dir. Buzz Kulik. CBS. Season 2, Episode 23, April 7, 1961.

Shinabery, Michael. "Destination Moon." Moonandback.com, July 10, 2011. http://moonandback.com/2011/07/10/destination-moon-this-week-in-space-history/.

Sonnichsen, C. L. *Tularosa: Last of the Frontier West*. Albuquerque: University of New Mexico Press, 1980.

Strong, Ray, and Paul Karlstrom. "Oral History Interview with Ray Strong." September 14, 1993. Archives of American Art, Smithsonian Institution. http://www.aaa.si.edu/collections/interviews/oral-history-interview-ray-strong-11668.

"TV-Movies Eye Range for Public." *Wind & Sand* (newspaper of the White Sands Missile Range), May 15, 1959: 6B. http://www.wsmrhistoric.com/files/1959%20Wind%20and%20Sand%20V10%20Issue%207.pdf.

US Fish and Wildlife Service. "Mexican Wolves in the Wild: The Blue Range Wolf Reintroduction Project." http://www.fws.gov/southwest/es/mexicanwolf/brwrp_home.cfm.

Walker, Steven James, Tim Church, and Deni J. Seymour. *Basin and Fan: Evaluation of 41 Prehistoric Sites in the Doña Ana Firing Groups B, E, & F, Doña Ana Range, Fort Bliss, New Mexico*. Historic and Natural Resources Report, no. 02–09. Lone Mountain Archaeological Services Report, 560–002. El Paso, TX: Lone Mountain Archaeological Services, 2004.

Welsh, Michael. *Dunes and Dreams: A History of White Sands National Monument*. Intermountain Cultural Resources Center Professional Paper No. 55. Santa Fe, NM: National Park Service, Division of History, Intermountain Cultural Resources Center, 1995.

CRAIG VARJABEDIAN

Varjabedian, Craig. *As the Spirit Stands Still*. Essay by Gussie Fauntleroy. Limited edition. Santa Fe, NM: Cirrus Editions Limited, 1998.

———. *By the Grace of Light: Images of Faith from Catholic New Mexico*. Essays by the Most Reverend Michael J. Sheehan, Archbishop of Santa Fe; Mag Dimond; and Cathy Wright. Colorado Springs, CO: Colorado Springs Fine Arts Center, 1998.

———. *Craig Varjabedian: Photographs and Words*. Edited by Cindy L. Lane. Santa Fe, NM: Eloquent Light Editions, 2014.

———. *Eloquence of Trees*. Essay by Jaima Chevalier. Santa Fe, NM: Athenon Editions, 2010.

———. *En Divina Luz: The Penitente Moradas of New Mexico*. Essay by Michael Wallis. Albuquerque: University of New Mexico Press, 1994.

———. *Four and Twenty Photographs: Stories from Behind the Lens*. Text by Robin Jones. Afterword by Jay Packer. Albuquerque: University of New Mexico Press, 2007.

———. *Ghost Ranch and the Faraway Nearby*. Essays by Belden C. Lane, Rob Craig, Douglas Fairfield, and Marin Sardy. Albuquerque: University of New Mexico Press, 2009.

———. *Landscape Dreams, A New Mexico Portrait*. Essays by Marin Sardy and Jeanetta Calhoun Mish. Foreword by Hampton Sides. Albuquerque: University of New Mexico Press, 2012.

———. *Places of power*. Essay by Daniel Pearlman. Santa Fe, NM, 1986.

———. *This Enchanted Land*. Essay by Marc Simmons. Seguin, TX: Texas Lutheran University, 2001.

JEANETTA CALHOUN MISH

Mish, Jeanetta Calhoun. *Ain't Nobody That Can Sing Like Me: New Oklahoma Writing*. Norman, OK: Mongrel Empire Press, 2010.
———. *Oklahomeland: Essays*. Beaumont, TX: Lamar University Press, 2015.
———. *Tongue Tied Woman*. Sarasota, FL: SOULSPEAK/Sarasota Poetry Theater, 2002.
———. *What I Learned at the War*. Albuquerque, NM: West End Press, 2016.
———. *Work Is Love Made Visible: Collected Family Photographs*. Albuquerque, NM: West End Press, 2009.

JIM ECKLES

Eckles, Jim. *Deming, New Mexico's Camp Cody: A World War One Training Camp*. CreateSpace Independent Publishing Platform, 2017.
———. *Pocketful of Rockets: History and Stories Behind White Sands Missile Range*. Las Cruces, NM: Fiddlebike Partnership, 2013.
———. *Trinity: The History of an Atomic Bomb National Historic Landmark*. Las Cruces, NM: Fiddlebike Partnership, 2015.

Photographs © 2018 by Craig Varjabedian

Text © 2018 by Jeanetta Calhoun Mish, Dennis
    Ditmanson, Jim Eckles, and Craig Varjabedian

Published 2018

Printed in Canada

First paperback edition, 2026

Paperback ISBN: 978-0-8263-6898-0

Library of Congress Cataloging-in-Publication Data
Names: Varjabedian, Craig, 1957– | Mish, Jeanetta Calhoun,
    author. | Ditmanson, Dennis, author. | Eckles, Jim, author.
Title: Into the great White Sands / photographs by Craig
    Varjabedian ; essays by Jeanetta Calhoun Mish, Dennis
    Ditmanson, and Jim Eckles.
Description: Albuquerque: University of New Mexico Press,
    2018. | Includes bibliographical references. |
Identifiers: LCCN 2017026644 (print) | LCCN 2017029764
    (ebook) | ISBN 9780826358318 (E–book) |
    ISBN 9780826358301 (cloth: alk. paper)
Subjects: LCSH: White Sands National Monument (N.M.)—
    Pictorial works. | Natural history—New Mexico—
    White Sands—Pictorial works. | Sand dune ecology—
    New Mexico—Pictorial works. | White Sands Missile Range
    (N.M.)—Pictorial works.
Classification: LCC QH105.N6 (ebook) | LCC QH105.N6 V37
    2018 (print) | DDC 577.5/8309789—dc23
LC record available at https://lccn.loc.gov/2017026644

Cover photographs: *Yucca in Bloom, Spring (front)* and *Farewell
    Sunset, Spring (back)* by Craig Varjabedian
Designed by Lisa C. Tremaine